MW01516292

I Choose Low-Glycemic Living

(I Choose Healthy Living - Volume 11)

Reach 365 Happy and Healthy Days!

Mia Safra

Contents

Introduction

Hi my dear friends,

I let the first part to tell you some interesting stories that you can understand partly the reason why the book "I Choose Low-Glycemic Living", as well as the series "I Choose Healthy Living" was born!

1. *My Journey towards Low-Glycemic Diet Due to my Baby's Dairy Sensitivity – And How it Transformed my Life*

When your baby's health is at risk, as a mom, you can do everything! Yes, I said goodbye to my favorite dairies. Bye, butter! Bye, ice cream! Bye, cheese! I never imagined that I can do something as radical as this in my life since I have always been a fussy eater. You can never ever make me eat something unfamiliar to me.

But, when my son was born last 2009, a dairy sensitivity is detected on him. And since the proteins in breastmilk are being passed to the baby during breastfeeding, dairy foods became suddenly a no-no in my life!

I started to browse for some blog entries related to Low-Glycemic diet. To be honest, my situation is very challenging and I don't know how to deal with it at first. But surprisingly, there are a lot of fellow mothers out there with the same experiences and who generously shared their resources. I am now a master of label evaluation in grocery stores. "Hasta la vista" to casein, milk, whey and lactose. I also planned to gamble on those Low-Glycemic counterparts of some of my favorites that's why I already prepared a list of them, just in case. So, the next time I visited the grocery store, I (timidly) bought a bar of rice milk chocolate, an ice cream made of almond milk, a coconut milk, a yogurt made of coconut milk, a Low-Glycemic pancake mix, a plant-based butter and the best of all... a vanilla coffee creamer made of coconut milk! Coffee is a new mother's BFF. I never expected that life can go back to (somehow) normal this soon.

With the new lifestyle, I noticed that my skin is smoother and radiant. My digestive problems that bugged me forever also vanished. Moreover, I lost all my pregnancy weight gain and more.

To top it all, my son's indications to dairy sensitivity is gone! Wow! Who would have thought that I will be accustomed to this way of life? I adapted Low-Glycemic living for another 3 years. Instead of being overwhelmed during parties and celebrations, they became even more exciting events for me since it will open opportunities to share my regimen and inspire others to go for it, too.

If you ask me, besides my son's health, the next best thing was my own personal growth. We are often afraid of changes but they are actually closed doors of opportunities waiting for us to open them. Now, I take pride that I can sacrifice anything for my children. Also, I now understand that the foods I "want" are just cravings and I should not rely on them to make me feel fulfilled. Until now, I still prefer the Low-Glycemic substitutes of some foods that I consume. Why? Because I feel healthier without dairy! Don't get me wrong, I will never be thankful for my son's dairy sensitivity and distresses because of it, but where the situation took me is what I am thankful for.

2. *The Journey of Lili Safra's daughter – Celiac Disease*

Lili Safra is my best friend forever. And the following is the journey of her daughter about Celiac Disease.

My impeccable Zoey was born five weeks premature and she was really small at 4 pounds and 6 ounces. It was a very challenging pregnancy. Three years have passed and she still has minimal weight gain, which led her Pediatrician to order a test for Celiac Disease. How can we be so unaware that our child has the disease and we often gave her pizza and pasta!

The results, in fact, turn out positive. She had endoscopy and blood test to confirm. When I finally absorbed everything, I cried so hard. We were thankful that we are now aware why she was not growing right, but, I also began to worry for her. She would miss a lot and she might feel that she did not belong. She has to bring her own food during birthday celebrations and there is a constant worry that the foods she will consume will take a toll on her health. A few weeks after starting the gluten-free diet, an enthusiastic and a positive Zoey was what we've got. Since she was still young, she was never able to verbalize the discomfort she felt before and cannot also describe that she did felt better after the diet. I became very optimistic that she can be 100% well if we continue this regimen. After three more years, we are still very blessed as Zoey remains to thrive and she is even imparting her knowledge on gluten-free lifestyle with her friends.

This life challenge made me realize that I want to contribute more not only to my family but also to my dear friends around me, as well as the community. That is why I am sharing the recipe collections, knowledge and experiences that I gained during the process. I am praying that this will reach out to many families and help them the way I was helped out by those blog entries some years ago.

3. *The Journey of Chloe (Recipe Developer of our team) – How She Reached to a Healthy Life*

Actually, I have always had a huge passion for health and nutrition. Since I was young, I am already a foodie. I have always been fanatical of well-being and nourishment BUT the road I took is not balanced and healthy. I became addicted to junk foods – sweets and chips. Then, when I was in secondary school, I followed these unmaintainable and famous low-calorie regimens. These diet crazes were advertised as hip and trendy and they will make you believe that this is the only approach to cut those extra weight. As a teenager, I was obsessed to be thin. Back then, I have been a believer that to achieve it, I should starve myself. Unknown to me, consuming very low amounts of food will just make me very hungry and as a result, will make me consume too much food…. Then, the cycle repeats again, making my health unbalanced and my weight at its heaviest!

Tired of my unhealthy life, I just gave up dieting altogether. I prayed to God and begun studying the situation. What I am doing with my body not only

harms me but it also disgraces Him. So, I stopped these "fad diets" and started eating the right kinds of foods. It worked! I am not craving anymore and a total of 35 pounds was gradually lost in 1.5 years. This regimen is something I can endure and continue.

I now understand that the road to losing weight has no shortcuts. You have to have realistic goals and really vow to change your lifestyle. I should know, it worked for me. Bye, 40 pounds! I am also glad to share that those pounds never came back.

"I Choose Healthy Living" – the tagline of this series, is one of my much-loved quotes. Eating well and having a balanced diet is never easy but if you look at what you will reap after the challenges, you will know that all is worth it. Hello, Healthy Eating!

Replace your favorite sweets with fruit. Apples, strawberries, cantaloupe and grapes – to name a few of my top favorites. Or you may have an organic salted chocolate bar, or a scoop of ice cream made of coconut milk. Name it! You can still fulfill your cravings.

Eating a well-balanced diet is the key. You don't need to consume all types of food to achieve it. But you don't have to deprive yourself, too. I noticed that my food preference changed and I feel so light and positive. Eating healthy equals feeling better and feeling better equals wanting to eat healthier to feel much better. A good cycle compared to the one I had before. Try it to believe it. Because you choose healthy living, say hello healthy eating and goodbye unhealthy dieting.

In conclusion, through three stories I told you above, I want to share you the reasons and the purposes of the book and the series as well. The series "I Choose Healthy Living" firstly is for my dear family, friends around me. Most of them have problems about health and want to find a suitable diet to follow in a long journey of their life. So I really want to present them this gift and wish them always be healthy and happy. Second reason, I also want to send you, my dear friends all around the world! Because I myself got a terrible time to struggle with my baby's dairy sensitivity, I deeply understand with you and want to support you partly. Therefore, I want to inspire you through the recipes in this series. The series contain many different subjects that are done by our team with all the warm heart

- ✓ *Gluten-Free*
- ✓ *Low-Carb*
- ✓ *Paleo Diet*
- ✓ *Clean Eating*
- ✓ *...*

I really hope that each book in the series will be useful and always your best friend in your little kitchen.

Live Happy and Eat Healthy!

Enjoy the book,

List of Abbreviations

I Choose
Healthy Living

LIST OF ABBREVIATIONS

Tbsp(s).	Tablespoon(s)
Tsp(s).	Teaspoon(s)
C	Cup

Chapter 1: Low-Glycemic Diet: A Simple Guide For Beginners

***

Also known as low-GI diet, the low-glycemic diet is based on the glycemic index (GI). Research has proved the many health benefits of this diet, including lower blood glucose levels, decreased risk of type 2 diabetes and heart disease, and weight loss. But critics oppose the way the glycemic index ranks foods—they believe GI isn't reliable because it doesn't reflect overall health.

This section presents an in-depth review of the low-glycemic diet: What it's all about, how to use it, as well as its advantages and disadvantages.

I. What is GI?

A vital component of healthy eating, carbohydrates are present in fruits, dairy products, breads, vegetables, and cereals. Eating any kind of carbs causes your digestive system to break it down into simple sugars that go into the bloodstream. Different kinds of carbohydrates affect blood sugar in different ways.

The glycemic index or GI is a number used to rank foods based on their effect on blood glucose levels in the body. Dr. David Jenkins, a Canadian professor, developed this food ranking system in the early '80s. The GI ranks the rates at which various foods increase blood glucose levels compared with the absorption of 50 grams of pure glucose with a GI value of 100.

Here are the three GI ratings:

- ✓ Low GI: 55 or lower
- ✓ Medium GI: 56 to 69
- ✓ High GI: 70 or higher

A low-GI value means a certain food is a healthy option because the body digests and absorbs it slowly, resulting in the blood sugar levels getting a smaller and slower increase. In contrast, a high-GI value means a food should be limited in intake because they're digested and absorbed fast, leading to quick fluctuations of blood glucose levels.

Foods are given a GI value only if they have carbs. Thus, no-carb foods like eggs, spices and herbs, beef, fish, and chicken aren't listed on GI food ranking.

1. *What Affects a Food's Glycemic Index?*

The GI value of a meal or food is driven by the following factors:

- ✓ **The kind of sugar:** Not all sugars have a high glycemic index. In fact, the GI of sugar goes from as low as 19 for fructose to as high as 105 for maltose. Thus, a food's GI somewhat depends on the kind of sugar it has.
- ✓ **Structure of the starch**: Being a carbohydrate, starch consists of amylopectin and amylose. Amylopectin is easy to digest, while amylose is hard to digest. So foods with a lower GI are those that contain more amylose.
- ✓ **How refined the carbs is**: Rolling, grinding, and other food processing methods alter the structure of amylopectin and amylose, and this causes the food's GI to increase. Typically, higher-GI foods are the processed ones.
- ✓ **Nutrients in foods**: Acid and fats slow down the digestion and absorption of food in the body.

This decreases the GI. To lower your meal's GI, add acids like lemon juice or fats like avocado to your meals.

- ✓ **Cooking techniques**: How you prepare and cook your food can also affect the GI. Most of the time, the GI goes higher if you cook a food longer, as it will cause quicker digestion and absorption of sugars in the body.
- ✓ **The ripeness of fruits**: Unripe fruits have complex carbs that break down into sugars as the fruit becomes ripe. Ripe fruits have a higher GI. For instance, an overripe banana has a GI of 48, while an unripe banana has a GI of 30.

2. The Carbohydrate Amount Counts, Too

Three things affect the rate at which foods increase blood glucose levels: the amount of foods you eat, the type of carbohydrates they have, and the nutrients they contain. The glycemic index, however, doesn't factor in the amount of food intake. This is why critics are skeptical about it.

To address this issue, the glycemic load or GL rating was created. It measures how a carbohydrate raises or lowers blood glucose levels. The GL considers both the quantity (grams per serving) and type (GI) of foods. Similar to the GI, the GL is categorized into three groups:

- ✓ Low GL: 10 or lower
- ✓ Medium GL: 11 to 19
- ✓ High GL: 20 or higher

When you're on a low-GI diet, the GI still holds the most importance. But the recommendation of the Glycemic Index Foundation (an Australia-based organization that promotes awareness of the low-GI diet) is to still keep track of your GL. It advises people to make it a goal to keep their total daily GL below 100. Feel free to use this database to refer to the GL and GI of common foods.

If possible, go for low-GI foods and eat them in moderate amounts. It's the easiest way to achieve a GL that's lower than 100.

II. What are the Benefits of Low-GI Diet?

1. Low-GI Diet and How It Helps Control Diabetes

Diabetes affects millions of people in the world. This complex health condition causes the body's failure to process sugars effectively, making it hard to keep normal blood sugar levels. But the ability to control blood glucose well can help delay and prevent the start of kidney failure, stroke, heart disease, nerve damage, and other complications of diabetes.

Various studies show that low-GI diets effectively lower blood sugar levels of diabetes patients.

A study conducted in almost 3,000 diabetics examined the impact of high-GI and low-GI diets on the study participants' glycated hemoglobin levels (HbA1c), which are an average measure of blood glucose levels in a span of three months.

The study found that HbA1c levels were 6% to 11% lower in people with diabetes who followed the lowest-GI diets (GI of 58 to 79) compared to others who had the highest-GI diets (GI of 86 to 112). The findings associated the lower-GI diets with long-term reduced blood glucose levels.

Additionally, several studies found that higher-GI diets can possibly raise the risk of type 2 diabetes by 8% to 40%.

In a systematic review of 24 studies, it was concluded that for every five GI points, the risk of type 2 diabetes went up by 8%.

Also, a low-GI diet may result in better pregnancy in women with gestational diabetes mellitus (GDM), which is a form of diabetes that happens to pregnant patients.

A low-GI diet has been found to lower the risk of macrosomia by 73%. Macrosomia occurs when babies have a birth weight of higher than 8 pounds and 13 ounces. This condition is associated with many short-term and long-term complications for both the mother and newborn.

2. Other benefits of low-GI diet

The low-GI diet may also provide these other health

benefits, studies have found:

- ✓ **Lower cholesterol levels**: Low-GI diets lowers LDL cholesterol by 8.6% and total cholesterol by 9.6%. LDL or bad cholesterol raises the risk of stroke and heart disease.
- ✓ **May help in weight loss**: Healthy adults on low-GI diets lost 1.5 to 4.2 lbs. (0.7 to 1.9 kg) over five to 10 weeks. When it comes to long-term weight loss, there is limited research on the effect of low-GI diets.
- ✓ **May lower the risk of cancer**: Compared to low-GI diets, high-GI diets make people more susceptible to colorectal, endometrial, breast cancer, and other types of cancer.
- ✓ **May lower the risk of heart disease**: According to a review of 37 studies, people who follow high-GI diets were 25% more prone to heart disease than those who follow low-GI diets. To confirm these findings, the medical community needs more evidence.

III. Must-Eat and Must-Avoid Foods on a Low-GI Diet

1. What to eat

When you're on a low-GI diet, you don't have to monitor your intake of carbohydrates, fat, and protein or count calories of foods. Rather, it entails replacing foods with a high glycemic index with foods that have a low glycemic index. You have so many healthy, low-GI foods to choose from. Base your diet on these low-GI foods:

- ✓ Bread: Rye, whole grain, sourdough, and multigrain varieties
- ✓ Breakfast cereals: Porridge that consists of All-Bran, bircher muesli, and rolled oats
- ✓ Fruits: Peaches, kiwi, apples, pears, strawberries, plums, and apricots
- ✓ Vegetables: Celery, zucchini, carrots, tomatoes, broccoli, and cauliflower
- ✓ Starchy vegetables: Sweet potatoes with an orange flesh, yams, Nicola and Carisma potato varieties, and corn
- ✓ Legumes: Baked beans, kidney beans, lentils, butter beans, and chickpeas

- ✓ Noodles and pasta: Vermicelli noodles, pasta, rice noodles, and soba noodles
- ✓ Rice: Long-grain, basmati, brown rice, and Doongara
- ✓ Grains: Buckwheat, semolina, quinoa, freekeh, barley, and pearl couscous
- ✓ Dairy: Custard, almond milk, cheese, soy milk, yogurt, and milk

These foods don't have a GI value because they have zero or few carbs, and they can be added to a low-GI diet:

- ✓ Meat: Eggs, pork, beef, lamb, and chicken
- ✓ Seafood and fish: Salmon, tuna, prawns, sardines, and trout
- ✓ Nuts: Pistachios, macadamia nuts, almonds, walnuts, and cashews
- ✓ Oils and fats: Butter, margarine, olive oil, and rice bran oil
- ✓ Spices and herbs: Garlic, dill, salt, basil, and pepper

Use this GI search tool to find foods that aren't listed above.

2. What to Avoid

The low-GI diet doesn't prohibit eating any food.

Nevertheless, as often as you can, try to swap these high-GI foods with low-GI substitutes.

- ✓ Bread: Naan bread, Lebanese bread, white bread, French baguettes, Turkish bread, and bagels
- ✓ Breakfast cereals: Corn Flakes, Froot Loops, instant oats, Cocoa Krispies, and Rice Krispies
- ✓ Starchy vegetables: Instant mashed potatoes, Red Pontiac, and Désirée potatoes
- ✓ Noodles and pasta: Instant noodles and corn pasta
- ✓ Rice: Calrose, Jasmine, medium-grain white rice, and Arborio rice (typically used in risotto)
- ✓ Dairy replacements: Oat milk and rice milk
- ✓ Fruit: Watermelon

- ✓ Flavorful snacks: Rice cakes, corn chips, rice crackers, pretzels, and corn thins
- ✓ Biscuits and cakes: Cookies, pikelets, scones, waffles, doughnuts, and cupcakes
- ✓ Others: Gatorade, jelly beans, Lucozade, and licorice

3. *Healthy Snack Ideas for a Low-GI Diet*

Try these healthy and low-GI snacks when you go hungry in between meals:

- ✓ A handful of nuts (unsalted)
- ✓ Fruit
- ✓ Carrot sticks with hummus
- ✓ A cup of grapes or berries
- ✓ Greek yogurt
- ✓ Sliced apple with peanut butter or almond butter
- ✓ A hard-boiled egg
- ✓ Leftover foods from last night

To sum it up, the low-GI diet is all about eating foods with a low glycemic index and avoiding those with a high GI. Low-GI diets provide an array of health benefits such as weight loss, lower blood glucose levels, and reduced risk of type 2 diabetes and heart disease.

Finally, make sure to eat a healthy and balanced diet based on a selection of unprocessed and whole foods, notwithstanding their GI values.

Chapter 2: 365 Amazing Low-Glycemic Recipes

***

1. A Jerky Chicken

"This dish is native to Jamaica. The spicy combination of habanero pepper, herbs and vinegar make this chicken dish fantastic. You can serve along with rice!"

Servings: 4 | Prep: 1 m | Ready In: 1 h 15 m

Ingredients

- 1 tsp. onion, finely chopped
- 3 tbsps. brown sugar
- 4 tbsps. soy sauce
- 4 tbsps. red wine vinegar
- 2 tsps. chopped fresh thyme
- 1 tsp. sesame oil
- 3 cloves garlic, chopped
- 1/2 tsp. ground allspice
- 1 habanero pepper, sliced
- 4 skinless, boneless chicken breast halves - cut into 1 inch strips

Directions

- Into the container of a blender or food processor, mix onion, habanero pepper, brown sugar, garlic, soy sauce, allspice, sesame oil, vinegar and thyme and then process until the mixture is smooth. Transfer chicken to a large bag that is resealable and add 3/4 of the sauce. Remove excess air by squeezing and then seal. Place in a fridge for a minimum of one hour to marinate.
- Preheat the broiler of oven.
- Take out chicken from the bag and get rid of the marinade. Let the chicken to broil for about 10 to 15 minutes and flip once to cook evenly. Heat the sauce remaining in a pan and spread on top of chicken when serving.

Nutrition Information

- Nutritionist's Calories: 197 kcal 10%
- Total Fat: 2.7 g 4%
- Carbohydrates: 13.5g 4%
- Protein: 28.5 g 57%
- Cholesterol: 68 mg 23%
- Sodium: 982 mg 39%

2. Albino Pasta

"A wonderful pasta sauce!"

Servings: 8 | Prep: 15 m | Ready In: 25 m

Ingredients

- 1 (16 ounce) package dry penne pasta
- 4 tbsps. olive oil
- 1 tsp. minced garlic
- 1/3 c grated Parmesan cheese

Directions

- Bring to boil lightly salted water in a pot and add penne pasta. Cook until al dente or for about 8 to 10 minutes. Drain.
- Sauté garlic a little amount of oil in a saucepan. In a bowl, mix pasta, garlic and olive oil. Add parmesan cheese.

Nutrition Information

- Nutritionist's Calories: 275 kcal 14%
- Total Fat: 9 g 14%
- Carbohydrates: 41g 13%
- Protein: 8.8 g 18%
- Cholesterol: 3 mg < 1%
- Sodium: 54 mg 2%

3. Alison's Gluten-Free Bread

"This is delicious bread that is gluten-free."

Servings: 12

Ingredients

- 1 egg
- 1/3 c egg whites
- 1 tbsp. apple cider vinegar
- 1/4 c canola oil
- 1/4 c honey
- 1 1/2 c warm skim milk
- 1 tsp. salt
- 1 tbsp. xanthan gum
- 1/2 c tapioca flour
- 1/4 c garbanzo bean flour
- 1/4 c millet flour
- 1 c white rice flour
- 1 c brown rice flour
- 1 tbsp. active dry yeast

Directions

- In the pan of bread machine, put the ingredients by following the order recommended by manufacturer. Choose cycle and press Start. Check the dough consistency after 5 minutes into the cycle. Pour in more liquid or rice flour if need be.
- Once the bread is done, allow to cool for about 10 to 15 minutes prior to taking out from pan.

Nutrition Information

- Nutritionist's Calories: 225 kcal 11%
- Total Fat: 6 g 9%
- Carbohydrates: 38g 12%
- Protein: 5.2 g 10%
- Cholesterol: 16 mg 5%
- Sodium: 255 mg 10%

4. Amatriciana

"Authentic Italian pasta dish. When in season, add fresh basil and during off-season add fresh flat-leaf parsley."

Servings: 4 | Prep: 15 m | Ready In: 35 m

Ingredients

- 4 slices bacon, diced
- 1/2 c chopped onion
- 1 tsp. minced garlic
- 1/4 tsp. crushed red pepper flakes
- 2 (14.5 ounce) cans stewed tomatoes
- 1 pound linguine pasta, uncooked
- 1 tbsp. chopped fresh basil
- 2 tbsps. grated Parmesan cheese

Directions

- Over medium high heat, cook diced bacon for about 5 minutes in a saucepan until crisp. Drain off and reserve two tbsps. of the drippings from pan.
- Over medium heat, add onions and then allow to cook for about three minutes. Add red pepper flakes and garlic and then cook 30 seconds. Stir in canned tomatoes that are undrained and let to simmer for ten minutes to breaking up the tomatoes.
- In the meantime, in a pot containing four quarts of boiling salted water, cook pasta until al dente and drain.
- Mix basil into sauce and combine with the cooked pasta. You can serve together with grated Parmesan cheese.

Nutrition Information

- Nutritionist's Calories: 529 kcal 26%
- Total Fat: 7.5 g 12%

- Carbohydrates: 97.6g 31%
- Protein: 21.5 g 43%
- Cholesterol: 12 mg 4%
- Sodium: 702 mg 28%

5. Amazing Pork Tenderloin in the Slow Cooker

"A very delicious meal! When cooking, the pork tenderloin soak up the delicious juices. You can use the au jus on the side! Very easy recipe and you'll like it!"

Servings: 6 | Prep: 15 m | Ready In: 4 h 15 m

Ingredients

- 1 (2 pound) pork tenderloin
- 1 (1 ounce) envelope dry onion soup mix
- 1 c water
- 3/4 c red wine
- 3 tbsps. minced garlic
- 3 tbsps. soy sauce
- freshly ground black pepper to taste

Directions

- In a slow cooker, put pork tenderloin along with contents of soup packet. Add soy sauce, water and wine on top and flip the pork to coat. Gently, add garlic on top of pork and leave lots of them on roast's top when cooking. Drizzle pepper on top, cover and then let to cook for 4 hours on low setting. You can serve together with the cooking liquid on the side as au jus.

Nutrition Information

- Nutritionist's Calories: 180 kcal 9%
- Total Fat: 3.7 g 6%
- Carbohydrates: 5.8g 2%

- Protein: 24.5 g 49%
- Cholesterol: 65 mg 22%
- Sodium: 918 mg 37%

6. Amy's Spicy Beans and Rice

"This vegan dish is quick, simple and delicious and feel free to add sausage or chicken if desired!"

Servings: 6 | Prep: 5 m | Ready In: 45 m

Ingredients

- 1 1/2 c water
- 1/2 c uncooked brown rice
- 2 (15 ounce) cans black beans, undrained
- 2 fresh jalapeno peppers, seeded and chopped
- 1 tsp. ground cumin, or to taste
- 1 tbsp. chili powder, or to taste
- black pepper to taste
- 1/2 c shredded sharp Cheddar cheese
- 2 fresh green onions, chopped
- 1/2 (2 ounce) can sliced black olives, drained

Directions

- Preheat an oven to 175 degrees C (350 degrees F).
- Bring to boil water in a saucepan and stir in rice. Decrease the heat, cover the pan and allow to simmer for 40 minutes.
- In the meantime, transfer beans to a two quart casserole. Drizzle with black pepper, cumin, jalapenos, and chili powder.
- Bake for about 30 minutes. Drizzle with olives, cheese and green onions. Bake for about 5 to 10 more minutes.
- Serve the beans on top of the cooked rice.

Nutrition Information

- Nutritionist's Calories: 96 kcal 5%
- Total Fat: 4.3 g 7%
- Carbohydrates: 11.2g 4%
- Protein: 3.7 g 7%
- Cholesterol: 10 mg 3%
- Sodium: 114 mg 5%

7. Anaheim Fish Tacos

"I developed this for those who like sweet things. Fish tacos are my favorite and hate fried versions or cabbage. This isn't so good for kids since it's a little flavorful. You can serve together with sour cream, authentic Mexican cheese, lime, lettuce and fresh cilantro."

Servings: 6 | Prep: 15 m | Ready In: 45 m

Ingredients

- 1 tsp. vegetable oil
- 1 Anaheim chile pepper, chopped
- 1 leek, chopped
- 2 cloves garlic, crushed
- salt and pepper to taste
- 1 c chicken broth
- 2 large tomatoes, diced
- 1/2 tsp. ground cumin
- 1 1/2 pounds halibut fillets
- 1 lime
- 12 corn tortillas

Directions

- Over medium heat, heat oil in a skillet and then sauté garlic, chile and leek until browned lightly and tender. Add pepper and salt to taste.
- Into the skillet, combine tomatoes and chicken broth and then season using cumin. Heat to boil. Decrease the heat to low. Add halibut to

the mixture and drizzle lime juice on top. Allow to cook for about 15 to 20 minutes until halibut flakes easily with a fork. Use warmed corn tortillas to wrap and then serve.

Nutrition Information

- Nutritionist's Calories: 273 kcal 14%
- Total Fat: 5.1 g 8%
- Carbohydrates: 29.9g 10%
- Protein: 27.7 g 55%
- Cholesterol: 36 mg 12%
- Sodium: 286 mg 11%

8. Andouille and Chicken Creole Pasta

"Very spicy dish!!! This is for those who like it hot!! To make it spicier, add more cayenne pepper!"

Servings: 8 | Prep: 15 m | Ready In: 45 m

Ingredients

- 2 tbsps. margarine
- 1/2 pound andouille sausage, diced
- 2 skinless, boneless chicken breast halves - cut into strips
- 3 tbsps. Creole seasoning
- 1 green bell pepper, seeded and sliced into strips
- 1 red bell pepper, seeded and sliced into strips
- 8 ounces fresh mushrooms, sliced
- 4 green onions, chopped
- 1 (14.5 ounce) can fat-free chicken broth
- 1 c 2% milk
- 2 tsps. lemon pepper
- 2 tsps. garlic powder
- 1/4 c cornstarch
- 1/2 c cold water
- 1 (16 ounce) package linguine pasta

Directions

- Over medium-high heat, heat margarine in a skillet and stir in chicken along with Creole seasoning and sausage. Cook until meat is about halfway cooked. Pour in red pepper, mushrooms, green pepper and green onion. Over medium heat, sauté for about 10 minutes until mushrooms start to shrink.
- Add milk and chicken broth and then season with garlic powder and lemon pepper. Decrease the heat to medium-low. (At this time, start boiling water for pasta.) Combine cold water and cornstarch together until dissolved - I usually use a coffee mug. Mix into skillet. Let to cook while stirring slowly until sauce returns to a boil. Allow to boil for 1 minute, take out from the heat source and reserve. You can serve while hot on top of cooked pasta.
- In a pot of lightly salted water, add pasta and then let to boil for about 8 to 10 minutes or until the pasta becomes al dente and drain.

Nutrition Information

- Nutritionist's Calories: 410 kcal 20%
- Total Fat: 13.4 g 21%
- Carbohydrates: 51.5g 17%
- Protein: 21.6 g 43%
- Cholesterol: 36 mg 12%
- Sodium: 1059 mg 42%

9. Andrea's Pasta Fagioli

"My grandma's recipe that I have adapted. It is simple and great for a Sunday afternoon alongside fresh Italian bread."

Servings: 8 | Prep: 10 m | Ready In: 1 h 40 m

Ingredients

- 3 tbsps. olive oil
- 1 onion, quartered then halved
- 2 cloves garlic, minced
- 1 (29 ounce) can tomato sauce
- 5 1/2 c water
- 1 tbsp. dried parsley
- 1 1/2 tsps. dried basil
- 1 1/2 tsps. dried oregano
- 1 tsp. salt
- 1 (15 ounce) can cannellini beans
- 1 (15 ounce) can navy beans
- 1/3 c grated Parmesan cheese
- 1 pound ditalini pasta

Directions

- Over medium heat, cook onion in olive oil in a pot until translucent. Add garlic and then cook until tender. Decrease the heat and mix in basil, tomato sauce, navy beans, water, oregano, parsley, cannelini beans, salt and Parmesan. Let to simmer for one hour.
- Bring to boil lightly salted water in a pot and add pasta. Cook until al dente or for about 8 to 10 minutes. Drain and then mix into soup.

Nutrition Information

- Nutritionist's Calories: 403 kcal 20%
- Total Fat: 7.6 g 12%
- Carbohydrates: 68g 22%
- Protein: 16.3 g 33%
- Cholesterol: 3 mg < 1%
- Sodium: 1223 mg 49%

10. Angel's Pasta

"This is a simple vegan pasta entrée that is light and delicate!"

Ingredients

- 8 ounces angel hair pasta
- 1 tbsp. crushed garlic
- 1 tbsp. olive oil
- 2 zucchini, sliced
- salt and pepper to taste
- 3 tomatoes, chopped
- 12 leaves fresh basil
- 4 ounces mozzarella cheese, shredded

Directions

- Bring to boil lightly salted water in a pot and add pasta. Cook until al dente or for about 8 to 10 minutes and drain.
- In the meantime, over medium heat, heat a skillet and add oil. Sauté garlic until it's golden. Mix in pepper, zucchini and salt and then sauté for two minutes. Stir in tomato and then cook for several minutes. Cut basil and then add to the veggies right before combining with pasta.
- Mix the pasta and veggies. Top with mozzarella and serve.

Nutrition Information

- Nutritionist's Calories: 201 kcal 10%
- Total Fat: 6.6 g 10%
- Carbohydrates: 26.9g 9%
- Protein: 10.1 g 20%
- Cholesterol: 12 mg 4%
- Sodium: 202 mg 8%

Ingredients

- 1 (1 ounce) package dry onion soup mix
- 4 bone-in chicken breast halves, skinless
- 1 (.6 ounce) package cream of chicken soup mix
- 2 tbsps. soy sauce
- 2 cloves crushed garlic
- 1 c apple juice
- 1 c orange juice
- salt and pepper to taste

Directions

- Preheat an oven to 175 degrees C (350 degrees F).
- Into a baking dish that is lightly greased of 9x13 inch, put pieces of chicken.
- Mix soy sauce, onion soup mix, garlic, cream of chicken soup mix, pepper, salt and apple and orange juice in a bowl. Combine together and spread the mixture on top of chicken. Cover and then bake for one hour. Uncover and continue baking for 1/2 an hour to brown chicken.

Nutrition Information

- Nutritionist's Calories: 230 kcal 12%
- Total Fat: 2.7 g 4%
- Carbohydrates: 21.4g 7%
- Protein: 29.1 g 58%
- Cholesterol: 69 mg 23%
- Sodium: 1351 mg 54%

---

11. Apple and Orange Chicken

"This is a wonderful apple and orange chicken recipe!"

---

12. Apple Butter Pork Loin

"My favorite pork recipe. Pork that is seasoned with spiced apple butter and then roasted in apple juice. It's a perfect Sunday dish when served warm and cozy."

Ingredients

- 2 (2 pound) boneless pork loin roast
- seasoning salt to taste
- 2 c apple juice
- 1/2 c apple butter
- 1/4 c brown sugar
- 2 tbsps. water
- 1/4 tsp. ground cinnamon
- 1/4 tsp. ground cloves

Directions

- Preheat an oven to 175 degrees C (350 degrees F).
- Use seasoning salt to season pork loins and then transfer them to a small roasting pan or 9x13 inch baking dish. Add apple juice on top of pork and then use a lid or aluminum foil to cover the dish.
- Bake for one hour. As the pork roasts, combine together cloves, cinnamon, water, apple butter and brown sugar. Take out pork roasts from oven and smear with the mixture of apple butter.
- Cover and then bake for two hours or until fork-tender.

Nutrition Information

- Nutritionist's Calories: 607 kcal 30%
- Total Fat: 25.4 g 39%
- Carbohydrates: 25.7g 8%
- Protein: 64.9 g 130%
- Cholesterol: 194 mg 65%
- Sodium: 151 mg 6%

---

13. Apricot Lentil Soup

"This apricot lentil soup has a sweet-tangy twist. Perfect together with a slice of black bread that is warm and slathered with creamy butter."

Servings: 6 | Prep: 15 m | Ready In: 1 h 5 m

Ingredients

- 3 tbsps. olive oil
- 1 onion, chopped
- 2 cloves garlic, minced
- 1/3 c dried apricots
- 1 1/2 c red lentils
- 5 c chicken stock
- 3 roma (plum) tomatoes - peeled, seeded and chopped
- 1/2 tsp. ground cumin
- 1/2 tsp. dried thyme
- salt to taste
- ground black pepper to taste
- 2 tbsps. fresh lemon juice

Directions

- Sauté apricots, onion and garlic in olive oil. Stir in stock and lentils. Heat to boil, low the heat and allow to simmer for 30 minutes.
- Mix in tomatoes and season with pepper, salt, cumin and thyme. Allow to simmer for ten minutes.
- Add lemon juice. In a blender, puree half of the soup and return to pot and serve.

Nutrition Information

- Nutritionist's Calories: 263 kcal 13%
- Total Fat: 7.4 g 11%
- Carbohydrates: 37.2g 12%
- Protein: 13.2 g 26%
- Cholesterol: 0 mg 0%
- Sodium: 7 mg < 1%

14. Asian Carryout Noodles

"You can experiment this when you desire carry food on the go. You will receive lots of requests for this recipe."

Servings: 2 | Prep: 20 m | Ready In: 50 m

Ingredients

- 1 (8 ounce) package angel hair pasta
- 1 tsp. canola oil
- 1 tsp. sesame oil
- 1/2 onion, chopped
- 1 clove garlic, minced
- 1 skinless, boneless chicken breast half - cut into bite-size pieces
- 1 tbsp. grated fresh ginger
- 2 leaves bok choy, diced
- 1/4 c chicken broth
- 2 tbsps. dry sherry
- 1 tbsp. soy sauce
- 1 1/2 tbsps. hoisin sauce
- 1/8 tsp. salt
- 2 green onions, minced

Directions

- Cook angel hair pasta in a pot containing boiling salted water until al dente and then drain.
- In the meantime, over medium high heat, heat sesame oil and canola in a nonstick skillet and add garlic and onion. Sauté until softened. Add sliced chicken and then cook until the chicken turns brown and the juice flows clear. Add sherry, ginger, hoisin sauce, bok choy, chicken stock and soy sauce. Low the heat and continue to cook for ten minutes.
- Mix pasta together with the chicken mixture until coated well. Add salt to taste. Serve while warm topped with minced green onions.

Nutrition Information

- Nutritionist's Calories: 499 kcal 25%
- Total Fat: 9.2 g 14%
- Carbohydrates: 75.4g 24%
- Protein: 28.1 g 56%
- Cholesterol: 35 mg 12%
- Sodium: 1257 mg 50%

15. Asian Tuna Patties

"This is a tasty, quick and new way to enjoy tuna. Those who have had it have requested for the recipe."

Servings: 6 | Prep: 15 m | Ready In: 35 m

Ingredients

- 2 (5 ounce) cans tuna, drained and flaked
- 1 egg, beaten
- 3/4 c dry bread crumbs
- 3 green onions, minced
- 1 clove garlic, peeled and minced
- 1 tbsp. soy sauce
- 1 tbsp. teriyaki sauce
- 1 tbsp. ketchup
- 1 tsp. sesame oil
- 1 tsp. black pepper
- 1/2 c cornmeal
- 2 tbsps. vegetable oil

Directions

- Combine garlic, green onions, tuna, egg and bread crumbs in a bowl. Combine sesame oil, soy sauce, pepper, teriyaki sauce and ketchup into the mixture. Shape about 6 patties out of the mixture of about one inch thick. Drizzle cornmeal lightly onto each patty on all sides.
- Over medium heat, heat oil in a skillet and then fry every patty for approximately five minutes per side until golden brown.

Nutrition Information

- Nutritionist's Calories: 214 kcal 11%
- Total Fat: 7.5 g 11%
- Carbohydrates: 21.1g 7%
- Protein: 15 g 30%
- Cholesterol: 44 mg 15%
- Sodium: 427 mg 17%

16. Asparagus, Chicken and Penne Pasta

"A slightly spicy dish. Its tastes is different and fantastic!"

Servings: 8 | Prep: 15 m | Ready In: 35 m

Ingredients

- 1 (16 ounce) package dry penne pasta
- 2 tbsps. olive oil, divided
- 3/4 pound skinless, boneless chicken breast meat - cut into bite-size pieces
- 4 cloves garlic, minced
- 12 ounces asparagus, trimmed and cut into 1 inch pieces
- 1 tsp. crushed red pepper flakes
- salt and pepper to taste
- 1/2 c grated Parmesan cheese

Directions

- Bring to boil lightly salted water in a pot and add pasta. Cook until al dente or for about 8 to 10 minutes. Drain and place in a bowl.
- Over medium heat, heat one tbsp. of olive oil in a skillet and add chicken. Sauté until browned lightly and firm. Take out from the pan. Pour in a tbsp. of olive oil into skillet. Cook while stirring red pepper flakes, garlic and

asparagus in oil until the asparagus becomes tender. Add chicken and then cook for two minutes to blend flavors. Add pepper and salt.
- Combine the pasta together with chicken and asparagus mixture. Drizzle Parmesan cheese on top.

Nutrition Information

- Nutritionist's Calories: 311 kcal 16%
- Total Fat: 6.8 g 10%
- Carbohydrates: 43.2g 14%
- Protein: 20.3 g 41%
- Cholesterol: 29 mg 10%
- Sodium: 113 mg 5%

17. Aunt Jewel's Chicken Dressing Casserole

"This is a real Southern chicken and dressing casserole. My great-great-aunt used to make it and has been passed on to me. It's simple and tasty."

Servings: 12 | Prep: 15 m | Ready In: 1 h

Ingredients

- 3 pounds skinless, boneless chicken breast meat
- 1 (10.75 ounce) can condensed cream of chicken soup
- 1 (10.75 ounce) can condensed cream of celery soup
- 1 (10.75 ounce) can milk
- 1 1/2 c chicken broth
- 1 (6 ounce) package seasoned cornbread stuffing mix

Directions

- In a saucepan filled with lightly salted water, add chicken and heat to boil. Allow to boil for about 30 minutes or until the chicken becomes cooked through (the juice runs clear). Take out chicken from the pan and set aside the broth. Chop chicken into small pieces and transfer to a baking dish of 9x13 inch.

- Preheat an oven to 175 degrees C (350 degrees F).
- Combine cream of celery soup and cream of chicken soup together in a bowl. Into one empty soup can, add milk and then combine the milk with soups. Spread the mixture on top of chicken. Mix broth and stuffing in a bowl. Combine together and pour the mixture on top of casserole.
- Bake for about 45 minutes.

Nutrition Information

- Nutritionist's Calories: 236 kcal 12%
- Total Fat: 5.2 g 8%
- Carbohydrates: 15.8g 5%
- Protein: 29.5 g 59%
- Cholesterol: 73 mg 24%
- Sodium: 745 mg 30%

18. Autumn Apple Salad II

"This side dish is sweet, tart and crunchy and great in the fall."

Servings: 4 | Prep: 10 m | Ready In: 10 m

Ingredients

- 4 tart green apples, cored and chopped
- 1/4 c blanched slivered almonds, toasted
- 1/4 c dried cranberries
- 1/4 c chopped dried cherries
- 1 (8 ounce) container vanilla yogurt

Directions

- Combine together yogurt, cherries, almonds, apples and cranberries in a bowl until coated evenly.

Nutrition Information

- Nutritionist's Calories: 202 kcal 10%
- Total Fat: 4.1 g 6%
- Carbohydrates: 38.9g 13%
- Protein: 5.1 g 10%
- Cholesterol: 3 mg < 1%
- Sodium: 41 mg 2%

19. Awesome Broccoli Marinara

"An Italian side dish that is fast and used in our family. Feel free to add fresh basil and tomatoes. As a mom with four kids, I like the quick method and even other parents will like it. It's a favorite for the kids."

Servings: 4 | Prep: 5 m | Ready In: 25 m

Ingredients

- 2 tbsps. olive oil
- 1 (14.5 ounce) can diced tomatoes with balsamic vinegar, basil and olive oil
- 1 pound broccoli florets
- 2 cloves garlic, chopped
- salt and pepper to taste

Directions

- Over medium heat, heat olive oil in a skillet and add garlic. Cook for several minutes while stirring continuously. Add tomatoes along with their juices and allow to simmer until liquid reduces by about half. Put broccoli onto the tomatoes and add some salt and pepper to taste. Cover the skillet and allow to simmer at low heat for about ten minutes or until broccoli becomes tender. Avoid overcooking the broccoli, should look vibrant green. Transfer to a serving dish and stir to blend with sauce prior to serving.

Nutrition Information

- Nutritionist's Calories: 121 kcal 6%
- Total Fat: 7.2 g 11%
- Carbohydrates: 11.4g 4%
- Protein: 4.1 g 8%
- Cholesterol: 0 mg 0%
- Sodium: 197 mg 8%

20. Awesome Chicken and Yellow Rice Casserole

"For many generations, this Cuban inspired dish has been a favorite for the family. It made of chicken baked together with water chestnuts, onions and bell peppers. Makes a fantastic dish when added to prepared yellow rice!"

Servings: 8 | Prep: 30 m | Ready In: 2 h 15 m

Ingredients

- 1 medium onion, coarsely chopped
- 1 medium green bell pepper, coarsely chopped
- 1 (8 ounce) can water chestnuts, drained and chopped
- 2 tbsps. olive oil
- 1 whole chicken
- salt and pepper to taste
- seasoning salt to taste
- 1 (10 ounce) package yellow rice
- 1 (4 ounce) jar diced pimentos, drained

Directions

- Preheat an oven to 175 degrees C (350 degrees F).
- Mix green bell pepper, onion, water chestnuts and olive oil to coat in a Dutch oven. Brush chicken with seasoning salt, salt and pepper and spread on top of veggies in Dutch oven.
- Cover the oven and allow the chicken to cook for about 1 hour and 15 minutes or until the internal temperature is 85 degrees C (180 degrees F). Take out from heat and leaving veggies in Dutch oven. Take out the cooked chicken, let to cool, remove skin, debone and then shred the meat.
- As the chicken cooks, prepare yellow rice by following the package instructions.
- Combine the cooked rice and shredded chicken into Dutch oven containing the veggies. Return to 175 degrees C (350 degrees F) and continue to cook for 15 minutes prior to serving.

Nutrition Information

- Nutritionist's Calories: 353 kcal 18%
- Total Fat: 10.7 g 16%
- Carbohydrates: 32.8g 11%
- Protein: 30.8 g 62%
- Cholesterol: 85 mg 28%
- Sodium: 714 mg 29%

21. Baked Halibut Steaks

"This tasty baked halibut is topped with an Italian-style of vegetable and feta cheese."

Servings: 4 | Prep: 15 m | Ready In: 30 m

Ingredients

- 1 tsp. olive oil

- 1 c diced zucchini
- 1/2 c minced onion
- 1 clove garlic, peeled and minced
- 2 c diced fresh tomatoes
- 2 tbsps. chopped fresh basil
- 1/4 tsp. salt
- 1/4 tsp. ground black pepper
- 4 (6 ounce) halibut steaks
- 1/3 c crumbled feta cheese

Directions

- Preheat an oven to 230 degrees C (450 degrees F). Polish a baking dish lightly with grease.
- Over medium heat, heat olive oil in a saucepan and add garlic, zucchini and onion. Cook while stirring for five minutes or until tender. Take out the pan from the heat and add pepper, basil, tomatoes and salt.
- In the baking dish prepared, spread a single layer of halibut steaks. Add the same amounts of zucchini mixture onto each steak. Add feta cheese on top.
- Bake for about 15 minutes or until the fish flakes easily with a fork.

Nutrition Information

- Nutritionist's Calories: 259 kcal 13%
- Total Fat: 8 g 12%
- Carbohydrates: 6.7g 2%
- Protein: 38.5 g 77%
- Cholesterol: 66 mg 22%
- Sodium: 385 mg 15%

Ingredients

- 6 skinless, boneless chicken breast halves
- salt and pepper to taste
- 1/2 c honey
- 1/2 c prepared mustard
- 1 tsp. dried basil
- 1 tsp. paprika
- 1/2 tsp. dried parsley

Directions

- Preheat an oven to 175 degrees C (350 degrees F).
- Drizzle pepper and salt onto chicken breasts and transfer to a baking dish that is lightly greased of 9x13 inch. Mix well parsley, paprika, basil, honey and mustard in a small bowl. Spread half of this mixture on top of chicken and then polish to cover.
- Bake for about 30 minutes. Flip over the pieces of chicken and polish with the half of honey mustard mixture remaining. Bake for about 10 to 15 minutes or until the juice runs clear and the pink color of chicken disappears. Allow to cool for ten minutes prior to serving.

Nutrition Information

- Nutritionist's Calories: 232 kcal 12%
- Total Fat: 3.7 g 6%
- Carbohydrates: 24.8g 8%
- Protein: 25.6 g 51%
- Cholesterol: 67 mg 22%
- Sodium: 296 mg 12%

22. Baked Honey Mustard Chicken

"A fast and simple recipe and loved by kids!"

Servings: 6 | Prep: 15 m | Ready In: 1 h

23. Baked Sweet Potatoes

"These sweet potatoes are nutritious and delicious and perfect when added to any meal. Super simple!"

Servings: 4 | Prep: 10 m | Ready In: 1 h 15 m

Ingredients

- 2 tbsps. olive oil
- 3 large sweet potatoes
- 2 pinches dried oregano
- 2 pinches salt
- 2 pinches ground black pepper

Directions

- Preheat an oven to 175 degrees C (350 degrees F). Use olive oil to coat just enough bottom of a glass or non-stick baking dish.
- Clean and remove sweet potatoes skin. Chop into medium size pieces. Transfer the chopped sweet potatoes to the baking dish and roll to coat with olive oil. Moderately drizzle with pepper, salt and oregano.
- Bake for about 60 minutes at 175 degrees C (350 degrees F) or until soft.

Nutrition Information

- Nutritionist's Calories: 321 kcal 16%
- Total Fat: 7.3 g 11%
- Carbohydrates: 61g 20%
- Protein: 4.8 g 10%
- Cholesterol: 0 mg 0%
- Sodium: 92 mg 4%

24. Baked Tortilla Chips

"These are delicious homemade tortilla chips that are better compared to those bought in stores. You can serve alongside garnishes and salsas you like."

Servings: 6 | Prep: 10 m | Ready In: 25 m

Ingredients

- 1 (12 ounce) package corn tortillas
- 1 tbsp. vegetable oil
- 3 tbsps. lime juice
- 1 tsp. ground cumin
- 1 tsp. chili powder
- 1 tsp. salt

Directions

- Preheat an oven to 175 degrees C (350 degrees F).
- Chop every tortilla into 8 chip sized wedges and then spread a single layer of the wedges onto a cookie sheet.
- Mix lime juice and oil in a mister. Combine well and then spray every tortilla wedge until moist a little.
- In a bowl, mix salt, cumin and chili powder and drizzle onto the chips.
- Bake in oven for approximately seven minutes. Rotate pan and then continue baking for about 8 minutes or until chips become crispy and not too brown. Can serve together with guacamole, salsas and garnishes.

Nutrition Information

- Nutritionist's Calories: 147 kcal 7%
- Total Fat: 4.1 g 6%
- Carbohydrates: 26g 8%
- Protein: 3.3 g 7%
- Cholesterol: 0 mg 0%
- Sodium: 418 mg 17%

25. Barley and Mushrooms with Beans

"This vegan dish is easy and delicious. It's great as a side dish, meal or wrapped in tortilla together with cheese. I usually a lot and chill some."

Ingredients

- 1 tsp. olive oil
- 3 c sliced fresh mushrooms
- 1 c chopped onion
- 1/2 c chopped celery
- 2 cloves garlic, minced
- 1/2 c uncooked barley
- 3 c vegetable broth
- 1 (15.5 ounce) can white beans, drained

Directions

- Over medium heat, heat oil in a saucepan, mix in garlic, onion, celery and mushrooms and sauté until tender.
- Into the saucepan, combine vegetable broth and barley. Heat to boil, cover the pan and decrease the heat. Allow to simmer for about 45 to 50 minutes until the barley becomes tender.
- Add white beans to the mixture of barley and continue to cook for approximately five minutes until the beans are heated.

Nutrition Information

- Nutritionist's Calories: 202 kcal 10%
- Total Fat: 2.1 g 3%
- Carbohydrates: 39g 13%
- Protein: 9.1 g 18%
- Cholesterol: 0 mg 0%
- Sodium: 245 mg 10%

Ingredients

- 1 (8 ounce) package angel hair pasta
- 2 tsps. olive oil
- 1/2 c finely chopped onion
- 1 clove garlic, chopped
- 2 1/2 c chopped tomatoes
- 2 c boneless chicken breast halves, cooked and cubed
- 1/4 c chopped fresh basil
- 1/2 tsp. salt
- 1/8 tsp. hot pepper sauce
- 1/4 c Parmesan cheese

Directions

- Cook angel hair pasta in a pot containing salted boiling water for about 8 to 10 minutes until al dente. Drain and reserve.
- Over medium-high heat, heat oil in a skillet, add garlic and onions and then sauté. Add hot pepper sauce, basil, tomatoes, salt and chicken. Decrease the heat to medium and then cover the skillet. Allow to simmer for approximately five minutes while stirring occasionally until the tomatoes become soft and the mixture becomes hot.
- Combine the sauce together with the hot cooked angel hair pasta to coat. Add Parmesan cheese on top.

Nutrition Information

- Nutritionist's Calories: 362 kcal 18%
- Total Fat: 10.8 g 17%
- Carbohydrates: 37.8g 12%
- Protein: 28.4 g 57%
- Cholesterol: 57 mg 19%
- Sodium: 536 mg 21%

26. Basil Chicken over Angel Hair

"This is a delicious chicken and pasta dish."

*Servings: 4 | **Prep:** 15 m | **Ready In:** 35 m*

27. BBQ Chicken Salad

"A perfect way to make use of leftover of grilled chicken. Can serve over a layer of greens."

Servings: 4 | Prep: 15 m | Ready In: 50 m

Ingredients

- 2 skinless, boneless chicken breast halves
- 4 stalks celery, chopped
- 1 large red bell pepper, diced
- 1/2 red onion, diced
- 1 (8.75 ounce) can sweet corn, drained
- 1/4 c barbeque sauce
- 2 tbsps. fat-free mayonnaise

Directions

- Preheat the grill over high heat.
- Polish grate lightly with oil. Grill the chicken for about ten minutes per side or until the juice runs clear. Take out from the heat, allow to cool and then cube.
- Combine together corn, onion, chicken, celery and red bell pepper in a large bowl.
- Combine mayonnaise and barbeque sauce together in a small bowl. Spread on top of the chicken and vegetables. Toss and freeze until when ready to serve.

Nutrition Information

- Nutritionist's Calories: 168 kcal 8%
- Total Fat: 2.2 g 3%
- Carbohydrates: 23.6g 8%
- Protein: 14.7 g 29%
- Cholesterol: 34 mg 11%
- Sodium: 473 mg 19%

28. BBQ Chili Pasta

"If you love high flavor foods, pasta and barbecue, this recipe is for you. The dish is fast, simple to prepare and tasty. You will definitely like it. For variation, add wagon wheel pasta."

Servings: 6

Ingredients

- 1 (8 ounce) package rotini pasta
- 1 tbsp. olive oil
- 1 onion, chopped
- 8 ounces ground turkey
- 1 green bell pepper, chopped
- 1 (15 ounce) can whole kernel corn, drained
- 1 tbsp. chili powder
- 1 tbsp. dried oregano
- 1/2 tsp. salt
- 1 (8 ounce) can tomato sauce
- 3/4 c barbecue sauce

Directions

- Cook rotelle pasta in a pot containing boiling salted water until al dente and then drain.
- In the meantime, over medium-high heat, heat oil in a non-stick skillet and stir in onion. Cook for two minutes or until softened. Stir in ground turkey and then cook for 3 to 4 minutes until no longer pink. Add tomato sauce, chopped green bell pepper, dried oregano, corn, BBQ sauce, chili powder and salt. Heat the mixture to boil. Decrease the heat to medium and allow to simmer while stirring frequently for about 3 to 4 minutes until thickened slightly.
- Mix pasta with the turkey mixture in a large serving bowl and serve right away.

Nutrition Information

- Nutritionist's Calories: 340 kcal 17%

- Total Fat: 7.4 g 11%
- Carbohydrates: 57.5g 19%
- Protein: 14.4 g 29%
- Cholesterol: 29 mg 10%
- Sodium: 1000 mg 40%

29. Bean Quesadillas

"Simple and delicious! The recipe is made of beans, cheese and vegetables sandwiched in tortillas. Feel free to add or replace the veggies you prefer. You can serve together with rice and sour cream."

Servings: 12 | Prep: 15 m | Ready In: 45 m

Ingredients

- 1 tbsp. vegetable oil
- 1 onion, finely diced
- 2 cloves garlic, minced
- 1 (15 ounce) can black beans, rinsed and drained
- 1 green bell pepper, chopped
- 2 tomatoes, chopped
- 1/2 (10 ounce) package frozen corn
- 12 (12 inch) flour tortillas
- 1 c shredded Cheddar cheese
- 1/4 c vegetable oil

Directions

- Over medium heat, heat one tbsp. of oil in a skillet, stir in garlic and onion and then sauté until soft. Add corn, tomatoes, beans and bell pepper and cook until the ingredients are heated through.
- Arrange six tortillas with the same amounts of the mixture of bean and vegetable. Drizzle the same amounts of Cheddar cheese and place the tortillas remaining on top to form quesadillas.
- Over medium-high heat, heat 1/4 c of oil in a skillet and add quesadillas. Cook and flip once

until the both sides turn brown lightly and cheese has melted.

Nutrition Information

- Nutritionist's Calories: 504 kcal 25%
- Total Fat: 18.3 g 28%
- Carbohydrates: 69.7g 22%
- Protein: 14.7 g 29%
- Cholesterol: 10 mg 3%
- Sodium: 913 mg 37%

30. Beef Tips and Noodles

"A simple meal that is great and uses a few ingredients. Works well with rolls of any kind. My mom passed this recipe to me and it's liked by the family."

Servings: 8 | Prep: 10 m | Ready In: 1 h 15 m

Ingredients

- 1 pound sirloin tips, cubed
- 1 (10.75 ounce) can condensed cream of mushroom soup
- 1 (1.25 ounce) package beef with onion soup mix
- 1 (4.5 ounce) can mushrooms, drained
- 1 c water
- 1 (16 ounce) package wide egg noodles

Directions

- Preheat an oven to 200 degrees C (400 degrees F).
- Mix canned mushrooms, water, mushroom and beef onion soups in a casserole dish of 13x9 inch. Combine well and stir in beef tips. Flip to coat thoroughly.
- Bake for one hour in oven.
- As the beef tips bake, bring to boil lightly salted water in a pot and add pasta. Cook until al

dente or for about 8 to 10 minutes and drain. You can serve the beef tips and sauce on top of noodles.

Nutrition Information

- Nutritionist's Calories: 314 kcal 16%
- Total Fat: 8.8 g 14%
- Carbohydrates: 41.1g 13%
- Protein: 17.4 g 35%
- Cholesterol: 65 mg 22%
- Sodium: 673 mg 27%

31. Beer Chops I

"I got this recipe from my mother. It's a good, simple and slow cooked recipe."

Servings: 4 | Prep: 10 m | Ready In: 8 h 10 m

Ingredients

- 1 onion, sliced
- 2 pork chops butterfly cut
- 1 (12 fluid ounce) can or bottle beer
- 2 cubes chicken bouillon

Directions

- At the bottom of the slow-cooker, spread slices of onion. Slice butterfly chops in half and spread over onions. Add beer and then cubes of chicken bouillon. Cover and allow to cook for about 6 to 8 hours on low.

Nutrition Information

- Nutritionist's Calories: 112 kcal 6%

- Total Fat: 3.3 g 5%
- Carbohydrates: 6.5g 2%
- Protein: 7.9 g 16%
- Cholesterol: 19 mg 6%
- Sodium: 591 mg 24%

32. Best Black Beans

"A simple side dish for black beans that is great with Cuban and Mexican meals."

Servings: 4 | Prep: 10 m | Ready In: 15 m

Ingredients

- 1 (16 ounce) can black beans
- 1 small onion, chopped
- 1 clove garlic, chopped
- 1 tbsp. chopped fresh cilantro
- 1/4 tsp. cayenne pepper
- salt to taste

Directions

- Mix garlic, beans and onion in a saucepan and heat to boil. Decrease the heat to medium-low. Add salt, cilantro and cayenne to taste. Allow to simmer for about five minutes and then serve.

Nutrition Information

- Nutritionist's Calories: 112 kcal 6%
- Total Fat: 0.4 g < 1%
- Carbohydrates: 20.8g 7%
- Protein: 7.1 g 14%
- Cholesterol: 0 mg 0%
- Sodium: 510 mg 20%

33. Better Slow Cooker Robust Chicken

"This is a combo of nice flavors that blend to form a lovely rich sauce for chicken! For a feast, you can serve together with focaccia and a simple green salad!"

Servings: *6* | ***Prep:*** *5 m* | ***Ready In:*** *8 h 5 m*

Ingredients

- 1 1/2 pounds skinless, boneless chicken breast halves - cut into 1 inch strips
- 2 tbsps. bacon bits
- 1/4 c chopped green olives
- 1 (14.5 ounce) can diced tomatoes, drained
- 1 (4.5 ounce) can sliced mushrooms, drained
- 1 (1.25 ounce) envelope dry chicken gravy mix
- 1/2 c red wine
- 3 tbsps. Dijon mustard
- 1/4 c balsamic vinegar

Directions

- Mix together mushrooms, chicken, wine, bacon bits, vinegar, olives, tomatoes, mustard and gravy mix in a slow cooker.
- Cover the slow cooker and then cook for 6 to 8 hours on Low setting.

Nutrition Information

- Nutritionist's Calories: 198 kcal 10%
- Total Fat: 4.7 g 7%
- Carbohydrates: 10.1g 3%
- Protein: 24.5 g 49%
- Cholesterol: 62 mg 21%
- Sodium: 946 mg 38%

34. Black Bean and Corn Pasta with Chicken

"This is a nice fast dinner that is great for summer corn leftovers. You can get a c of kernels from two ears of corn. Add shredded cheese on top."

Servings: *8* | ***Prep:*** *5 m* | ***Ready In:*** *20 m*

Ingredients

- 1 (16 ounce) package jumbo pasta shells
- 1 c fresh corn kernels
- 1 (15 ounce) can black beans, rinsed and drained
- 1 (14.5 ounce) can diced tomatoes with juice
- salt and pepper to taste
- 1 dash hot pepper sauce
- 1 dash Worcestershire sauce
- 2 boneless chicken breast halves, cooked and cut into bite-sized pieces

Directions

- Bring to boil lightly salted water in a pot and add pasta. Cook until al dente or for about 8 to 10 minutes and drain.
- Over low heat, cook black beans and corn for two minutes in a skillet. Add in tomatoes and reserve their juice and stir. Add pepper and salt to taste and then cook for two more minutes. Cover with some tomato juice and then season with Worcestershire and hot pepper sauce. Raise the heat a little, add in chicken and stir and then heat through for about 3 to 5 minutes. Pour on top of cooked pasta.

Nutrition Information

- Nutritionist's Calories: 341 kcal 17%
- Total Fat: 3.3 g 5%
- Carbohydrates: 57.7g 19%
- Protein: 19.2 g 38%
- Cholesterol: 21 mg 7%

- Sodium: 309 mg 12%

- Carbohydrates: 49.5g 16%
- Protein: 11.7 g 23%
- Cholesterol: 0 mg 0%
- Sodium: 1084 mg 43%

35. Black Bean and Corn Salad I

"A nice easy salad that is perfect as a main course when served with cornbread or tortillas or great for potlucks. You can add sweet red peppers only or combine sweet and hot peppers depending on what you family loves. Chills well for a few days."

Servings: 6 | Prep: 15 m | Ready In: 12 h 15 m

Ingredients

- 1/2 c balsamic vinaigrette salad dressing
- 1/4 tsp. seasoned pepper
- 1/4 tsp. dried cilantro
- 1/8 tsp. ground cayenne pepper
- 1/4 tsp. ground cumin
- 2 (15 ounce) cans black beans, rinsed and drained
- 2 (15 ounce) cans whole kernel corn, drained
- 1/2 c chopped onion
- 1/2 c chopped green onions
- 1/2 c red bell pepper, chopped

Directions

- Combine together cilantro, vinaigrette, cumin, seasoned pepper and cayenne pepper in a small bowl. Reserve the dressing.
- Combine together red bell pepper, beans, onion, corn and green onions in a large bowl. Combine with the dressing. Cover the bowl and chill overnight. Combine again prior to serving.

Nutrition Information

- Nutritionist's Calories: 304 kcal 15%
- Total Fat: 8.5 g 13%

36. Black Bean and Salsa Soup

"I developed this soup when in a hurry on one night. It is super easy and ready in about five minutes."

Servings: 4 | Prep: 10 m | Ready In: 20 m

Ingredients

- 2 (15 ounce) cans black beans, drained and rinsed
- 1 1/2 c vegetable broth
- 1 c chunky salsa
- 1 tsp. ground cumin
- 4 tbsps. sour cream
- 2 tbsps. thinly sliced green onion

Directions

- Mix cumin, salsa, beans and broth in a blender or electric food processor and then blend until the mixture is fairly smooth.
- Over medium heat, heat bean mixture in a saucepan until heated thoroughly.
- Spoon the soup into four individual bowls and add half tbsp. of green onion and one tbsp. of the sour cream onto each bowl.

Nutrition Information

- Nutritionist's Calories: 240 kcal 12%
- Total Fat: 5 g 8%
- Carbohydrates: 34.5g 11%
- Protein: 13.3 g 27%
- Cholesterol: 6 mg 2%
- Sodium: 1216 mg 49%

37. Black Bean Chili

"This chili is perfect when made with fresh veggies but it's also tasty with frozen or canned ones. You can serve on top of rice or as a whole meal."

Servings: 8 | Prep: 20 m | Ready In: 40 m

Ingredients

- 1 tbsp. olive oil
- 1 onion, chopped
- 2 red bell pepper, seeded and chopped
- 1 jalapeno pepper, seeded and minced
- 10 fresh mushrooms, quartered
- 6 roma (plum) tomatoes, diced
- 1 c fresh corn kernels
- 1 tsp. ground black pepper
- 1 tsp. ground cumin
- 1 tbsp. chili powder
- 2 (15 ounce) cans black beans, drained and rinsed
- 1 1/2 c chicken broth or vegetable broth
- 1 tsp. salt

Directions

- Over medium-high heat, heat oil in a saucepan. Sauté tomatoes, onion, red bell peppers, mushrooms, corn and jalapeno for about 10 minutes or until onions become translucent. Season with chili powder, cumin and black pepper. Add in salt, vegetable or chicken broth and black beans and stir. Heat to boil.
- Decrease the heat to medium low. Into a blender or food processor, add 1 1/2 c of the soup and then puree. Mix bean mixture back into soup. Can serve while hot alone or on top of rice.

Nutrition Information

- Nutritionist's Calories: 164 kcal 8%
- Total Fat: 2.8 g 4%
- Carbohydrates: 28g 9%
- Protein: 9 g 18%
- Cholesterol: < 1 mg < 1%
- Sodium: 897 mg 36%

38. Black Bean Salsa

"This salsa is lovely!! Contains onion, corn, black beans and tomatoes. I find it difficult making enough for a party!! If time allows, refrigerate for 24 hours prior to serving!! You can serve together with tortilla chips."

Servings: 40 | Prep: 15 m | Ready In: 8 h 15 m

Ingredients

- 3 (15 ounce) cans black beans, drained and rinsed
- 1 (11 ounce) can Mexican-style corn, drained
- 2 (10 ounce) cans diced tomatoes with green chile peppers, partially drained
- 2 tomatoes, diced
- 2 bunches green onions, chopped
- cilantro leaves, for garnish

Directions

- Combine together green onion stalks, black beans, Mexican-style corn, tomatoes and diced tomatoes along with green chile peppers in a large bowl. Decorate with the amount of cilantro leaves desired. Refrigerate for a minimum of 8 hours or overnight prior to serving.

Nutrition Information

- Nutritionist's Calories: 42 kcal 2%
- Total Fat: 0.2 g < 1%
- Carbohydrates: 8.3g 3%
- Protein: 2.5 g 5%
- Cholesterol: 0 mg 0%
- Sodium: 207 mg 8%

Nutrition Information

- Nutritionist's Calories: 272 kcal 14%
- Total Fat: 3.4 g 5%
- Carbohydrates: 48.5g 16%
- Protein: 12.5 g 25%
- Cholesterol: 0 mg 0%
- Sodium: 870 mg 35%

39. Black-Eyed Pea Gumbo

"My family loves this winter dish. We normally make it for New Year's Day and watch football! Can be served with corn bread and a tossed salad."

Servings: 8 | Prep: 15 m | Ready In: 1 h 10 m

Ingredients

- 1 tbsp. olive oil
- 1 medium onion, chopped
- 1 medium green bell pepper, chopped
- 5 stalks celery, chopped
- 2 c chicken broth
- 1 c brown rice
- 4 (15 ounce) cans black-eyed peas with liquid
- 1 (10 ounce) can diced tomatoes and green chiles
- 1 (14.5 ounce) can diced tomatoes
- 2 cloves garlic, finely chopped

Directions

- Over medium heat, heat olive oil in a saucepan and add celery, onion and pepper. Cook until tender. Add chicken broth and stir in garlic, rice, diced tomatoes, black-eyed peas with liquid and diced tomatoes and green chiles. Heat to boil, decrease the heat to low and allow to simmer for about 45 minutes or until the rice becomes tender. In case the soup is too thick, add water.

40. Black-Eyed Pea Salad

"A salad that works well with barbeque and great for New Year's Day."

Servings: 8 | Prep: 30 m | Ready In: 8 h 30 m

Ingredients

- 2 (15.5 ounce) cans black-eyed peas
- 1 large tomato, chopped
- 1 medium red bell pepper, chopped
- 1 medium green bell pepper, chopped
- 1/2 red onion, diced
- 1 stalk celery, chopped
- 1 tbsp. chopped fresh parsley
- 3 tbsps. balsamic vinegar
- 2 tbsps. olive oil
- salt and pepper to taste

Directions

- Combine together green bell pepper, black-eyed peas, celery, tomato, parsley, red bell pepper and red onion in a medium bowl.
- Combine olive oil and balsamic vinegar in a small bowl. Add pepper and salt to taste. Mix into the veggies. Cover the bowl and refrigerate for 8 hours or overnight.

Nutrition Information

- Nutritionist's Calories: 132 kcal 7%
- Total Fat: 4.1 g 6%
- Carbohydrates: 19g 6%
- Protein: 5.8 g 12%
- Cholesterol: 0 mg 0%
- Sodium: 478 mg 19%

41. Boston Baked Beans

"This baked bean flavor recipe is old-fashioned. It's my mother-in-law's recipe and has been made for many years in our family. The dish tastes awesome with honey and biscuits or fresh cornbread. It's a simple recipe and you need time for soaking and simmering the beans."

Servings: 6 | Prep: 30 m | Ready In: 5 h

Ingredients

- 2 c navy beans
- 1/2 pound bacon
- 1 onion, finely diced
- 3 tbsps. molasses
- 2 tsps. salt
- 1/4 tsp. ground black pepper
- 1/4 tsp. dry mustard
- 1/2 c ketchup
- 1 tbsp. Worcestershire sauce
- 1/4 c brown sugar

Directions

- Soak the beans in cold water overnight. Allow the beans to simmer in the same water for about 1 to 2 hours until tender. Drain and set the liquid aside.
- Preheat an oven to 165 degrees C (325 degrees F).
- Into a 2 quart casserole dish or bean pot, spread the beans by putting some of beans at the bottom of the dish and then lay them together with onion and bacon.
- Mix brown sugar, molasses, Worcestershire sauce, salt, ketchup, pepper and dry mustard in a saucepan. Heat the mixture to boil and spread on top of beans. Add plenty of the bean water reserved to cover beans. Use aluminum foil or lid to cover dish.
- Bake for about 3 to 4 hours until the beans become tender. Uncover about halfway through cooking and pour in extra liquid if need be to keep beans from getting too dry.

Nutrition Information

- Nutritionist's Calories: 382 kcal 19%
- Total Fat: 6.3 g 10%
- Carbohydrates: 63.1g 20%
- Protein: 20.7 g 41%
- Cholesterol: 14 mg 5%
- Sodium: 1320 mg 53%

42. Bourbon Chicken

"This dish is named after the Bourbon Street in New Orleans in the state of Louisiana and the bourbon whiskey. Currently the dish is bought as Cajun-style cuisine across America and it's not a genuine Cajun or Creole! Ensure chicken remains a single layer when doubling the recipe."

Servings: 4

Ingredients

- 4 skinless, boneless chicken breast halves
- 1 tsp. ground ginger
- 4 ounces soy sauce
- 2 tbsps. dried minced onion
- 1/2 c packed brown sugar
- 3/8 c bourbon
- 1/2 tsp. garlic powder

Directions

- Into a baking dish of 9x13 inch, put chicken breasts. Mix garlic powder, ginger, bourbon, soy sauce, sugar and onion flakes in a small bowl. Combine together and then spread the mixture on top of chicken. Cover the dish and transfer to a fridge to marinate overnight.
- Preheat an oven to 165 degrees C (325 degrees F).
- Take out the dish from the fridge and uncover. Bake for about 1 ½ hours while basting occasionally or until the chicken browns well and the juice runs clear.

Nutrition Information

- Nutritionist's Calories: 313 kcal 16%
- Total Fat: 1.5 g 2%
- Carbohydrates: 31.2g 10%
- Protein: 29.3 g 59%
- Cholesterol: 68 mg 23%
- Sodium: 1664 mg 67%

---

43. Bow Tie Tuna Florentine

"This tuna meal is authentic. It's a pesto sauce containing tuna, spinach and bow tie pasta. For a classy meal, you can serve alongside wine and warm French bread."

Servings: 4 | Prep: 15 m | Ready In: 50 m

Ingredients

- 1 (8 ounce) package farfalle (bow tie) pasta
- 1 tbsp. margarine
- 1 1/4 c milk
- 1 (1.2 ounce) package creamy pesto sauce mix
- 2 c fresh spinach, rinsed and thinly sliced
- 1/2 c sliced fresh mushrooms
- 3 (5 ounce) cans tuna, drained

- 3 roma (plum) tomatoes, chopped

Directions

- Bring to boil lightly salted water in a pot and add pasta. Cook until al dente or for about 8 to 10 minutes and drain.
- Over medium-high heat, heat margarine in a large saucepan and then stir in pesto sauce mix and milk. Heat to boil while stirring continuously using a wire whisk until boiling and blended well. Decrease the heat and stir in mushrooms and spinach. Allow to simmer for about 3 to 4 minutes while stirring frequently.
- Pour in tomatoes, tuna and cooked pasta and stir slowly to coat. Allow to cook for about 3 to 5 minutes until heated thoroughly.

Nutrition Information

- Nutritionist's Calories: 437 kcal 22%
- Total Fat: 7.6 g 12%
- Carbohydrates: 53.4g 17%
- Protein: 37 g 74%
- Cholesterol: 34 mg 11%
- Sodium: 664 mg 27%

---

44. Braised Balsamic Chicken

"Chicken that is great with pasta or rice. The green beans make it a lovely side dish."

Servings: 6 | Prep: 10 m | Ready In: 35 m

Ingredients

- 6 skinless, boneless chicken breast halves
- 1 tsp. garlic salt
- ground black pepper to taste
- 2 tbsps. olive oil
- 1 onion, thinly sliced

- 1 (14.5 ounce) can diced tomatoes
- 1/2 c balsamic vinegar
- 1 tsp. dried basil
- 1 tsp. dried oregano
- 1 tsp. dried rosemary
- 1/2 tsp. dried thyme

Directions

- Use pepper and garlic salt to season each side of chicken breasts.
- Over medium heat, heat olive oil in a skillet and then cook the seasoned chicken breasts for 3 to 4 minutes on each side until the chicken turns brown. Stir in onion and then cook while stirring for 3 to 4 minutes until the onion turns brown.
- Spread balsamic vinegar and diced tomatoes on top of chicken. Add thyme, rosemary, basil, and oregano. Allow to simmer for about 15 minutes until no pink color remains of chicken and juice runs clear. The internal temperature should be at least 74 degrees C (165 degrees F).

Nutrition Information

- Nutritionist's Calories: 196 kcal 10%
- Total Fat: 7 g 11%
- Carbohydrates: 7.6g 2%
- Protein: 23.8 g 48%
- Cholesterol: 61 mg 20%
- Sodium: 511 mg 20%

45.Brazilian Black Bean Stew

"You can make this simple and nice stew any time you want. You can omit meat without interfering with the dish. Can serve while still hot along with spinach salad and bread."

Servings: 6 | Prep: 15 m | Ready In: 45 m

Ingredients

- 1 tbsp. canola oil
- 1/4 pound chorizo sausage, chopped
- 1/3 pound cooked ham, chopped
- 1 medium onion, chopped
- 2 cloves garlic, minced
- 2 (1 pound) sweet potatoes, peeled and diced
- 1 large red bell pepper, diced
- 2 (14.5 ounce) cans diced tomatoes with juice
- 1 small hot green chile pepper, diced
- 1 1/2 c water
- 2 (16 ounce) cans black beans, rinsed and drained
- 1 mango - peeled, seeded and diced
- 1/4 c chopped fresh cilantro
- 1/4 tsp. salt

Directions

- Over medium heat, heat the oil in a pot and then cook ham and chorizo for about 2 to 3 minutes. Add onion and then cook until tender. Mix in garlic and then cook until tender. Stir in chile pepper, sweet potatoes, water, bell pepper and tomatoes along with juice. Heat to boil, decrease the heat to low, cover the pot and allow to simmer for about 15 minutes until the sweet potatoes become tender.
- Mix beans to pot and then cook without covering until heated through. Stir in cilantro and mango and then add salt to taste.

Nutrition Information

- Nutritionist's Calories: 508 kcal 25%
- Total Fat: 15 g 23%
- Carbohydrates: 70.7g 23%
- Protein: 22.8 g 46%
- Cholesterol: 31 mg 10%
- Sodium: 1538 mg 62%

46. Broccoli Beef II

"This is a nice homemade dish that resembles a take-out. Strips of beef are marinated fast and sautéed with mushrooms and broccoli in a nutritious sauce."

***Servings:** 4 | **Prep:** 15 m | **Ready In:** 1 h*

Ingredients

- 2 tbsps. low-sodium soy sauce
- 2 tbsps. fat-free Italian dressing
- 1 tsp. cornstarch
- 1 tbsp. minced garlic
- 1 tsp. ground ginger
- 3/4 pound round steak, cut into strips
- 6 c water
- 5 cubes beef bouillon
- 4 ounces linguine pasta, uncooked
- 1/2 c fat free beef broth
- 1 c fresh mushrooms, sliced
- 1/2 c sliced green onion
- 1 pound broccoli, separated into florets

Directions

- Combine together ginger, soy sauce, garlic, Italian dressing and cornstarch in a shallow bowl or glass dish. Transfer the steak strips to the mixture for 15 minutes to marinate.
- As the beef marinates, in a saucepan, mix bouillon cubes in water. Heat to boil and then stir in pasta. Cook until al dente or for about 8 minutes and drain.
- Over medium-high heat, heat a skillet. Use a slotted spoon to take out the beef from the marinade and transfer to the hot skillet. Get rid of marinade. Cook the beef while stirring continuously for about 2 to 3 minutes or until it's mostly browned. Add green onions, beef broth and mushrooms and stir. Decrease the heat to medium-low, cover the skillet and

allow to simmer for approximately five minutes. Uncover, stir in broccoli and let to cook until the broccoli becomes bright green and tender but crispy. Pour in the drained linguine, mix and then serve.

Nutrition Information

- Nutritionist's Calories: 303 kcal 15%
- Total Fat: 7.1 g 11%
- Carbohydrates: 35.1g 11%
- Protein: 26.4 g 53%
- Cholesterol: 46 mg 15%
- Sodium: 1533 mg 61%

47. Burgundy Pork Tenderloin

"My hubby has no taste for pork but likes this dish. The dish is super simple to make and has a rich taste. Can be served along with baked potato."

***Servings:** 4 | **Prep:** 30 m | **Ready In:** 1 h 30 m*

Ingredients

- 2 pounds pork tenderloin
- 1/2 tsp. salt
- 1/2 tsp. ground black pepper
- 1/2 tsp. garlic powder
- 1/2 onion, thinly sliced
- 1 stalk celery, chopped
- 2 c red wine
- 1 (.75 ounce) packet dry brown gravy mix

Directions

- Preheat an oven to 175 degrees C (350 degrees F).
- Transfer pork to a baking dish of 9x13 inch and drizzle garlic powder, pepper and salt on

meat. Add celery and onion on top and add wine over all.

- Bake for about 45 minutes in oven.
- Once done with baking, take out the meat from the baking dish and transfer to a serving platter. Into the baking dish containing cooking juices and wine, add gravy mix and mix until thickened. Chop meat and then cover with gravy.

Nutrition Information

- Nutritionist's Calories: 400 kcal 20%
- Total Fat: 8.6 g 13%
- Carbohydrates: 8.2g 3%
- Protein: 47.8 g 96%
- Cholesterol: 148 mg 49%
- Sodium: 676 mg 27%

48.Busy Night Turkey Taco Soup with Avocado Cream

"Tex-Me meals are loved by my family. I like fast, versatile and nutritious meals and this soup suits my needs. Since the flavors combine nicely, nobody believes that the recipe simmers for a short while. You can combine green chiles with sour cream in case guacamole isn't available. You can serve together with tortilla chips!"

Servings: 4 | Prep: 10 m | Ready In: 30 m

Ingredients

- 1 (11 ounce) can Mexican-style corn
- 1 (16 ounce) can chili beans, undrained
- 2 (14.5 ounce) cans chicken broth
- 1 (16 ounce) jar chunky salsa
- 2 1/2 c cooked, chopped turkey meat
- salt and pepper to taste
- 1/4 c chopped fresh cilantro
- 1/2 c low-fat sour cream
- 2 tbsps. guacamole

Directions

- Over medium heat, mix salsa, broth, corn and chili beans in a large pot. Heat to boil, decrease the heat and add cooked turkey. Add pepper and salt to taste. Cover the pot and let to cook for about 5 to 10 minutes until heated through. Add cilantro and stir.
- Combine guacamole and sour cream together in a bowl until smooth.
- Spoon soup into bowls and add guacamole mixture on top.

Nutrition Information

- Nutritionist's Calories: 382 kcal 19%
- Total Fat: 10.2 g 16%
- Carbohydrates: 42.9g 14%
- Protein: 36.3 g 73%
- Cholesterol: 79 mg 26%
- Sodium: 1518 mg 61%

49.Butternut Squash Pizzas with Rosemary

"This is a very delicious dish!"

Servings: 4 | Prep: 20 m | Ready In: 50 m

Ingredients

- 1 c thinly sliced onion
- 1/2 butternut squash - peeled, seeded, and thinly sliced
- 1 tsp. chopped fresh rosemary
- salt and black pepper to taste
- 3 tbsps. olive oil, divided
- 1 (16 ounce) package refrigerated pizza crust dough, divided
- 1 tbsp. cornmeal

- 2 tbsps. grated Asiago or Parmesan cheese

Directions

- Preheat an oven to 205 degrees C (400 degrees F). In a roasting pan, put chopped onion and squash. Drizzle with 2 tbsps. of olive oil, rosemary, salt and pepper. Stir to coat.
- Bake for about 20 minutes or until the squash becomes tender and onions become browned lightly. Reserve.
- Raise the temperature of oven to 230 degrees C (450 degrees F). Roll each dough ball on a floured surface into an 8 inch round. Transfer the rounds to a baking sheet drizzled with cornmeal (may require two baking sheets but depends on their size). Spread the mixture of squash on top of the 2 rounds and continue to bake for about 10 minutes, keep checking frequently, or until crust becomes firm. Drizzle cheese and one tbsp. of olive oil. Chop into quarters and then serve.

Nutrition Information

- Nutritionist's Calories: 567 kcal 28%
- Total Fat: 13.7 g 21%
- Carbohydrates: 96.9g 31%
- Protein: 14.8 g 30%
- Cholesterol: 3 mg 1%
- Sodium: 948 mg 38%

---

50. Cajun Pasta Fresca

"I love this pasta dish! A recipe for those who like pasta and something with a little kick!"

Servings: 8 | Prep: 5 m | Ready In: 25 m

Ingredients

- 1 pound vermicelli pasta
- 2 tbsps. olive oil
- 1 tsp. minced garlic
- 13 roma (plum) tomatoes, chopped
- 1 tbsp. salt
- 1 tbsp. chopped fresh parsley
- 1 tbsp. Cajun seasoning
- 1/2 c shredded mozzarella cheese
- 1/2 c grated Parmesan cheese

Directions

- Bring to boil lightly salted water in a pot and add pasta. Cook until al dente or for about 8 to 10 minutes. Drain.
- As the pasta water boils, over medium heat, briefly sauté garlic in oil in a skillet. Mix in tomatoes along with their juice and drizzle with salt. Use a fork to mash the tomatoes slightly when they become bubbly. Add parsley, stir, low the heat and let to simmer for five minutes.
- Mix the hot pasta together with Cajun seasoning, tomato sauce, Parmesan and mozzarella.

Nutrition Information

- Nutritionist's Calories: 294 kcal 15%
- Total Fat: 7.5 g 12%
- Carbohydrates: 46.2g 15%
- Protein: 12.2 g 24%
- Cholesterol: 9 mg 3%
- Sodium: 1178 mg 47%

---

51. Cajun Style Baked Sweet Potato

"Try this recipe if you're tired of the old baked sweet potato. The sweet potatoes are herb and spice mixture and

perfect for barbecues and picnics."

Servings: 4 | Prep: 10 m | Ready In: 1 h 10 m

Ingredients

- 1 1/2 tsps. paprika
- 1 tsp. brown sugar
- 1/4 tsp. black pepper
- 1/4 tsp. onion powder
- 1/4 tsp. dried thyme
- 1/4 tsp. dried rosemary
- 1/4 tsp. garlic powder
- 1/8 tsp. cayenne pepper
- 2 large sweet potatoes
- 1 1/2 tsps. olive oil

Directions

- Preheat an oven to 190 degrees C (375 degrees F).
- Combine together paprika, onion powder, brown sugar, rosemary, black pepper, cayenne pepper, garlic powder and thyme in a small bowl.
- Chop sweet potatoes lengthwise in half. Use olive oil to rub each half. Brush seasoning mix onto the cut surface of every half. Transfer the sweet potatoes to a shallow pan or a baking sheet.
- Bake for about one hour until tender.

Nutrition Information

- Nutritionist's Calories: 229 kcal 11%
- Total Fat: 2.3 g 3%
- Carbohydrates: 49.1g 16%
- Protein: 4.8 g 10%
- Cholesterol: 0 mg 0%
- Sodium: 83 mg 3%

52. Carib Black Bean Soup

"This soup is creamy and has Caribbean flavor. Tips of Uncle Bill: in case you're adding canned beans, decrease time for cooking 40 minutes when you add the beans. For a unique flavor, add 2 (7.5 ounce) cans of flaked ham. When you add broth to the cooking pot, you can then add ham."

Servings: 12

Ingredients

- 2 1/2 c dry black beans
- 6 c water
- 3 tbsps. olive oil
- 2 onions, chopped
- 3 cloves garlic, chopped
- 6 stalks celery, chopped, with leaves
- 2 c water
- 8 c chicken broth
- 1/2 tsp. ground cayenne pepper
- 1 1/2 tsps. ground cumin
- 2 tbsps. balsamic vinegar
- 1/4 c sherry
- 1 tbsp. soy sauce
- 1/2 tsp. ground black pepper
- 1/4 c sour cream
- 1/4 c chopped green onions

Directions

- Pour six c of water and dried black beans in a medium-size stock pot, cover the pot and allow to soak overnight.
- Heat olive oil in a separate large stock pot and add sliced celery, onion and minced garlic Sauté until the veggies become soft.
- Drain the soaked beans and then rinse. Stir drained and rinsed canned beans or pre-soaked beans into the vegetable mixture and add broth and two c of water. Heat to boil, low the heat and allow to simmer.
- Pour in ground cumin and cayenne pepper. Cover the pot partially and allow to simmer

for about 2 to 2 ½ hours at low heat or until the beans become soft.

- In a blender or food processor, puree the soup in batches. Take back the pureed soup into the stock pot and let to simmer.
- Stir in pepper, vinegar, soy sauce and sherry. Serve while still hot together with a dollop of yogurt or sour cream and sliced green onions.

Nutrition Information

- Nutritionist's Calories: 199 kcal 10%
- Total Fat: 5.1 g 8%
- Carbohydrates: 29.6g 10%
- Protein: 9.5 g 19%
- Cholesterol: 2 mg <1%
- Sodium: 128 mg 5%

53. Carol's Chicken Chili

"This is a great white chili dish made of beans, onion, chicken breast and chile peppers. It's is great recipe for cold nights. You can serve together with a salad and crusty French bread. Season as desired (others like it spicier.)"

Servings: 6 | Prep: 5 m | Ready In: 35 m

Ingredients

- 1 tbsp. olive oil
- 6 skinless, boneless chicken breast halves - chopped
- 1 c chopped onion
- 1 1/2 c chicken broth
- 1 (4 ounce) can chopped green chile peppers
- 1 tsp. garlic powder
- 1 tsp. ground cumin
- 1/2 tsp. dried oregano
- 1/2 tsp. dried cilantro
- 1/8 tsp. crushed red pepper
- 2 (19 ounce) cans cannellini beans, drained and rinsed

- 2 green onions, chopped
- 3/4 c shredded Monterey Jack cheese

Directions

- Over medium high heat, heat oil in a pot and add onion and chicken. Sauté for about 4 to 5 minutes. Mix in cilantro, cumin, broth, chile peppers, red pepper, garlic powder and oregano. Decrease the heat to low and allow to simmer for about 15 minutes.
- Add beans, stir and allow to simmer for about 10 minutes. Add green onion and cheese on top and then serve.

Nutrition Information

- Nutritionist's Calories: 447 kcal 22%
- Total Fat: 11.1 g 17%
- Carbohydrates: 43g 14%
- Protein: 43.8 g 88%
- Cholesterol: 86 mg 29%
- Sodium: 608 mg 24%

54. Carrie's Garlic Pesto Tuna Salad Sandwiches

"Making different tuna sandwiches is my thing. I served this to my hubby for lunch and he want this again for dinner that same day! I never measured anything when making this dish and you can adjust the ingredients to suit your taste."

Servings: 4 | Prep: 10 m | Ready In: 10 m

Ingredients

- 2 (5 ounce) cans tuna in water, drained
- 2 tbsps. mayonnaise
- 1 tbsp. prepared mustard
- 2 tbsps. basil pesto

- 2 cloves garlic, minced
- 8 slices rye bread
- 8 leaves lettuce
- 1 large ripe tomato, sliced

Directions

- Combine together garlic, pesto, tuna, mayonnaise and mustard in a medium bowl.
- Form 4 sandwiches by layering slices of tomato, tuna and lettuce in between bread slices and serve.

Nutrition Information

- Nutritionist's Calories: 342 kcal 17%
- Total Fat: 11.9 g 18%
- Carbohydrates: 34.6g 11%
- Protein: 23.8 g 48%
- Cholesterol: 24 mg 8%
- Sodium: 600 mg 24%

55. Catherine's Spicy Chicken Soup

"A wonderful recipe that you can adjust to suit your taste. It becomes better the longer it simmers. Add shredded cheese and crushed tortilla chips on top."

Servings: 8 | Prep: 15 m | Ready In: 45 m

Ingredients

- 2 quarts water
- 8 skinless, boneless chicken breast halves
- 1/2 tsp. salt
- 1 tsp. ground black pepper
- 1 tsp. garlic powder
- 2 tbsps. dried parsley
- 1 tbsp. onion powder
- 5 cubes chicken bouillon
- 3 tbsps. olive oil

- 1 onion, chopped
- 3 cloves garlic, chopped
- 1 (16 ounce) jar chunky salsa
- 2 (14.5 ounce) cans peeled and diced tomatoes
- 1 (14.5 ounce) can whole peeled tomatoes
- 1 (10.75 ounce) can condensed tomato soup
- 3 tbsps. chili powder
- 1 (15 ounce) can whole kernel corn, drained
- 2 (16 ounce) cans chili beans, undrained
- 1 (8 ounce) container sour cream

Directions

- Over medium heat, mix bouillon cubes, water, chicken, onion powder, salt, pepper, parsley and garlic powder in a large pot. Heat to boil, decrease heat and allow to simmer for one hour or until the chicken juice runs clear. Take out the chicken and set broth aside. Shred the chicken.
- Over medium heat, cook garlic and onion in olive oil in a pot until browned slightly. Mix in chili powder, salsa, chili beans, diced tomatoes, 5 c of broth, whole tomatoes, corn, sour cream, shredded chicken and tomato soup. Allow to simmer for about 30 minutes.

Nutrition Information

- Nutritionist's Calories: 473 kcal 24%
- Total Fat: 15.3 g 24%
- Carbohydrates: 50.3g 16%
- Protein: 39.6 g 79%
- Cholesterol: 82 mg 27%
- Sodium: 2436 mg 97%

56. Cavatelli and Broccoli

"A fast meal to prepare. You can serve together with garlic bread."

Servings: 12 | Prep: 10 m | Ready In: 35 m

Ingredients

- 3 heads fresh broccoli, cut into florets
- 1/2 c olive oil
- 3 cloves garlic, minced
- 1 1/2 pounds cavatelli pasta
- 1 tsp. salt
- 1 tsp. crushed red pepper flakes
- 2 tbsps. grated Parmesan cheese

Directions

- Blanch broccoli in a pot containing boiling water for about five minutes. Drain broccoli and reserve.
- Over medium heat, heat olive oil in a skillet, add garlic and sauté until golden a little and take care not to burn it. Stir in the broccoli. Sauté while stirring frequently for approximately ten minutes. The broccoli should be crispy when bitten and tender.
- In the meantime, in a pot containing boiling salted water, cook cavatelli until al dente or for about 8 to 10 minutes. Drain and transfer to a serving bowl. Combine with broccoli and then add hot pepper flakes and salt to taste. Top with parmesan cheese and serve.

Nutrition Information

- Nutritionist's Calories: 317 kcal 16%
- Total Fat: 10.3 g 16%
- Carbohydrates: 47.6g 15%
- Protein: 10.2 g 20%
- Cholesterol: < 1 mg < 1%
- Sodium: 234 mg 9%

---

57. Ceviche

"A Mexican recipe. Lime juice cooks raw seafood!

Nobody would know that seafood isn't cooked when serving. You should use fresh ingredients in this recipe! Feel free to replace scallops with other types of seafood such as swordfish, flounder, halibut or red snapper."

Servings: 4 | Prep: 20 m | Ready In: 8 h 20 m

Ingredients

- 1 pound bay scallops
- 8 limes, juiced
- 2 tomatoes, diced
- 5 green onions, minced
- 2 stalks celery, sliced
- 1/2 green bell pepper, minced
- 1/2 c chopped fresh parsley
- freshly ground black pepper
- 1 1/2 tbsps. olive oil
- 1/8 c chopped fresh cilantro

Directions

- Transfer rinsed scallops to a medium sized bowl. Add lime juice on top of scallops. Lime juice should cover the scallops completely. Refrigerate the scallops and lime juice overnight or the whole until the scallops become opaque (light doesn't pass through them).
- Remove half of lime juice from bowl. Stir in cilantro, tomatoes, green bell pepper, green onions, olive oil, black pepper, celery and parsley to the scallop mixture. Combine slowly. You can transfer to fancy glasses along with a piece of lime hanging on the rim and then serve.

Nutrition Information

- Nutritionist's Calories: 211 kcal 11%
- Total Fat: 6.5 g 10%
- Carbohydrates: 22.4g 7%
- Protein: 21.4 g 43%
- Cholesterol: 37 mg 12%

- Sodium: 213 mg 9%

58. Cheesy Tuna Noodle Casserole

"I loved this casserole when I was a kid and it's a family favorite. Currently, I usually double the recipe to feed my family. For variation, you can add 1/8 tsp. of cayenne and canned chopped green chilies, add pasta shells or spirals or add chopped cheddar or American cheese on top instead of adding breadcrumbs."

Servings: 6 | Prep: 10 m | Ready In: 1 h 5 m

Ingredients

- 1 (12 ounce) package egg noodles
- 2 tbsps. vegetable oil
- 1/4 c chopped onion
- 1/4 c chopped green bell pepper
- 1/4 c red bell pepper, chopped
- 1 (11 ounce) can condensed cream of Cheddar cheese soup
- 1 (5 ounce) can tuna, drained
- 1/4 c milk
- 1/4 tsp. salt
- ground black pepper to taste
- 1/4 c Italian seasoned bread crumbs

Directions

- Preheat an oven to 175 degrees C (350 degrees F).
- Bring to boil salted water to boil in a pot and stir in noodles. Heat to boil again. Let to cook until al dente and then drain thoroughly.
- As the noodles cook, sauté green and red bell peppers, onion and vegetable oil in a saucepan until tender.
- Into the saucepan, add tuna, soup, milk, black pepper and salt. Over medium-low heat, combine thoroughly.
- Roll noodles into saucepan.

- Transfer the whole mixture to a casserole of two quart. Drizzle bread crumbs on top of the mixture. Bake for about 20 to 30 minutes or until top turns golden brown and crispy.

Nutrition Information

- Nutritionist's Calories: 373 kcal 19%
- Total Fat: 12 g 18%
- Carbohydrates: 49.4g 16%
- Protein: 16.7 g 33%
- Cholesterol: 66 mg 22%
- Sodium: 600 mg 24%

59. Chicken and Broccoli Pasta

"This tomato-garlic sauce is tasty and made with broccoli and boneless chicken. Add pasta you love- shells and penne work great."

Servings: 8 | Prep: 10 m | Ready In: 20 m

Ingredients

- 3 tbsps. olive oil
- 1 pound skinless, boneless chicken breast halves - cut into 1 inch pieces
- 1 tbsp. chopped onion
- 2 cloves garlic, chopped
- 2 (14 5 ounce) cans diced tomatoes
- 2 c fresh broccoli florets
- salt and pepper to taste
- 1 pinch dried oregano
- 18 ounces dry penne pasta
- 1/4 c fresh basil leaves, cut into thin strips
- 2 tbsps. grated Parmesan cheese

Directions

- Over medium heat, warm oil in a skillet and stir in chicken. Cook until browned a little. Stir in garlic and onion and let to cook for approximately five minutes or until the onions become translucent and garlic turns golden.

- Stir in oregano, pepper, salt, tomatoes and broccoli. Combine well and heat to boil. Cover the skillet and reduce the heat to simmer for approximately 10 minutes.
- In the meantime, bring to boil lightly salted water in a pot and add pasta. Let to cook for about 8 to 10 minutes or until tender. Drain and return to the pot. Into the pot, add chicken sauce and then combine thoroughly.
- Add basil and mix thoroughly. Top with Parmesan cheese and serve.

Nutrition Information

- Nutritionist's Calories: 368 kcal 18%
- Total Fat: 7.7 g 12%
- Carbohydrates: 51g 16%
- Protein: 23.5 g 47%
- Cholesterol: 34 mg 11%
- Sodium: 296 mg 12%

60.Chicken and Corn Chili

"This simple meal is slow cooked and adjust the seasoning as you wish. Perfect for cold winter nights! You can serve this meal together with flour tortillas, chopped cilantro, sour cream, grated cheese and green onions on the side."

Servings: 6 | Prep: 15 m | Ready In: 12 h 15 m

Ingredients

- 4 skinless, boneless chicken breast halves
- 1 (16 ounce) jar salsa
- 2 tsps. garlic powder
- 1 tsp. ground cumin
- 1 tsp. chili powder
- salt to taste
- ground black pepper to taste

- 1 (11 ounce) can Mexican-style corn
- 1 (15 ounce) can pinto beans

Directions

- Into a slow cooker, put salsa and chicken the night before you wish to enjoy this chili. Season with pepper, salt, cumin, garlic powder and chili powder. Let to cook on Low setting for about 6 to 8 hours.
- Use two forks to shred chicken in around 3 to 4 hours before serve. Take back the meat to pot and continue to cook.
- Into the slow cooker, mix the pinto beans and corn and let to simmer until when serving.

Nutrition Information

- Nutritionist's Calories: 188 kcal 9%
- Total Fat: 2.3 g 4%
- Carbohydrates: 22.6g 7%
- Protein: 20.4 g 41%
- Cholesterol: 41 mg 14%
- Sodium: 1012 mg 40%

61. Chicken and Red Wine Sauce

"This delicious dish is made with paprika, red wine sauce, garlic, brown sugar, pepper and salt. These braised chicken breasts have a very good taste."

Servings: 12 | Prep: 10 m | Ready In: 55 m

Ingredients

- 1 tbsp. olive oil
- 1 tbsp. minced garlic
- 3 pounds skinless, boneless chicken breast halves

- 1 tbsp. paprika
- 1 c brown sugar
- 1 c red wine
- salt and pepper to taste

Directions

- Over medium high heat, heat oil in a skillet, add garlic and cook until tender. Transfer chicken to the skillet and let it cook for approximately 10 minutes per side until the juice runs clear and no pink color remains.
- Drain off oil from the skillet. Drizzle one c of brown sugar and paprika onto the chicken. Spread red wine over the chicken. Cover and let to simmer for approximately 15 to 20 minutes while basting the chicken lightly with the wine sauce as you cook. Add pepper and salt to taste.

Nutrition Information

- Nutritionist's Calories: 214 kcal 11%
- Total Fat: 3.5 g 5%
- Carbohydrates: 19g 6%
- Protein: 22.2 g 44%
- Cholesterol: 59 mg 20%
- Sodium: 248 mg 10%

62. Chicken and Sausage with Bowties

"I developed this recipe due to the long hours I often travelled to work. My 2 teenage boys need a nice meal that can keep them for a minimum of 1 hour or less. You can add pork Italian sausage if desired but cook longer or use veal or pork cutlets or cubes and make sure to cook thoroughly. Omit pasta, serve as a sandwich, combine with cooked rice leftovers and pour in some broccoli and green peas. I'm sure everything will work well!"

Servings: 8 | Prep: 15 m | Ready In: 1 h

Ingredients

- 1 (16 ounce) package uncooked farfalle pasta
- 2 skinless, boneless chicken breasts
- 1 pound hot Italian turkey sausage, casings removed
- 1 tbsp. olive oil
- 2 cloves garlic, sliced
- 1 (14.5 ounce) can crushed tomatoes
- 1/2 c red wine
- 2 tbsps. chopped fresh basil
- 1 tsp. dried rosemary

Directions

- Bring to boil lightly salted water in a pot and add pasta. Cook until al dente or for about 8 to 10 minutes and then drain.
- Clean chicken breasts and then chop into large pieces. Slice sausages into large sizes. Over medium low heat, mix garlic and oil in a deep skillet and then cook for a while enough to flavor oil. Take out garlic from the oil.
- Into the skillet, pour in sausage and chicken and then lightly brown both of them until they become opaque. Pour in wine and tomatoes. Heat to boil and allow to simmer for around 20 minutes. Add pepper, salt, basil and rosemary to the sauce mixture. Transfer the cooked and drained pasta to the mixture in skillet. Mix and then serve.

Nutrition Information

- Nutritionist's Calories: 382 kcal 19%
- Total Fat: 9.1 g 14%
- Carbohydrates: 47.6g 15%
- Protein: 24 g 48%
- Cholesterol: 51 mg 17%
- Sodium: 526 mg 21%

63. Chicken Chili Soup

"A delicious soup that is great on a cold day."

Servings: 18 | Prep: 30 m | Ready In: 1 h

Ingredients

- 1 3/4 pounds diced chicken breast meat
- 2 green bell peppers, diced
- 2 red bell peppers, diced
- 1 onion, diced
- 1/2 c frozen corn kernels
- 4 (15 ounce) cans kidney beans with liquid
- 2 (14.5 ounce) cans diced tomatoes
- 1 (15 ounce) can tomato sauce
- 2 c water
- 2 tsps. chili powder
- 1 tbsp. dried parsley
- 1 tsp. garlic powder
- 1/2 tsp. ground cayenne pepper
- 1/2 tsp. ground cumin

Directions

- Use cooking spray to coat a large pot and then put it on a medium-high heat. Cook while stirring onion, chicken and bell peppers until the peppers become just tender and the chicken turns brown. Mix in tomato sauce, corn, tomatoes, water and beans. Add cumin, chili powder, cayenne, parsley and garlic powder to taste. Low the heat, cover the pot and let to simmer for 30 minutes.

Nutrition Information

- Nutritionist's Calories: 160 kcal 8%
- Total Fat: 1.1 g 2%
- Carbohydrates: 21g 7%
- Protein: 16.5 g 33%
- Cholesterol: 26 mg 9%

64. Chicken Costa Brava

"A dish inspired by cuisine of the Spain's Costa Brava region that blends the sweet tropical pineapple flavors and the saltiness of olives. You can serve on top rice."

Servings: 10

Ingredients

- 1 (20 ounce) can pineapple chunks
- 10 skinless, boneless chicken breast halves
- 1 tbsp. vegetable oil
- 1 tsp. ground cumin
- 1 tsp. ground cinnamon
- 2 cloves garlic, minced
- 1 onions, quartered
- 1 (14.5 ounce) can stewed tomatoes
- 2 c black olives
- 1/2 c salsa
- 2 tbsps. cornstarch
- 2 tbsps. water
- 1 red bell pepper, thinly sliced
- salt to taste

Directions

- Drain off pineapple and set the juice aside. Drizzle some salt.
- Brown chicken in oil in a frying pan. Mix cinnamon and cumin and then drizzle on top of chicken. Pour in onion and garlic and then cook until the onion becomes soft. Pour in the reserved pineapple juice, salsa, olives and tomatoes. Cover the pan and allow to simmer for 25 minutes.
- Combine cornstarch together with water and then mix into the pan juices. Pour in bell pepper and let to simmer until the sauce

becomes thick and boils. Add in pineapple chunks, stir and then heat through.

Nutrition Information

- Nutritionist's Calories: 239 kcal 12%
- Total Fat: 6.1 g 9%
- Carbohydrates: 17.6g 6%
- Protein: 28.6 g 57%
- Cholesterol: 68 mg 23%
- Sodium: 495 mg 20%

---

65. Chicken Creole

"This creole is delicious and simple!"

Servings: 4

Ingredients

- 1 tbsp. olive oil
- 1 clove garlic, minced
- 1 onion, thinly sliced
- 1 stalk celery, sliced thin
- 1 green bell pepper, minced
- 2 (16 ounce) cans diced tomatoes
- 1 bay leaf
- 1/2 tsp. salt
- 1/8 tsp. cayenne pepper
- 4 skinless, boneless chicken breasts

Directions

- Preheat an oven to 175 degrees C (350 degrees F).
- Over medium heat, heat oil in a skillet. Pour in bell pepper, celery, onion and garlic. Cook while stirring at intervals for about 4 minutes until tender. Pour in cayenne pepper, salt, tomatoes and bay leaf. Let this Creole sauce to

cook for three 3 minutes longer as you stirring occasionally.
- Into a baking dish of 8x11 inch, spread the chicken breasts. Add Creole sauce on top of chicken.
- Bake for about 15 to 20 minutes until chicken becomes tender and is white all over.

Nutrition Information

- Nutritionist's Calories: 225 kcal 11%
- Total Fat: 4.9 g 8%
- Carbohydrates: 11.8g 4%
- Protein: 29.7 g 59%
- Cholesterol: 68 mg 23%
- Sodium: 901 mg 36%

---

66. Chicken, Feta Cheese, and Sun-Dried Tomato Wraps

"You can easily adjust the ingredients in this recipe to suit your needs. Cook in the grill to make a simple summertime treat. Use the oven in the winter. The end product is just similar to that of a restaurant!"

Servings: 4 | Prep: 15 m | Ready In: 3 h 45 m

Ingredients

- 2 (4 ounce) skinless, boneless chicken breast halves
- 1/4 c sun-dried tomato dressing
- 8 sun-dried tomatoes (not oil packed)
- 1 c boiling water
- 1/3 c crumbled feta cheese
- 4 c loosely packed torn fresh spinach
- 4 (10 inch) whole wheat tortillas
- 1/4 c sun-dried tomato dressing

Directions

- Mix 1/4 c of dressing and chicken breasts in a large plastic bag that is resealable. Seal and then chill for a few hours.
- Preheat the grill over high heat. In a small bowl, mix hot water and sun-dried tomatoes. Reserve for about 10 minutes, then drain and chop the tomatoes into thin pieces.
- Polish grill grate lightly with oil. Get rid of the marinade and put the chicken onto the grill. Let it cook for about 12 to 15 minutes, flip once, or until cooked.
- Chop the chicken into strips and then transfer to a medium bowl containing spinach, feta and chopped tomatoes. Mix with the 1/4 c of dressing remaining. Subdivide the mixture into 4 tortillas and then wrap. You can chop in ½ and serve cold or put on the grill for a short while until tortilla become crispy and warm.

Nutrition Information

- Nutritionist's Calories: 324 kcal 16%
- Total Fat: 14.2 g 22%
- Carbohydrates: 34.1g 11%
- Protein: 20.7 g 41%
- Cholesterol: 44 mg 15%
- Sodium: 902 mg 36%

67. Chicken Fiesta Salad

"This dish is both zesty and attractive. Contains chicken, vegetables and rich with flavor. It's fast to make. Add tortilla chips and shredded cheese on top if desired."

Servings: 4 | Prep: 10 m | Ready In: 40 m

Ingredients

- 2 skinless, boneless chicken breast halves

- 1 (1.27 ounce) packet dry fajita seasoning, divided
- 1 tbsp. vegetable oil
- 1 (15 ounce) can black beans, rinsed and drained
- 1 (11 ounce) can Mexican-style corn
- 1/2 c salsa
- 1 (10 ounce) package mixed salad greens
- 1 onion, chopped
- 1 tomato, cut into wedges

Directions

- Use 1/2 of the fajita seasoning to brush chicken evenly. Over medium heat, heat oil in a skillet and then cook chicken for about 8 minutes per side or until the juice runs clear. Reserve.
- Combine the other 1/2 of fajita seasoning, salsa, beans and corn in a large saucepan. Over medium heat, heat until the contents are warm.
- Make salad by mixing tomato, greens and onion. Add chicken on top of salad and then dress with the mixture of bean and corn.

Nutrition Information

- Nutritionist's Calories: 311 kcal 16%
- Total Fat: 6.4 g 10%
- Carbohydrates: 42.2g 14%
- Protein: 23 g 46%
- Cholesterol: 36 mg 12%
- Sodium: 1606 mg 64%

68. Chicken in a Pot

"You just need one skillet to make this dish. Fast, simple and tasty. The combo of chicken broth and tomato paste form a delicious sauce. Add fresh parsley for decoration."

Servings: 4 | Prep: 20 m | Ready In: 40 m

Ingredients

- 3/4 c chicken broth
- 1 1/2 tbsps. tomato paste
- 1/4 tsp. ground black pepper
- 1/2 tsp. dried oregano
- 1/8 tsp. salt
- 1 clove garlic, minced
- 4 boneless, skinless chicken breast halves
- 3 tbsps. dry bread crumbs
- 2 tsps. olive oil
- 2 c fresh sliced mushrooms

Directions

- Mix garlic, oregano, salt, broth, tomato paste and ground black pepper in a medium bowl. Combine well and reserve.
- Into bread crumbs, dredge chicken and coat well. Over medium high heat, heat oil in a large skillet and then sauté the chicken for about two minutes on each side or until browned lightly.
- Pour mushrooms and the broth mixture reserved into skillet and heat to boil. Cover the skillet, decrease the heat to low and let to simmer for about 20 minutes. Take out the chicken, reserve and cover to keep it warm.
- Bring to boil the broth mixture and let to cook for four minutes or until it reaches the thickness desired. Pour the sauce on top of chicken and then serve.

Nutrition Information

- Nutritionist's Calories: 206 kcal 10%
- Total Fat: 6.6 g 10%
- Carbohydrates: 6.9g 2%
- Protein: 28.7 g 57%
- Cholesterol: 73 mg 24%
- Sodium: 402 mg 16%

69. Chicken Marinade

"This grilled chicken recipe is unique due to addition of sherry. It has an Asian flair."

Servings: 4 | Prep: 15 m | Ready In: 4 h 30 m

Ingredients

- 1 c soy sauce
- 1/2 c vegetable oil
- 1 tbsp. cooking sherry
- 3 tbsps. brown sugar
- 3 cloves garlic, crushed
- 4 boneless, skinless chicken breast halves

Directions

- Combine garlic, sherry, soy sauce, brown sugar and vegetable oil in a medium bowl. Transfer to a large bag that is resealable. Add chicken to bag and then shake to coat. Place in a fridge to marinate for a minimum of 4 hours.
- Preheat the outdoor grill over high heat and polish grate lightly with oil.
- Onto the grill prepared, put chicken. Let it cook for about 6 to 8 minutes per side or until the juice runs clear and no pink remains. Get rid of the marinade remaining.

Nutrition Information

70. Chicken Pasta I

"This is a different way to serve veggies, pasta and chicken. It's tasty and low in calories and fat. Feel free to add pasta you like. We prefer using mostaccioli pasta. If desired, pour in the vegetables you like."

Servings: 8 | Prep: 30 m | Ready In: 45 m

Ingredients

- 3 c mostaccioli
- 3 skinless, boneless chicken breast halves
- 1/4 onion, chopped
- 3 fresh mushrooms, sliced
- 2 tbsps. Italian seasoning
- 1 (14.5 ounce) can diced tomatoes
- salt and pepper to taste
- 2 tbsps. grated Parmesan cheese

Directions

- Bring to boil lightly salted water in a pot and add pasta. Cook until al dente or for about 8 to 10 minutes. Drain and then set aside.
- In the meantime, over medium heat, cook chicken for 15 minutes in a lightly greased skillet and take out from the pan. Let to cool and then dice.
- Over medium heat, mix Italian seasoning, onion, mushrooms, pepper, salt and tomatoes along with juice in a large skillet. Cook until the onions become translucent. Take out from the heat source and pour in pasta and chicken. Top with Parmesan cheese and serve.

Nutrition Information

- Nutritionist's Calories: 185 kcal 9%
- Total Fat: 1.8 g 3%
- Carbohydrates: 26.1g 8%
- Protein: 15.7 g 31%
- Cholesterol: 27 mg 9%
- Sodium: 165 mg 7%

71. Chicken Pepper Steak

"This recipe is made of chicken breast that is simmered with spices, soy sauce, tomatoes, onion and bell pepper. It's then served together with pepper steak style gravy. You can use chicken in case you love the taste of pepper steak but dislike red meat."

*Servings: 4 | **Prep:** 15 m | **Ready In:** 45 m*

Ingredients

- 1 tbsp. vegetable oil
- 4 boneless, skinless chicken breasts
- 1 tsp. seasoning salt
- 1/2 tsp. onion powder
- 2 tsps. minced garlic
- 1/2 c soy sauce, divided
- 1 large onion, cut into long slices
- 2 tbsps. cornstarch
- 2 1/2 c water
- 1 green bell pepper, sliced
- 4 roma (plum) tomatoes, seeded and chopped

Directions

- Over medium heat, heat oil in a large skillet. Season the chicken using onion powder and salt and then transfer to the skillet. Let to cook for around 5 to 7 minutes before adding half of the chopped onion, garlic and 4 tbsps. of soy sauce. Let to cook until the juice runs clear and no pink color remains.
- In a small bowl, dissolve cornstarch in water and them combine with chicken mixture. Add in the onion remaining, tomatoes, bell pepper, and 4 tbsps. of soy sauce and stir. Let to simmer until the gravy reaches the consistency desired.

Nutrition Information

- Nutritionist's Calories: 248 kcal 12%
- Total Fat: 7.5 g 11%
- Carbohydrates: 15.1g 5%
- Protein: 29.9 g 60%
- Cholesterol: 72 mg 24%
- Sodium: 2101 mg 84%

72. Chicken Pot Pie Soup

"This soup is simple, good and contains low calories. Top with crumbled crackers for decoration."

Servings: 4

Ingredients

- 2 c cubed cooked chicken breast meat
- 1 (16 ounce) package frozen mixed vegetables, thawed
- 1 (10.75 ounce) can condensed cream of potato soup
- 1 (10.75 ounce) can condensed cream of chicken soup
- 2 c skim milk

Directions

- Mix milk, chicken, cream of chicken soup, mixed veggies and cream of potato soup in a medium sauce pan. Heat through, top with crumbled crackers and serve.

Nutrition Information

- Nutritionist's Calories: 367 kcal 18%
- Total Fat: 11.5 g 18%
- Carbohydrates: 35.9g 12%
- Protein: 30.1 g 60%
- Cholesterol: 64 mg 21%
- Sodium: 1133 mg 45%

73. Chicken Satay

"There's no need to buy Thai food and you can prepare it at home. Thai-style chicken satay that are tasty and consist of chicken that is first marinated in a peanutty sauce before grilling."

Servings: 12 | Prep: 2 h 10 m | Ready In: 2 h 40 m

Ingredients

- 2 tbsps. creamy peanut butter
- 1/2 c soy sauce
- 1/2 c lemon or lime juice
- 1 tbsp. brown sugar
- 2 tbsps. curry powder
- 2 cloves garlic, chopped
- 1 tsp. hot pepper sauce
- 6 skinless, boneless chicken breast halves - cubed

Directions

- Mix curry powder, peanut butter, brown sugar, soy sauce, garlic, hot pepper sauce and lime juice in a mixing bowl. Put chicken breasts into marinade and chill. Marinate chicken for a minimum of two hours but overnight is better.
- Preheat the grill over high heat.
- Onto the skewers, weave chicken and then let to grill for five minutes on each side.

Nutrition Information

- Nutritionist's Calories: 162 kcal 8%
- Total Fat: 3 g 5%
- Carbohydrates: 4.1g 1%
- Protein: 28.8 g 58%
- Cholesterol: 68 mg 23%
- Sodium: 694 mg 28%

74. Chicken Scampi I

"This is a nice and simple way to enjoy chicken. It's great on top of rice."

Servings: 5

Ingredients

- 5 (4 ounce) skinless, boneless chicken breast halves - cut into 1 inch strips
- 1/4 tsp. ground black pepper
- 3 tbsps. grated Parmesan cheese
- 1 tbsp. dried parsley
- 1 clove garlic, minced
- 1/4 tsp. salt
- 1 tsp. dried oregano
- 3 tbsps. lemon juice
- 3 tbsps. Worcestershire sauce
- 1/4 c white wine

Directions

- In a shallow bowl, mix cheese, garlic, lemon juice, oregano, wine, Worcestershire sauce, chicken with ground pepper, parsley and salt. Place in a fridge to marinate for a few hours (overnight is best).
- Preheat the broiler. Take out chicken from the marinade (reserve the marinade) and transfer to a shallow pan. Let to broil 8 inches away from the heat source for about 15 minutes, flip once until the chicken's pink color inside disappears.
- Bring to boil the marinade in a small saucepan. Add on top of chicken, mix and then serve.

Nutrition Information

- Nutritionist's Calories: 179 kcal 9%
- Total Fat: 4.5 g 7%
- Carbohydrates: 4.2g 1%
- Protein: 26.8 g 54%
- Cholesterol: 72 mg 24%
- Sodium: 324 mg 13%

75. Chicken Tortilla Soup IV

"This soup is full of beans and corn and can be served as a main meal. Reduce prep time by add store bough tortilla chips on top."

Servings: 6

Ingredients

- 2 1/2 tsps. vegetable oil
- 6 (6 inch) corn tortillas, cut into 1/2 inch strips
- 3 c chicken broth
- 1/2 tsp. ground cumin
- 1/2 tsp. chili powder
- 1/2 tsp. dried oregano
- 1 (15 ounce) can black beans, rinsed and drained
- 1 (15 ounce) can whole kernel corn, drained
- 2 skinless, boneless chicken breast halves, cut into bite size pieces
- 1/2 c salsa
- 1/2 c chopped fresh cilantro

Directions

- Over medium heat, heat two tsps. of oil in a pot. Pour in ½ of tortilla strips while stirring frequently until crispy. Use paper towels to drain. Repeat this with the tortilla strips remaining and half of the tsp. oil remaining and reserve.
- Pour oregano, cumin, broth and chili powder into the pot. Increase the heat to high and heat to boil. Pour in salsa, chicken, beans and corn. Decrease the heat to low, mix and let to simmer for approximately two minutes or until the pink color of chicken inside disappears and cooked through.
- Pour in ½ of the tortilla strips reserved and cilantro. Spoon into individual bowls and decorate each with the strips remaining.

Nutrition Information

- Nutritionist's Calories: 257 kcal 13%
- Total Fat: 5.5 g 8%
- Carbohydrates: 36.1g 12%
- Protein: 17.6 g 35%
- Cholesterol: 20 mg 7%
- Sodium: 968 mg 39%

76. Chickpea Curry

"You can either prepare beans at home or add canned chickpeas to have a quick and simple dish."

Servings: 8 | Prep: 10 m | Ready In: 40 m

Ingredients

- 2 tbsps. vegetable oil
- 2 onions, minced
- 2 cloves garlic, minced
- 2 tsps. fresh ginger root, finely chopped
- 6 whole cloves
- 2 (2 inch) sticks cinnamon, crushed
- 1 tsp. ground cumin
- 1 tsp. ground coriander
- salt
- 1 tsp. cayenne pepper
- 1 tsp. ground turmeric
- 2 (15 ounce) cans garbanzo beans
- 1 c chopped fresh cilantro

Directions

- Over medium heat, heat oil in a frying pan and then fry onions until they are tender.
- Add in cayenne, garlic, ginger, turmeric, cloves, coriander, cinnamon, cumin and salt and stir. Over medium heat, let to cook for one minute while stirring continuously. Stir in the garbanzo beans along with their liquid. Continue cooking while stirring until the

ingredients are heated through and blended well. Take out from the heat source. Mix in cilantro prior to serving and set aside one tbsp. for decorating.

Nutrition Information

- Nutritionist's Calories: 135 kcal 7%
- Total Fat: 4.5 g 7%
- Carbohydrates: 20.5g 7%
- Protein: 4.1 g 8%
- Cholesterol: 0 mg 0%
- Sodium: 289 mg 12%

77. Chickpea Salad II

"An authentic Mediterranean salad that is delicious and hearty."

Servings: 4 | Prep: 20 m | Ready In: 1 h 5 m

Ingredients

- 1 (15 ounce) can chickpeas (garbanzo beans), drained and rinsed
- 1 cucumber, peeled and finely chopped
- 1 c grape tomatoes, halved
- 1/4 c finely chopped sweet onion
- 1 tbsp. minced garlic
- 1/2 tsp. dried parsley flakes
- 1/4 tsp. dried basil
- 1 tbsp. grated Parmesan cheese
- 1 tbsp. olive oil
- 3 tbsps. balsamic vinegar
- 1/4 tsp. salt

Directions

- Mix together dried basil, chickpeas, onion, cucumber, parsley flakes, tomatoes, Parmesan cheese and garlic in a large bowl. Sprinkle balsamic vinegar and olive oil on top and then add salt to taste. Mix until combined well. Adjust the seasoning as desired. Cover the bowl and chill for a minimum of 45 minutes prior to serving. Serve while chilled.

Nutrition Information

- Nutritionist's Calories: 149 kcal 7%
- Total Fat: 4.8 g 7%
- Carbohydrates: 22.9g 7%
- Protein: 4.9 g 10%
- Cholesterol: 1 mg < 1%
- Sodium: 382 mg 15%

78. Chili Chicken

"These type of drumsticks are delicious and have a little of sweetness and spiciness. The Asian flair is added by the Thai sweet chili sauce."

Servings: 12 | Prep: 10 m | Ready In: 1 h 30 m

Ingredients

- 2 tbsps. honey
- 5 tbsps. sweet chili sauce
- 3 tbsps. soy sauce
- 12 chicken drumsticks, skin removed

Directions

- Combine together soy sauce, honey and sweet chili sauce in a large bowl. Reserve marinade in a small dish for basting. Transfer chicken drumsticks to bowl. Cover the bowl and chill for a minimum of one hour.
- Preheat the outdoor grill over medium-high heat.
- Polish grill grate lightly with oil. Onto the grill, spread the drumsticks and let to cook for

about 10 minutes on each side or until the juice runs clear. Use the sauce reserved to baste occasionally on the final 5 minutes.

Nutrition Information

- Nutritionist's Calories: 142 kcal 7%
- Total Fat: 4.1 g 6%
- Carbohydrates: 5.9g 2%
- Protein: 19.6 g 39%
- Cholesterol: 62 mg 21%
- Sodium: 353 mg 14%

79. Chinese Cold Pasta Salad

"This cold pasta recipe is tasty when served alongside a spicy peanut sauce."

Servings: 4 | Prep: 10 m | Ready In: 1 h 20 m

Ingredients

- 8 ounces dry fettuccine pasta
- 2 tbsps. natural peanut butter
- 1/2 c vegetable broth
- 2 tbsps. soy sauce
- 3 cloves garlic, minced
- 2 tsps. crushed red pepper flakes
- 1 red bell pepper, chopped
- 2 green onions, chopped
- 1/2 c chopped fresh cilantro

Directions

- In a pot containing boiling water, cook pasta until al dente. Rinse the pasta, drain and reserve.
- Mix peanut butter, crushed red pepper, broth, garlic and soy sauce in a large bowl. Combine well. Pour in cilantro, scallions, pasta and

chopped red pepper. Stir to combine and refrigerate.

Nutrition Information

- Nutritionist's Calories: 275 kcal 14%
- Total Fat: 5.6 g 9%
- Carbohydrates: 47.5g 15%
- Protein: 10.8 g 22%
- Cholesterol: 0 mg 0%
- Sodium: 537 mg 21%

80.Chinese Pork Tenderloin

"This marinade is tasty and simple to make. It uses ingredients easily available at a Chinese grocery store. Don't be fooled by the ingredients because this meal will be loved by everyone."

Servings: 6 | Prep: 5 m | Ready In: 2 h 40 m

Ingredients

- 2 (1 1/2 pound) pork tenderloins, trimmed
- 2 tbsps. light soy sauce
- 2 tbsps. hoisin sauce
- 1 tbsp. sherry
- 1 tbsp. black bean sauce
- 1 1/2 tsps. minced fresh ginger root
- 1 1/2 tsps. packed brown sugar
- 1 clove garlic
- 1/2 tsp. sesame oil
- 1 pinch Chinese five-spice powder

Directions

- In a shallow glass dish, put tenderloins. Whisk together sherry, soy sauce, black bean sauce hoisin sauce, sesame oil, ginger, five-spice powder, sugar and garlic in a small bowl. Add the marinade on top of pork and flip to coat.

Cover and then chill for a minimum of two hours or up to 24 hours.
- Preheat an oven to 190 degrees C (375 degrees F). Take out the tenderloins from the fridge as oven preheats.
- Bake the pork for about 30 to 35 minutes or to the doneness desired. Allow to rest for about 10 minutes and cut into thin slices diagonally.

Nutrition Information

- Nutritionist's Calories: 222 kcal 11%
- Total Fat: 5.5 g 8%
- Carbohydrates: 5g 2%
- Protein: 35.8 g 72%
- Cholesterol: 98 mg 33%
- Sodium: 373 mg 15%

---

81. Cider Vinegar Chicken

"These are chicken breasts that are baked together with garlic salt and cider vinegar."

Servings: 6

Ingredients

- 6 skinless, boneless chicken breasts
- 5 tsps. garlic salt
- 1 c cider vinegar

Directions

- Preheat an oven to 175 degrees C (350 degrees F).
- Into a baking dish of 9x13 inch, put chicken breasts. Drizzle garlic salt on top and spread vinegar on top of all.
- Bake for about 35 minutes at 175 degrees C (350 degrees F) or until the chicken is cooked through, browned and the juice run clear.

Nutrition Information

- Nutritionist's Calories: 141 kcal 7%
- Total Fat: 2.8 g 4%
- Carbohydrates: 0.9g < 1%
- Protein: 24.6 g 49%
- Cholesterol: 67 mg 22%
- Sodium: 1571 mg 63%

82. Cincinnati-Style Chili

"This spaghetti has hot chili on top and has all the food groups!"

Servings: 4

Ingredients

- 8 ounces spaghetti
- 1 tbsp. olive oil
- 1 (12 ounce) package frozen burger-style crumbles
- 1 onion, chopped
- 1 tbsp. minced garlic
- 1 c tomato sauce
- 1 c water
- 1 (14.5 ounce) can diced tomatoes
- 2 tbsps. red wine vinegar
- 2 tbsps. chili powder
- 1/2 tsp. ground cinnamon
- 1/2 tsp. paprika
- 1/2 tsp. ground allspice
- 1 tbsp. light brown sugar
- 1 tbsp. unsweetened cocoa powder
- 1 tsp. hot pepper sauce
- 1 c kidney beans, drained and rinsed
- 1 c shredded Cheddar cheese (optional)

Directions

- In a large frying pan, heat olive oil and then sauté onion until it's tender. Stir in garlic and burger-style crumbles and then cook until crumbles become browned.
- Mix in chopped tomatoes, tomato sauce, cinnamon, water, vinegar, hot sauce, chili powder, paprika, allspice, cocoa and light brown sugar. Over medium-high heat, heat until mixture starts to boil. Decrease the heat to low, cover the pan and allow to simmer for about 15 to 20 minutes until the sauce becomes thick.
- As the sauce thickens, bring to boil salted water in a pot and add spaghetti into the boiling water. Heat to boil again. Let to cook until al dente and then drain thoroughly.
- Into the chili, mix beans and combine lightly.
- Into bowl, spoon the cooked spaghetti and add chili on top. If desired, drizzle cheese on top.

Nutrition Information

- Nutritionist's Calories: 769 kcal 38%
- Total Fat: 17.7 g 27%
- Carbohydrates: 74.8g 24%
- Protein: 88.4 g 177%
- Cholesterol: 30 mg 10%
- Sodium: 1787 mg 71%

83. Cinnamon Chicken

"These are chicken breasts that are baked together with cinnamon and some seasonings. I developed this dish when I was working at a flight kitchen. There was plenty of cinnamon in the spice collection, I decided to make use of it on chicken because nobody used it. It's liked by my family and flight crews!"

Servings: 4 | Prep: 10 m | Ready In: 40 m

Ingredients

- 4 skinless, boneless chicken breast halves
- 1 tsp. ground cinnamon
- 2 tbsps. Italian-style seasoning
- 1 1/2 tsps. garlic powder
- 3 tsps. salt
- 1 tsp. ground black pepper

Directions

- Preheat an oven to 175 degrees C (350 degrees F).
- Into a baking dish of 9x13 inch that is lightly greased, put chicken. Drizzle with pepper, salt, garlic powder, seasoning and ground cinnamon evenly. (Keep in mind that you can be liberal with pepper, salt, seasoning and garlic powder and cinnamon should just be a dusting and shouldn't be clumped.)
- Bake for about 30 minutes at 175 degrees C (350 degrees F) or until the juices run clear and chicken is done.

Nutrition Information

- Nutritionist's Calories: 143 kcal 7%
- Total Fat: 1.7 g 3%
- Carbohydrates: 3g < 1%
- Protein: 27.7 g 55%
- Cholesterol: 68 mg 23%
- Sodium: 1822 mg 73%

84. Cinnamon-Curry Tuna Salad

"This lovely tuna salad is versatile and super easy to make. It's great for hors d'oeuvres and makes a good snack or sandwich."

Servings: 4 | Prep: 10 m | Ready In: 10 m

Ingredients

- 2 (5 ounce) cans water packed tuna, drained and flaked
- 2 tsps. mayonnaise
- 1 tsp. Dijon mustard
- 1 tbsp. sweet pickle relish
- 2 tsps. lemon juice
- 1 1/2 tsps. ground cinnamon
- 1 tsp. curry powder
- 1 tsp. ground black pepper
- salt to taste

Directions

- Combine tuna, cinnamon, lemon juice, mayonnaise, curry powder, mustard, pepper, salt and relish in a bowl. Cover the bowl and chill until when ready to serve.

Nutrition Information

- Nutritionist's Calories: 101 kcal 5%
- Total Fat: 2.5 g 4%
- Carbohydrates: 3.2g 1%
- Protein: 16.3 g 33%
- Cholesterol: 20 mg 7%
- Sodium: 146 mg 6%

85. Cod with Italian Crumb Topping

"A recipe for cod that is fast and low in fat."

Servings: 4 | Prep: 15 m | Ready In: 25 m

Ingredients

- 1/4 c fine dry bread crumbs
- 2 tbsps. grated Parmesan cheese
- 1 tbsp. cornmeal
- 1 tsp. olive oil

- 1/2 tsp. Italian seasoning
- 1/8 tsp. garlic powder
- 1/8 tsp. ground black pepper
- 4 (3 ounce) fillets cod fillets
- 1 egg white, lightly beaten

Directions

- Preheat an oven to 230 degrees C (450 degrees F).
- Combine together bread crumbs, Italian seasoning, pepper, cheese, garlic powder, cornmeal and oil in a small shallow bowl. Reserve.
- Use cooking spray to coat the rack of a broiling pan. Put cod onto the rack and fold any thin edges of the filets under. Use egg white to brush and then pour the mixture crumb evenly at the top.
- Bake for about 10 to 12 minutes or until fish easily flakes with a fork and becomes opaque throughout.

Nutrition Information

- Nutritionist's Calories: 131 kcal 7%
- Total Fat: 2.9 g 4%
- Carbohydrates: 7g 2%
- Protein: 18.1 g 36%
- Cholesterol: 39 mg 13%
- Sodium: 148 mg 6%

86. Cold Macaroni and Tuna Salad

"This recipe is easy and nice and good when served on hot summer days. You can make it ahead of time and enjoy it while cold the following day. My hubby never had it before we got married and he asks for it every week. Feel free to replace chicken with tuna. You can serve this over a lettuce leaf along some crackers."

Servings: 6 | Prep: 25 m | Ready In: 1 h 58 m

Ingredients

- 3 eggs
- 2 3/4 c macaroni
- 1/2 (10 ounce) package frozen English peas
- 2 (5 ounce) cans tuna, drained
- 3 tbsps. mayonnaise
- 1/4 tsp. salt
- 1/8 tsp. ground black pepper

Directions

- Into a saucepan, put eggs and add enough water to cover. Heat to boil, take out from the heat source and allow to eggs to stand in the hot water for about 15 minutes. Take out from the hot water, use cold running water to cool and then peel.
- Bring to boil lightly salted water in a pot and add macaroni pasta. Cook until al dente or for about 8 to 10 minutes. Drain and then use cold water to rinse.
- Into a colander, place frozen peas and then use hot water to rinse. Drain thoroughly.
- In a large bowl, put the peas and macaroni. Dice the eggs and pour into the bowl. Add tuna into bowl and then flake it apart.
- Add mayonnaise into the mixture little by little and mix such that mixture becomes moist and not soggy. Drizzle pepper and salt and stir for the last time. Cover and chill for a minimum of one hour or overnight.

Nutrition Information

- Nutritionist's Calories: 342 kcal 17%
- Total Fat: 9.5 g 15%
- Carbohydrates: 40.8g 13%
- Protein: 22.1 g 44%
- Cholesterol: 108 mg 36%
- Sodium: 220 mg 9%

87. Corn Tortillas

"You can have the best corn tortillas by combining water and a mixture of masa harina. The key is using a cast iron pan! Masa harina is available at Mexican grocery stores or large supermarkets."

Servings: 5 | Prep: 20 m | Ready In: 1 h 5 m

Ingredients

- 1 3/4 c masa harina
- 1 1/8 c water

Directions

- Combine together hot water and masa harina in a medium bowl until combined thoroughly. Onto a clean surface, turn dough and then knead until smooth and pliable. Add extra masa harina in case the dough is too sticky. Drizzle some water in case it starts to dry out. Use plastic wrap to cover the dough tightly and let to rest for 30 minutes.
- Preheat a cast iron griddle or skillet over medium-high.
- Subdivide the dough into 15 equal-size balls. Push every dough ball flat in between 2 sheets of plastic wrap with either your hands, a rolling pin or a tortilla press.
- In the pan preheated, put tortilla right away and let to cook for about 30 seconds or until slightly puffy and browned. Flip over tortilla to brown the other side for about 30 seconds and place onto a plate. Repeat this process with the other dough balls. Keep the tortillas moist and warm by covering with a towel until when ready to serve.

Nutrition Information

- Nutritionist's Calories: 146 kcal 7%
- Total Fat: 1.5 g 2%
- Carbohydrates: 30.4g 10%
- Protein: 3.7 g 7%
- Cholesterol: 0 mg 0%
- Sodium: 4 mg < 1%

88. Country Style Barbecued Chicken

"This is a tasty baked chicken recipe with flavors of barbeque."

Servings: 6 | Prep: 15 m | Ready In: 55 m

Ingredients

- 1/2 c chopped onions
- 1 c ketchup
- 1/2 c distilled white vinegar
- 1/4 c brown sugar
- 1 tbsp. dry mustard
- 3/4 tsp. salt
- 1/4 tsp. pepper
- 6 skinless, boneless chicken breast halves

Directions

- Over medium heat, in a saucepan, combine dry mustard, brown sugar, onions, ketchup, pepper, salt and vinegar. Let to cook for 15 minutes while stirring at intervals.
- Preheat an oven to 175 degrees C (350 degrees F). Polish a baking dish lightly with grease.
- Spread chicken into baking dish and add the sauce on top of chicken.
- Bake for about 25 minutes or until the chicken juice is clear.

Nutrition Information

- Nutritionist's Calories: 218 kcal 11%

- Total Fat: 3.5 g 5%
- Carbohydrates: 20.7g 7%
- Protein: 25.8 g 52%
- Cholesterol: 67 mg 22%
- Sodium: 798 mg 32%

89. Crab Ceviche

"Ceviche is usually a hit in my house. Great as an appetizer when served with tortilla chips or on tostadas. Chill first before serving because it tastes better when frozen. For a filling lunch, I usually serve over tostadas along with a layer of mayonnaise."

Servings: 8 | Prep: 40 m | Ready In: 40 m

Ingredients

- 1 (8 ounce) package imitation crabmeat, flaked
- 2 large tomatoes, chopped
- 1 red onion, finely chopped
- 1/2 bunch cilantro, chopped
- 2 limes, juiced
- 3 serrano peppers, finely chopped
- 1 tbsp. olive oil
- salt and pepper to taste

Directions

- Into a porcelain or glass bowl, put shredded imitation crab. It's not recommended to use metal or plastic ones. Mix olive oil into crabmeat until coated well. Mix in serrano peppers, cilantro, tomato and onion. Pour lime juice on top of all and combine well. Add enough pepper and salt. Chill for approximately one hour prior to serving.

Nutrition Information

- Nutritionist's Calories: 62 kcal 3%

- Total Fat: 2 g 3%
- Carbohydrates: 9.3g 3%
- Protein: 2.9 g 6%
- Cholesterol: 6 mg 2%
- Sodium: 241 mg 10%

90. Craig's Cocktail Sauce

"I have been preparing this cocktail sauce for many years. Transfer sauce back to ketchup bottle with a kitchen funnel. Lasts for a long period of time."

Servings: 20 | Prep: 5 m | Ready In: 5 m

Ingredients

- 1 (36 ounce) bottle ketchup
- 3 tbsps. steak sauce
- 3 tbsps. Worcestershire sauce
- 6 tbsps. lemon juice concentrate
- 3 tbsps. prepared horseradish
- 15 drops hot pepper sauce, or to taste
- 1 tsp. salt

Directions

- Into a bowl, squeeze ketchup. Add in lemon juice, steak sauce and Worcestershire sauce. Mix in salt, horseradish and hot pepper sauce and combine well.

Nutrition Information

- Nutritionist's Calories: 55 kcal 3%
- Total Fat: 0.2 g < 1%
- Carbohydrates: 14.3g 5%
- Protein: 1 g 2%
- Cholesterol: 0 mg 0%
- Sodium: 757 mg 30%

91. Cream of Chicken Breasts

"A baked dish for boneless chicken tenders or chicken breasts that is topped with cream of chicken soup. You serve on top of egg noodles if desired."

Servings: 4

Ingredients

- 4 skinless, boneless chicken breast halves
- 1 pinch poultry seasoning
- 1 (10.75 ounce) can condensed cream of chicken soup
- 1 (10.75 ounce) can milk

Directions

- Preheat an oven to 175 degrees C (350 degrees F).
- Into a baking dish of 9x13 inch, put chicken and then season to suit your taste.
- Combine soup together with the soup can of water/half-and-half/milk (you can add two cans to thicken the sauce if desired). Spread the soup mixture evenly on top of the chicken and then bake for approximately 1 1/2 hours or until the chicken becomes tender and no pink color remains.

Nutrition Information

- Nutritionist's Calories: 237 kcal 12%
- Total Fat: 7.4 g 11%
- Carbohydrates: 9.1g 3%
- Protein: 31.6 g 63%
- Cholesterol: 81 mg 27%
- Sodium: 607 mg 24%

92. Creamy Chicken

"A recipe for chicken that is creamy and super simple to prepare!"

Servings: 4

Ingredients

- 4 skinless, boneless chicken breast halves
- 1/2 tsp. salt
- 1/2 tsp. ground black pepper
- 1/2 tsp. garlic powder
- 1 (10.75 ounce) can condensed cream of chicken soup

Directions

- Preheat an oven to 190 degrees C (375 degrees F).
- Wash chicken breasts and then season using garlic powder, pepper and salt (or seasonings you desire) on each side of the chicken pieces.
- Bake in oven for about 25 minutes, then pour in cream of the chicken soup and continue baking for about 10 minutes or until done. Spread on top of egg noodles or rice and serve.

Nutrition Information

- Nutritionist's Calories: 200 kcal 10%
- Total Fat: 5.9 g 9%
- Carbohydrates: 5.9g 2%
- Protein: 29.1 g 58%
- Cholesterol: 75 mg 25%
- Sodium: 867 mg 35%

93. Creamy Italian White Bean Soup

"My family and friends love this healthy soup. Seems hard than it is. You will like it. Top with grated Parmesan cheese and serve."

Servings: 4 | Prep: 20 m | Ready In: 50 m

Ingredients

- 1 tbsp. vegetable oil
- 1 onion, chopped
- 1 stalk celery, chopped
- 1 clove garlic, minced
- 2 (16 ounce) cans white kidney beans, rinsed and drained
- 1 (14 ounce) can chicken broth
- 1/4 tsp. ground black pepper
- 1/8 tsp. dried thyme
- 2 c water
- 1 bunch fresh spinach, rinsed and thinly sliced
- 1 tbsp. lemon juice

Directions

- Heat oil in a saucepan and add celery and onion. Cook in the hot oil for about 5 to 8 minutes or until tender. Pour in garlic and then cook for around 30 seconds while stirring constantly. Mix in beans, two c of water, thyme, chicken broth and pepper. Heat to boil, low the heat and let to simmer for about 15 minutes.
- Take out two c of the vegetable and bean mixture with slotted spoon and reserve.
- Combine the soup remaining in small batches in a blender at low speed until smooth (this enables steam to escape by taking out the center piece of blender lid). When combined, return the soup into the stock pot, add the beans reserved and stir.
- Heat to boil while stirring at intervals. Add in spinach, stir and then cook for one minute or until the spinach has wilted. Pour in lemon juice, stir and take out from the heat source.

Top with fresh grated Parmesan cheese and serve.

Nutrition Information

- Nutritionist's Calories: 245 kcal 12%
- Total Fat: 4.9 g 8%
- Carbohydrates: 38.1g 12%
- Protein: 12 g 24%
- Cholesterol: 2 mg < 1%
- Sodium: 1014 mg 41%

94. Creole Okra

"This is a simple and tasty vegan side dish. Adding frozen okra makes it a family favorite throughout the year."

Servings: 4 | Prep: 10 m | Ready In: 40 m

Ingredients

- 2 tbsps. olive oil
- 1/2 large onion, chopped
- 2 cloves garlic, minced
- 1/2 green bell pepper, chopped
- 1 (16 ounce) can diced tomatoes in juice
- 3/8 tsp. dried thyme
- 2 tbsps. chopped fresh parsley
- 1/4 tsp. cayenne pepper
- salt and pepper to taste
- 1 (16 ounce) package frozen cut okra

Directions

- Over medium heat, heat olive oil in a skillet, add garlic and onion and then saute until limp. Pour in green pepper and then cook while stirring until tender. Drain off tomatoes and set the juice aside. Add the tomatoes to skillet. Season with pepper, salt, cayenne, thyme and parsley. Let to simmer for about 5 minutes at a medium heat.

- Pour in frozen okra and then cover the pan's bottom with the reserved tomato juice. Cover the skillet and let to cook for about 15 minutes or until the okra becomes tender.

Nutrition Information

- Nutritionist's Calories: 133 kcal 7%
- Total Fat: 7.2 g 11%
- Carbohydrates: 14.2g 5%
- Protein: 4 g 8%
- Cholesterol: 0 mg 0%
- Sodium: 184 mg 7%

95. Cuban Black Beans I

"You can serve these Cuban beans with a loaf of bread, as a sauce for pasta or on top of rice."

Servings: 6 | Prep: 20 m | Ready In: 13 h 50 m

Ingredients

- 1 pound black beans, washed
- 1 onion, chopped
- 1 red bell pepper, chopped
- 1 green bell pepper, chopped
- 2 bay leaves
- 1 1/2 tsps. paprika
- 1 1/2 tsps. ground cumin
- 1 tbsp. dried oregano
- 2 minced hot green chile peppers
- 3 cloves garlic, minced
- 1/4 c balsamic vinegar
- salt to taste
- ground black pepper to taste

Directions

- Soak beans covered in water in a bowl overnight.
- Rinse the beans and place in a stock pot. Pour in chile peppers, onion, cumin, bell peppers, paprika, oregano, bay leaves and cover with water. Heat to boil, low the heat and allow to simmer for about 1 1/2 hours.
- Check the tenderness of beans and once they're tender, pour in balsamic vinegar and garlic. Season with pepper and salt.

Nutrition Information

- Nutritionist's Calories: 296 kcal 15%
- Total Fat: 1.5 g 2%
- Carbohydrates: 55.5g 18%
- Protein: 17.6 g 35%
- Cholesterol: 0 mg 0%
- Sodium: 11 mg < 1%

96. Cucumber and Tomato Salad

"This salad is light and hearty for a hot and humid day on summer! Makes a nice vegan main dish with tofu and kidney beans. Can replace basil with mint or fresh parsley. You can prepare this salad prior to serving."

Servings: 4 | Prep: 15 m | Ready In: 15 m

Ingredients

- 1 tomato, chopped
- 1 cucumber, seeded and chopped
- 1/4 c thinly sliced red onion
- 1/4 c canned kidney beans, drained
- 1/4 c diced firm tofu
- 2 tbsps. chopped fresh basil
- 1/4 c balsamic vinaigrette salad dressing
- salt and pepper to taste

Directions

- Mix tofu, basil, red onion, tomato, cucumber and kidney beans in a large bowl. Before you serve, mix together with the balsamic vinaigrette salad dressing and then add pepper and salt to taste.

Nutrition Information

- Nutritionist's Calories: 98 kcal 5%
- Total Fat: 6.1 g 9%
- Carbohydrates: 8.6g 3%
- Protein: 4.1 g 8%
- Cholesterol: 0 mg 0%
- Sodium: 312 mg 12%

97. Curry Chicken Salad

"This recipe for chicken salad spread is great for a sandwich. You can serve over bread along with lettuce."

Servings: 6 | Prep: 10 m | Ready In: 10 m

Ingredients

- 3 cooked skinless, boneless chicken breast halves, chopped
- 3 stalks celery, chopped
- 1/2 c low-fat mayonnaise
- 2 tsps. curry powder

Directions

- Combine together curry powder, chicken, celery and mayonnaise in a medium bowl.

Nutrition Information

- Nutritionist's Calories: 77 kcal 4%

- Total Fat: 1.6 g 2%
- Carbohydrates: 1g < 1%
- Protein: 14 g 28%
- Cholesterol: 37 mg 12%
- Sodium: 46 mg 2%

98. Deer Chop Hurry

"Wild meat isn't my thing but my hubby loves it! This recipe has no 'gamey' taste and so tender."

Servings: 4 | Prep: 15 m | Ready In: 6 h 15 m

Ingredients

- 2 pounds deer chops (venison)
- 1 c ketchup
- 1/2 c water
- 1 medium onion, chopped
- 1/2 c packed brown sugar
- 1 (1 ounce) envelope dry onion soup mix

Directions

- Cut deer chops thinly and then brown the chops in a skillet at a medium-high heat. Into the slow cooker, put the meat. Stir in dry onion soup mix, brown sugar, onion, ketchup and water. Cook for about 6 hours on LOW or until tender. In case you wish to cook in the toaster, bake it for one hour at 350 degrees F.

Nutrition Information

- Nutritionist's Calories: 435 kcal 22%
- Total Fat: 5.3 g 8%
- Carbohydrates: 49.2g 16%
- Protein: 48.2 g 96%
- Cholesterol: 171 mg 57%
- Sodium: 1353 mg 54%

- Sodium: 941 mg 38%

99. Delicious and Easy Mock Risotto

"This a nice and simple way for those who like a creamy risotto but dislike the energy needed to make it! This cool side dish works well with the chicken recipe you love."

Servings: 4 | Prep: 5 m | Ready In: 25 m

Ingredients

- 2 tbsps. extra-virgin olive oil
- 2 cloves garlic, minced
- 1/2 small onion, finely chopped
- 2 (14 ounce) cans chicken broth
- 2 c uncooked orzo pasta
- salt and pepper to taste

Directions

- Over medium heat, heat a saucepan. The moments it's not becoming hotter, add olive oil. Pour in onion and garlic. Cook while stirring for about 3 minutes until tender. Stir in chicken broth to loosen the bits at the pan's bottom. .
- Once the broth starts to boil, add orzo pasta and stir. Decrease the heat to low, cover and let to simmer for about 15 minutes or until the pasta absorbs all the liquid. Mix frequently to keep from sticking particularly at the end. Add pepper and salt prior to serving.

Nutrition Information

- Nutritionist's Calories: 476 kcal 24%
- Total Fat: 9.6 g 15%
- Carbohydrates: 79.4g 26%
- Protein: 15.7 g 31%
- Cholesterol: 5 mg 2%

100. Doreen's Ham Slices on the Grill

"A family favorite for many years including the peaky ones! Made of cooked ham basted with zesty sauce when grilling. Can replace slices of smoked turkey with ham."

Servings: 4 | Prep: 10 m | Ready In: 25 m

Ingredients

- 1 c packed brown sugar
- 1/4 c lemon juice
- 1/3 c prepared horseradish
- 2 slices ham

Directions

- Preheat the outdoor grill over high heat and polish grate lightly with oil.
- Combine prepared horseradish, brown sugar and lemon juice in a small bowl.
- Microwave the mixture of brown sugar for about one minute on high or until warm.
- Score each side of ham pieces. Transfer to the grill prepared. As you grill, use the brown sugar mixture to baste continuously. Let to grill for about 6 to 8 minutes on each side or to the doneness desired.

Nutrition Information

- Nutritionist's Calories: 245 kcal 12%
- Total Fat: 1.3 g 2%
- Carbohydrates: 58g 19%
- Protein: 2.7 g 5%
- Cholesterol: 8 mg 3%
- Sodium: 260 mg 10%

101. D's Famous Salsa

"A recipe from Texas I created and adjusted it for many years. The recipe is super-fast, simple and ingredients are easily available. I usually bring it as a gift to family."

Servings: 16 | Prep: 10 m | Ready In: 10 m

Ingredients

- 2 (14.5 ounce) cans stewed tomatoes
- 1/2 onion, finely diced
- 1 tsp. minced garlic
- 1/2 lime, juiced
- 1 tsp. salt
- 1/4 c canned sliced green chiles, or to taste
- 3 tbsps. chopped fresh cilantro

Directions

- In a food processor or blender, add cilantro, green chile, lime juice, tomatoes, salt, onion and garlic and then blend on low to the consistency desired.

Nutrition Information

- Nutritionist's Calories: 16 kcal < 1%
- Total Fat: 0.1 g < 1%
- Carbohydrates: 3.9g 1%
- Protein: 0.6 g 1%
- Cholesterol: 0 mg 0%
- Sodium: 283 mg 11%

102. Easiest Eggplant

"I noted that some great recipes are super simple to make! Experiment this and you'll make it more often. Note: in case you add low-fat mayonnaise, you will be saving calories and fat usually absorbed while frying eggplant."

Servings: 6 | Prep: 10 m | Ready In: 55 m

Ingredients

- 1 medium eggplant, peeled and sliced into 1/2 inch rounds
- 4 tbsps. mayonnaise, or as needed
- 1/2 c seasoned bread crumbs

Directions

- Preheat an oven to 350° F. Line aluminum foil onto a baking sheet.
- Into a shallow dish, put bread crumbs. Use mayonnaise to coat every piece of eggplant on each side. Push into bread crumbs so as to coat. Transfer the coated slices of eggplant to the baking sheet prepared.
- Bake in oven for about 20 minutes until they turn golden brown. Turn over the slices and the cook for about 20 to 25 more minutes to brown the remaining side.

Nutrition Information

- Nutritionist's Calories: 126 kcal 6%
- Total Fat: 8 g 12%
- Carbohydrates: 12.3g 4%
- Protein: 2.4 g 5%
- Cholesterol: 4 mg 1%
- Sodium: 230 mg 9%

103. Easiest Spicy Cod

"This baked cod recipe is fast and simple and can be made by everyone. You can serve on top of warmed rice."

Servings: 4 | Prep: 5 m | Ready In: 35 m

Ingredients

- 1 1/2 pounds cod fillets
- 2 c salsa
- 2 tbsps. chopped fresh parsley
- salt and pepper to taste

Directions

- Preheat an oven to 175 degrees C (350 degrees F).
- Rinse cod fillets and then dry. Transfer the fillets in a casserole dish that is greased lightly. Spread salsa on top of fish. Drizzle pepper, parsley and salt.
- Bake for about 30 minutes and then serve while warm on top of rice.

Nutrition Information

- Nutritionist's Calories: 172 kcal 9%
- Total Fat: 1.3 g 2%
- Carbohydrates: 8.2g 3%
- Protein: 31.8 g 64%
- Cholesterol: 61 mg 20%
- Sodium: 884 mg 35%

104. Easy Baked Tilapia

"A simple tilapia recipe that is ready in no time, flavorful and has few ingredients."

Servings: 4 | Prep: 5 m | Ready In: 35 m

Ingredients

- 4 (4 ounce) fillets tilapia
- 2 tsps. butter
- 1/4 tsp. Old Bay Seasoning TM, or to taste
- 1/2 tsp. garlic salt, or to taste
- 1 lemon, sliced
- 1 (16 ounce) package frozen cauliflower with broccoli and red pepper

Directions

- Preheat an oven to 190 degrees C (375 degrees F). Polish a baking dish of 9x13 inch with grease.
- At the baking dish's bottom, put tilapia fillets and then use butter to dot. Add garlic salt and Old Bay seasoning. Add on top of each, one or two slices of lemon. Spread the frozen mixed veggies all-round the fish and then lightly season with pepper and salt.
- Cover and then bake for about 25 to 30 minutes until the fish easily flakes with a fork and the veggies become tender.

Nutrition Information

- Nutritionist's Calories: 172 kcal 9%
- Total Fat: 3.6 g 6%
- Carbohydrates: 7.3g 2%
- Protein: 24.8 g 50%
- Cholesterol: 46 mg 15%
- Sodium: 354 mg 14%

105. Easy Cajun Grilled Veggies

"This recipe for marinated and grilled vegetables is fast and simple. You can serve over brown rice or as a whole meal. You can also marinate the vegetables in plastic bags that are sealable."

Servings: 8 | Prep: 10 m | Ready In: 45 m

Ingredients

- 1/4 c light olive oil

- 1 tsp. Cajun seasoning
- 1/2 tsp. salt
- 1/2 tsp. cayenne pepper
- 1 tbsp. Worcestershire sauce
- 2 zucchinis, cut into 1/2-inch slices
- 2 large white onions, sliced into 1/2-inch wedges
- 2 yellow squash, cut into 1/2-inch slices

Directions

- Combine together Worcestershire sauce, light olive oil, cayenne pepper, salt and Cajun seasoning in a small bowl. In a bowl, put yellow squash, zucchinis and white onions and then add the olive oil mixture to cover. Cover and refrigerate for a minimum of 30 minutes to marinate the veggies.
- Preheat the outdoor grill over high heat and polish grate lightly with oil.
- Transfer the marinated pieces of vegetable onto skewers or place directly over the grill. Let to cook for five minutes or to the doneness desired.

Nutrition Information

- Nutritionist's Calories: 95 kcal 5%
- Total Fat: 7.3 g 11%
- Carbohydrates: 7.7g 2%
- Protein: 1.5 g 3%
- Cholesterol: 0 mg 0%
- Sodium: 233 mg 9%

106. Easy Garlic and Rosemary Chicken

"My husband's favorite baked chicken! Perfect when served on top of rice."

Servings: 2

Ingredients

- 2 skinless, boneless chicken breasts
- 2 cloves garlic, chopped
- 2 tbsps. dried rosemary
- 1 tbsp. lemon juice
- salt and pepper to taste

Directions

- Preheat an oven to 190 degrees C (375 degrees F).
- Use garlic to cover chicken breasts and then drizzle with pepper, salt, rosemary and lemon juice. Transfer to a baking dish of 9x13 inch and then bake for about 25 minutes or until the juice runs clear and done (the baking time varies depending on the thickness of the chicken).

Nutrition Information

- Nutritionist's Calories: 147 kcal 7%
- Total Fat: 2 g 3%
- Carbohydrates: 3.7g 1%
- Protein: 27.6 g 55%
- Cholesterol: 68 mg 23%
- Sodium: 79 mg 3%

107. Easy Garlic Ginger Chicken

"This is a flavorful and light recipe!"

Servings: 4

Ingredients

- 4 skinless, boneless chicken breast halves
- 3 cloves crushed garlic

- 3 tbsps. ground ginger
- 1 tbsp. olive oil
- 4 limes, juiced

Directions

- Pound chicken to half inch thickness. Mix lime juice, oil, garlic and ginger in a large plastic bag that is resealable. Seal the bag and then shake until combined. Open the bag and then put in chicken. Seal and then place in a fridge for a maximum for 20 minutes to marinate.
- Take out the chicken from the bag and broil or grill while basting with the marinade until the juice runs clear and cooked through. Get rid of the marinade remaining.

Nutrition Information

- Nutritionist's Calories: 197 kcal 10%
- Total Fat: 5.2 g 8%
- Carbohydrates: 10.7g 3%
- Protein: 28.2 g 56%
- Cholesterol: 68 mg 23%
- Sodium: 80 mg 3%

108. Easy Grilled Chicken Teriyaki

"A recipe for chicken breasts that are marinated in sesame oil, garlic, teriyaki sauce and lemon before grilling. Super simple and good for a hot evening on summer. The leftovers are awesome over a sandwich or green salad. Grill quickly while very hot!!"

Servings: 4 | Prep: 15 m | Ready In: 1 d 30 m

Ingredients

- 4 skinless, boneless chicken breast halves
- 1 c teriyaki sauce
- 1/4 c lemon juice

- 2 tsps. minced fresh garlic
- 2 tsps. sesame oil

Directions

- In a large plastic bag that is resealable, put garlic, lemon juice, chicken, sesame oil and teriyaki sauce. Seal and then shake to coat. Chill for 24 hours and turn occasionally.
- Preheat the grill over high heat.
- Polish grill grate lightly with oil. Take out the chicken from the bag and get rid of the marinade remaining. Let to grill for about 6 to 8 minutes per side or until the juice runs clear when you poke the chicken with a fork.

Nutrition Information

- Nutritionist's Calories: 240 kcal 12%
- Total Fat: 7.5 g 12%
- Carbohydrates: 16.6g 5%
- Protein: 25.2 g 50%
- Cholesterol: 67 mg 22%
- Sodium: 691 mg 28%

109. Easy Hummus

"I usually prepare this hummus. Ready in a few minutes and healthier with not oil. Adjust the ingredients as you wish particularly the jalapenos! You can serve together with fresh vegetable slices or pita chips. For a smoother dip, pour in more bean liquid."

Servings: 16 | Prep: 5 m | Ready In: 5 m

Ingredients

- 1 (15 ounce) can garbanzo beans, drained, liquid reserved
- 2 ounces fresh jalapeno pepper, sliced
- 1/2 tsp. ground cumin

- 2 tbsps. lemon juice
- 3 cloves garlic, minced

Directions

- Mix garlic, garbanzo beans, cumin, jalapeno, one tbsp. of reserved bean liquid and lemon juice in a food processor or blender and then blend until smooth.

Nutrition Information

- Nutritionist's Calories: 23 kcal 1%
- Total Fat: 0.2 g < 1%
- Carbohydrates: 4.5g 1%
- Protein: 1 g 2%
- Cholesterol: 0 mg 0%
- Sodium: 53 mg 2%

110. Easy Masoor Daal

"This daal uses red lentils and it's easy and quick."

Servings: 4 | Prep: 5 m | Ready In: 35 m

Ingredients

- 1 c red lentils
- 1 slice ginger, 1 inch piece, peeled
- 1/4 tsp. ground turmeric
- 1 tsp. salt
- 1/2 tsp. cayenne pepper, or to taste
- 4 tsps. vegetable oil
- 4 tsps. dried minced onion
- 1 tsp. cumin seeds

Directions

- Rinse the lentils properly and transfer to a medium saucepan and add cayenne pepper,

salt, ginger and turmeric. Add water to cover about one inch and then heat to boil. Any foam that forms on the surface of lentils, skim it off. Low the heat and let to simmer while stirring frequently until the beans are soupy and tender

- In the meantime, Mix cumin seeds, oil and dried onion in a microwave safe dish. Heat for about 45 seconds to 1 minute in microwave on high until onions are brown but not burned. Mix into the lentil mixture.

Nutrition Information

- Nutritionist's Calories: 185 kcal 9%
- Total Fat: 5.2 g 8%
- Carbohydrates: 25g 8%
- Protein: 11.1 g 22%
- Cholesterol: 0 mg 0%
- Sodium: 868 mg 35%

111. Easy Pizza Sauce III

"This pizza sauce is fast and simple. Fast to prepare without cooking."

Servings: 24 | Prep: 5 m | Ready In: 5 m

Ingredients

- 1 (15 ounce) can tomato sauce
- 1 (6 ounce) can tomato paste
- 1 tbsp. ground oregano
- 1 1/2 tsps. dried minced garlic
- 1 tsp. ground paprika

Directions

- Combine together tomato paste and tomato sauce in a medium bowl until smooth. Add in paprika, oregano and garlic and stir.

Nutrition Information

- Nutritionist's Calories: 11 kcal < 1%
- Total Fat: 0.1 g < 1%
- Carbohydrates: 2.6g < 1%
- Protein: 0.6 g 1%
- Cholesterol: 0 mg 0%
- Sodium: 148 mg 6%

Nutrition Information

- Nutritionist's Calories: 101 kcal 5%
- Total Fat: 3.4 g 5%
- Carbohydrates: 15.1g 5%
- Protein: 3.4 g 7%
- Cholesterol: 0 mg 0%
- Sodium: 318 mg 13%

112.Easy Red Pepper Hummus

"My friends' favorite red Pepper Hummus recipe. Simple to prepare! You can serve with vegetables, pita chips, chips, etc…"

Servings: 8 | Prep: 10 m | Ready In: 10 m

Ingredients

- 1 (16 ounce) can garbanzo beans, drained and rinsed
- 1 tbsp. olive oil
- 1 medium red bell pepper, cut into 1/2 inch pieces
- 1 tbsp. tahini
- 1 fresh lime, juiced
- 1 1/2 tbsps. water
- 1/2 tsp. salt
- 1/4 tsp. ground black pepper
- 1/4 tsp. garlic powder

Directions

- Combine tahini, garbanzo beans, lime juice, olive oil, garlic powder, red bell pepper, water, salt and black pepper in a blender or food processor and then blend until smooth.

113.Easy White Chili

"This chili is spicy, very delicious and has chicken in it. I love serving it along with a sweet corn bread."

Servings: 8 | Prep: 15 m | Ready In: 45 m

Ingredients

- 2 tbsps. olive oil
- 2 onions, chopped
- 4 cloves garlic, minced
- 4 cooked, boneless chicken breast half, chopped
- 3 (14.5 ounce) cans chicken broth
- 2 (4 ounce) cans canned green chile peppers, chopped
- 2 tsps. ground cumin
- 2 tsps. dried oregano
- 1 1/2 tsps. cayenne pepper
- 5 (14.5 ounce) cans great Northern beans, undrained
- 1 c shredded Monterey Jack cheese

Directions

- Over medium heat, heat oil in a pot, pour in garlic and onions and then sauté for about 10 minutes or until the onions become tender. Pour in chicken, cumin, chicken broth, cayenne pepper, oregano and green chile peppers and heat to a boil.
- Decrease the heat to low and pour in beans. Allow to simmer for about 20 to 30 minutes or

until heated thoroughly. Transfer to individual bowls and then add cheese on top.

Nutrition Information

- Nutritionist's Calories: 521 kcal 26%
- Total Fat: 13.9 g 21%
- Carbohydrates: 59.2g 19%
- Protein: 41.1 g 82%
- Cholesterol: 54 mg 18%
- Sodium: 935 mg 37%

114. Eggplant Parmesan II

"A popular dish that is delicious without frying!"

Servings: 10 | Prep: 25 m | Ready In: 1 h

Ingredients

- 3 eggplant, peeled and thinly sliced
- 2 eggs, beaten
- 4 c Italian seasoned bread crumbs
- 6 c spaghetti sauce, divided
- 1 (16 ounce) package mozzarella cheese, shredded and divided
- 1/2 c grated Parmesan cheese, divided
- 1/2 tsp. dried basil

Directions

- Preheat an oven to 175 degrees C (350 degrees F).
- Dunk slices of eggplant in egg and then dip in bread crumbs. In a baking sheet, put in a single layer and then bake for about 5 minutes per side.
- Pour spaghetti sauce to cover bottom of a baking dish of 9x13 inch. Add into the sauce, a layer of eggplant pieces. Drizzle Parmesan and mozzarella cheeses on top. Repeat this with

the ingredients remaining and top with the cheeses. Drizzle basil over all.
- Bake for about 35 minutes or until the final product is golden brown.

Nutrition Information

- Nutritionist's Calories: 487 kcal 24%
- Total Fat: 16 g 25%
- Carbohydrates: 62.1g 20%
- Protein: 24.2 g 48%
- Cholesterol: 73 mg 24%
- Sodium: 1663 mg 67%

115. Eggplant Tomato Bake

"This low-fat recipe is super easy to make."

Servings: 4

Ingredients

- 1 eggplant, sliced into 1/2 inch rounds
- 1 tomato, sliced
- 1/4 c grated fat-free Parmesan cheese

Directions

- Preheat an oven to 200 degrees C (400 degrees F).
- Use non-stick oil spray to coat a cookie sheet. Onto the cookie sheet, spread rounds of eggplant and drizzle Parmesan on top of eggplant. Spread a layer of a tomato slice on top of every round of eggplant. Drizzle Parmesan cheese on top.
- Bake in oven for about 10 to 15 minutes.

Nutrition Information

- Nutritionist's Calories: 55 kcal 3%
- Total Fat: 0.3 g < 1%
- Carbohydrates: 9.3g 3%
- Protein: 3.3 g 7%
- Cholesterol: 0 mg 0%
- Sodium: 105 mg 4%

116. Elegant Pork Loin Roast

"I got this recipe from my mother. Ready in a short while because it needs basting and it's worth the effort. It makes a classy meal when served together with green vegetable and mashed red potatoes."

Servings: 8 | Prep: 30 m | Ready In: 3 h 30 m

Ingredients

- 1 (4 pound) boneless pork loin roast
- 1/4 c Dijon mustard
- 2 tbsps. packed brown sugar
- 1 1/2 c apple juice, divided
- 1 c pitted prunes
- 1 c dried apricots
- 3/4 c red wine
- 1/4 c packed brown sugar
- 1/8 tsp. ground cloves
- 2 tsps. cornstarch

Directions

- Preheat an oven to 165 degrees C (325 degrees F).
- Into a shallow roasting pan, put roast. Combine together two tbsps. brown sugar and mustard and pour on top of the roast.
- Roast in oven for three hours as you baste with 1/4 c apple juice after every 30 minutes. The roast is cooked once the temperature at the center is 63 degrees C (145 degrees F).

- In the final hour of roasting, over medium heat, mix 3/4 c of juices from roasting pan, prunes, cloves, apricots, 1/4 c of brown sugar and red wine in a saucepan. Heat to boil, cover the pan and let to simmer for about 15 minutes. Spread fruit all-round the roast while still in roasting pan on the final 30 minutes of the cooking process.
- Once roast is cooked, transfer to a serving platter and pour fruit around it. Take out from the roasting pan, 1/4 c of drippings and then combine with cornstarch. Mix into pan containing the drippings and then let to cook while stirring gently at a medium-high heat for about 5 minutes until no longer cloudy and thickened. Place into a serving bowl or gravy boat.
- Chop roast and bring the sauce to the guests so that they can serve themselves.

Nutrition Information

- Nutritionist's Calories: 370 kcal 19%
- Total Fat: 9 g 14%
- Carbohydrates: 41.8g 13%
- Protein: 27.4 g 55%
- Cholesterol: 79 mg 26%
- Sodium: 241 mg 10%

117. Extra Easy Hummus

"This hummus has no tahini, ready in a few minutes and loved by kids."

Servings: 4 | Prep: 5 m | Ready In: 5 m

Ingredients

- 1 (15 ounce) can garbanzo beans, drained, liquid reserved
- 1 clove garlic, crushed
- 2 tsps. ground cumin

- 1/2 tsp. salt
- 1 tbsp. olive oil

Directions

- Mix olive oil, cumin, garbanzo beans, salt and garlic in a food processor or blender. Then blend on a low speed while slowly pouring in the bean liquid reserved until the consistency desired is achieved.

Nutrition Information

- Nutritionist's Calories: 118 kcal 6%
- Total Fat: 4.4 g 7%
- Carbohydrates: 16.5g 5%
- Protein: 3.7 g 7%
- Cholesterol: 0 mg 0%
- Sodium: 502 mg 20%

118.Fabulous Fajitas

"My children dislike peppers and onions but like these fajitas. You can replace pita breads with tortillas if available."

Servings: 10 | Prep: 15 m | Ready In: 30 m

Ingredients

- 2 green bell peppers, sliced
- 1 red bell pepper, sliced
- 1 onion, thinly sliced
- 1 c fresh sliced mushrooms
- 2 c diced, cooked chicken meat
- 1 (.7 ounce) package dry Italian-style salad dressing mix
- 10 (12 inch) flour tortillas

Directions

- Chop onion and peppers into thin slices. Avoid dicing and ensure the slices are long and thin.
- Sauté onion and peppers in a little amount of oil until tender. Pour in chicken and mushrooms. Continue cooking on low heat until the ingredients are heated through. Add in dry salad dressing mix, stir and then blend well.
- Fold the mixture inside warmed tortillas. You can add shredded lettuce, shredded cheddar cheese and diced tomato on top if desired.

Nutrition Information

- Nutritionist's Calories: 427 kcal 21%
- Total Fat: 10.3 g 16%
- Carbohydrates: 64.2g 21%
- Protein: 18 g 36%
- Cholesterol: 21 mg 7%
- Sodium: 1078 mg 43%

119. Fajita Marinade I

"This is a tasty fajita marinade that is prepared with soy sauce, olive oil and lime juice and then spiced with black pepper and cayenne. It yields marinade for two pounds of meat."

Servings: 16 | Prep: 15 m | Ready In: 15 m

Ingredients

- 1/4 c lime juice
- 1/3 c water
- 2 tbsps. olive oil
- 4 cloves garlic, crushed
- 2 tsps. soy sauce
- 1 tsp. salt
- 1/2 tsp. liquid smoke flavoring
- 1/2 tsp. cayenne pepper
- 1/2 tsp. ground black pepper

Directions

- Combine together soy sauce, lime juice, liquid smoke flavoring, water, garlic, olive oil and salt in a large plastic bag that is resealable. Add black pepper and cayenne and stir.
- Add your favorite meat into the marinade and chill for a minimum of two hours or overnight. Then cook as you wish.

Nutrition Information

120. Fantastic Black Bean Chili

"I discovered that I missed this recipe when my mother-in-law prepared it! She often gets requests for it. This recipe can easily feed a crowd. It's now my favorite dish! You can chill and then double to feed a large crowd. Add shredded cheese you like on top."

Servings: 6 | Prep: 20 m | Ready In: 1 h 35 m

Ingredients

- 1 tbsp. vegetable oil
- 1 onion, diced
- 2 cloves garlic, minced
- 1 pound ground turkey
- 3 (15 ounce) cans black beans, undrained
- 1 (14.5 ounce) can crushed tomatoes
- 1 1/2 tbsps. chili powder
- 1 tbsp. dried oregano
- 1 tbsp. dried basil leaves
- 1 tbsp. red wine vinegar

Directions

- Over medium heat, heat oil in a heavy pot, add garlic and onion and then cook until the

onions become translucent. Pour in turkey and then cook while stirring until the meat turns brown. Add in basil, vinegar, oregano, beans, tomatoes and chili powder and stir. Decrease the heat to low, cover the pot and allow to simmer for about 60 minutes or until the flavors blend well.

Nutrition Information

- Nutritionist's Calories: 366 kcal 18%
- Total Fat: 9.2 g 14%
- Carbohydrates: 44.1g 14%
- Protein: 29.6 g 59%
- Cholesterol: 56 mg 19%
- Sodium: 969 mg 39%

121. Fat Free Refried Beans

"Refried beans with no fat and work well with tacos, enchiladas or as a spread."

Servings: 4 | Prep: 10 m | Ready In: 25 m

Ingredients

- 2 c canned black beans, divided
- 1/2 c water
- 2 cloves garlic, minced
- 1 tsp. pepper
- 1 tsp. salt
- 1 tsp. liquid smoke flavoring
- 3/4 c diced onion

Directions

- Mash 2/3 c beans in a bowl to form a smooth paste.

- Over medium heat, mix the beans remaining with water in a saucepan. Once heated through, add in liquid smoke, salt, garlic and pepper and stir.
- Add bean paste to whole beans, stir and combine well. Add onion, stir and then cook for about 10 minutes or until the onions become coked a little.

Nutrition Information

- Nutritionist's Calories: 134 kcal 7%
- Total Fat: 1.5 g 2%
- Carbohydrates: 23.3g 8%
- Protein: 7.7 g 15%
- Cholesterol: 0 mg 0%
- Sodium: 1044 mg 42%

122. Favorite Barbecue Chicken

"This barbecue sauce is loved by all because it's neither too sweet nor tangy. Finished quickly and also, perfect on pork chops or ribs."

Servings: 2 | Prep: 5 m | Ready In: 40 m

Ingredients

- 1 1/2 tbsps. olive oil
- 1/4 c diced onion
- 2 cloves garlic, minced
- 5 tbsps. ketchup
- 3 tbsps. honey
- 3 tbsps. brown sugar
- 2 tbsps. apple cider vinegar
- 1 tbsp. Worcestershire sauce
- salt and pepper to taste
- 2 skinless, boneless chicken breast halves

Directions

- Preheat the grill over medium-high heat.
- Over medium heat, heat olive oil in a skillet, add garlic and onion and then sauté until tender. Add in Worcestershire sauce, ketchup, honey, apple cider vinegar, brown sugar, pepper and salt and stir. Let to cook for several minutes to thicken the sauce. Take out from the heat and let to cool.
- Polish grill grate lightly with oil. Dunk chicken into the sauce and flip to coat. Let to cook on the grill for about 10 to 15 minutes and flip once. Transfer the chicken to skillet containing the sauce. Over medium heat, let to simmer for approximately five minutes per side.

Nutrition Information

- Nutritionist's Calories: 452 kcal 23%
- Total Fat: 13.1 g 20%
- Carbohydrates: 60.1g 19%
- Protein: 25.7 g 51%
- Cholesterol: 67 mg 22%
- Sodium: 714 mg 29%

123. Festive Wild Rice

"This wild rice contains dried cranberries and peas and can be served as a whole meal!"

Servings: 4 | Prep: 5 m | Ready In: 25 m

Ingredients

- 1 (6 ounce) package uncooked wild rice
- 1 c frozen green peas, thawed
- 1/2 c dried cranberries

Directions

- Prepare the rice by following the package instructions.
- Heat peas in microwave for two minutes on high or until heated through.
- Into the cooked rice, roll the warm peas and cranberries.

Nutrition Information

- Nutritionist's Calories: 184 kcal 9%
- Total Fat: 0.5 g < 1%
- Carbohydrates: 40.1g 13%
- Protein: 6.2 g 12%
- Cholesterol: 0 mg 0%
- Sodium: 45 mg 2%

124. Fiery Fish Tacos with Crunchy Corn Salsa

"This recipe for grilled fish is spicy and made with fresh corn and a crunchy veggie salsa. The guests will come back for more in seconds!"

Servings: 6 | Prep: 30 m | Ready In: 40 m

Ingredients

- 2 c cooked corn kernels
- 1/2 c diced red onion
- 1 c peeled, diced jicama
- 1/2 c diced red bell pepper
- 1 c fresh cilantro leaves, chopped
- 1 lime, juiced and zested
- 2 tbsps. cayenne pepper, or to taste
- 1 tbsp. ground black pepper
- 2 tbsps. salt, or to taste
- 6 (4 ounce) fillets tilapia
- 2 tbsps. olive oil
- 12 corn tortillas, warmed
- 2 tbsps. sour cream, or to taste

Directions

- Preheat the grill over high heat.
- Combine together corn, cilantro, red bell pepper, red onion and jicama in a medium bowl. Add in zest and lime juice and stir.
- Mix salt, ground black pepper and cayenne pepper in a small bowl.
- Use olive oil to polish each fillet and drizzle with spices to suit your taste.
- Onto the grill grate, spread fillets and then cook for about three minutes on each side. Add 2 corn tortillas along with corn salsa, fish and sour cream on top of each fiery fish taco.

Nutrition Information

- Nutritionist's Calories: 351 kcal 18%
- Total Fat: 9.6 g 15%
- Carbohydrates: 40.3g 13%
- Protein: 28.7 g 57%
- Cholesterol: 43 mg 14%
- Sodium: 2416 mg 97%

125. Fig and Lemon Chicken

"These chicken thighs are roasted together with lemon slices and figs in a glaze of brown sugar, lemon and vinegar. Simple, tasty and you can easily double the sauce."

Servings: 12 | Prep: 10 m | Ready In: 1 h

Ingredients

- 1 lemon, juiced
- 1/4 c brown sugar
- 1/4 c white vinegar
- 1/4 c water
- 1 1/2 pounds dried figs
- 1 lemon, sliced

- 12 chicken thighs
- salt to taste
- 1 tbsp. chopped fresh parsley
- 1 tsp. dried parsley

Directions

- Preheat an oven to 200 degrees C (400 degrees F).
- Mix vinegar, water, lemon juice and brown sugar in a small bowl and reserve.
- At the bottom of a roasting or baking dish of 11x16 inch, put figs and lemon slices. Spread chicken thighs on top and add the mixture of vinegar on top of chicken. Lastly, drizzle dried parsley and salt on top.
- Roast or bake for 50 minutes at 200 degrees C (400 degrees F) while basting occasionally (in case the figs start to brown, turn them).
- Take out the figs, lemon slices and chicken from the baking dish using a slotted spoon and transfer to a warm platter. Skim the fat from the cooking juice and spread on top of chicken as the sauce. Sprinkle fresh parsley on top before serving.

Nutrition Information

- Nutritionist's Calories: 323 kcal 16%
- Total Fat: 10.5 g 16%
- Carbohydrates: 43.6g 14%
- Protein: 17.8 g 36%
- Cholesterol: 59 mg 20%
- Sodium: 62 mg 2%

126. Fra Diavolo Sauce With Pasta

"A sauce that has scallops and shrimp and great when served along with linguine pasta."

Servings: 8 | Prep: 20 m | Ready In: 1 h

Ingredients

- 4 tbsps. olive oil, divided
- 6 cloves garlic, crushed
- 3 c whole peeled tomatoes with liquid, chopped
- 1 1/2 tsps. salt
- 1 tsp. crushed red pepper flakes
- 1 (16 ounce) package linguine pasta
- 8 ounces small shrimp, peeled and deveined
- 8 ounces bay scallops
- 1 tbsp. chopped fresh parsley

Directions

- Over medium heat, heat two tbsps. of olive oil along with garlic in a saucepan. Add tomatoes once garlic begins to sizzle. Add pepper and salt to taste. Heat to boil. Decrease the heat and allow to simmer stirring at intervals for about 30 minutes.
- In the meantime, bring to boil lightly salted water in a pot and add pasta, Cook until al dente or for about 8 to 10 minutes. Drain.
- Over high heat, heat two tbsps. of olive oil in a skillet, add scallops and shrimp and then cook while stirring occasionally for about 2 minutes or until shrimp turns pink. Transfer the scallops and shrimp to the mixture of tomato, add parsley and stir. Let to cook for about 3 to 4 minutes or until sauce starts to bubble. Can serve the sauce on top of pasta.

Nutrition Information

- Nutritionist's Calories: 335 kcal 17%
- Total Fat: 8.9 g 14%
- Carbohydrates: 46.3g 15%
- Protein: 18.7 g 37%
- Cholesterol: 52 mg 17%
- Sodium: 655 mg 26%

127. Fresh California Salsa

"This salsa is famous and often asked for at potlucks. You can serve together with tortilla chips."

Servings: 16

Ingredients

- 4 large tomatoes, diced
- 1/2 large onion, minced
- 3 cloves garlic, chopped
- 2/3 c chopped fresh cilantro
- 1 jalapeno pepper, seeded and minced
- 2 tbsps. fresh lime juice
- salt to taste

Directions

- Mix lime juice, cilantro, garlic, tomatoes and onion in a small mixing bowl. Pour in two tsps. of jalapenos at a time and taste after every addition to check the hotness of salsa. Jalapeno peppers have varying hotness and hence, important to check salsa to make sure you can handle the hotness. Season with salt.

Nutrition Information

- Nutritionist's Calories: 12 kcal < 1%
- Total Fat: 0.1 g < 1%
- Carbohydrates: 2.7g < 1%
- Protein: 0.5 g 1%
- Cholesterol: 0 mg 0%
- Sodium: 3 mg < 1%

128. Fresh Tomato Salad

"A salad made with fresh cucumber, tomato, herbs, onion and green pepper."

Ingredients

- 5 tomatoes, diced
- 1 onion, chopped
- 1 cucumber, sliced
- 1 green bell pepper, chopped
- 1/2 c chopped fresh basil
- 1/2 c chopped parsley
- 2 tbsps. crushed garlic
- salt and pepper to taste
- 2 tbsps. white wine vinegar

Directions

- Mix garlic, basil, tomato, parsley, onion, vinegar, cucumber and bell pepper in a large bowl. Mix and season with pepper and salt. Refrigerate and then serve.

Nutrition Information

- Nutritionist's Calories: 39 kcal 2%
- Total Fat: 0.4 g < 1%
- Carbohydrates: 8.6g 3%
- Protein: 1.8 g 4%
- Cholesterol: 0 mg 0%
- Sodium: 10 mg < 1%

129. Fresh Tomato Salsa

"A tasty salsa made at home."

Servings: 4 | Prep: 10 m | Ready In: 1 h 10 m

Ingredients

- 3 tomatoes, chopped
- 1/2 c finely diced onion

- 5 serrano chiles, finely chopped
- 1/2 c chopped fresh cilantro
- 1 tsp. salt
- 2 tsps. lime juice

Directions

- Combine together lime juice, cilantro, salt, onion, tomatoes and chili peppers in a medium bowl. Refrigerate for 1 hour prior to serving.

Nutrition Information

- Nutritionist's Calories: 51 kcal 3%
- Total Fat: 0.2 g < 1%
- Carbohydrates: 9.7g 3%
- Protein: 2.1 g 4%
- Cholesterol: 0 mg 0%
- Sodium: 592 mg 24%

Directions

- In a large stockpot, bring Old Bay Seasoning and water to boil.
- Pour in potatoes and then cook for about 15 minutes. Pour in sausage and let to cook for about 5 minutes. Pour in corn and allow to cook for about five minutes. Add in shrimp, stir and then let to cook for about five minutes until the shrimp turns pink. Drain right away and serve.

Nutrition Information

- Nutritionist's Calories: 499 kcal 25%
- Total Fat: 15.5 g 24%
- Carbohydrates: 39.1g 13%
- Protein: 52.6 g 105%
- Cholesterol: 299 mg 100%
- Sodium: 2733 mg 109%

130. Frogmore Stew

"I have used this recipe for many years since I came to South Carolina. You can adjust to serve everyone. For each quart of water, add two tbsps. of the seasoning. In case hot smoked sausage isn't available, add any smoked sausage like kielbasa along with crushed hot red pepper."

*Servings: 12 | **Prep:** 10 m | **Ready In:** 40 m*

Ingredients

- 6 quarts water
- 3/4 c Old Bay Seasoning TM
- 2 pounds new red potatoes
- 2 pounds hot smoked sausage links, cut into 2 inch pieces
- 12 ears corn - husked, cleaned and quartered
- 4 pounds large fresh shrimp, unpeeled

131. Fruit Salad in Seconds

"I created this combo when unexpected guests showed up at a mealtime. It's now a family favorite. It's fast and simple. Can replace strawberry with lemon yogurt if desired."

*Servings: 12 | **Prep:** 10 m | **Ready In:** 10 m*

Ingredients

- 1 pint fresh strawberries, sliced
- 1 pound seedless green grapes, halved
- 3 bananas, peeled and sliced
- 1 (8 ounce) container strawberry yogurt

Directions

- Mix together strawberry yogurt, bananas, strawberries and grapes in a large bowl. Serve at once.

Nutrition Information

- Nutritionist's Calories: 81 kcal 4%
- Total Fat: 0.6 g < 1%
- Carbohydrates: 19.2g 6%
- Protein: 1.5 g 3%
- Cholesterol: 2 mg < 1%
- Sodium: 11 mg < 1%

132. Garbanzo Tomato Pasta Soup

"This is super simple vegan meal. The combo of pasta and garbanzo beans (chick peas) yields complex proteins needed by a vegan. Great for those who like tomato and garlic."

Servings: 4 | Prep: 15 m | Ready In: 30 m

Ingredients

- 3 (14.5 ounce) cans vegetable broth
- 3/4 c small seashell pasta
- 1 tbsp. olive oil
- 1 onion, chopped
- 2 cloves garlic, minced
- 1 (15 ounce) can garbanzo beans, drained and rinsed
- 1 (28 ounce) can whole peeled tomatoes, chopped, juice reserved
- 1/2 tsp. dried basil
- 1/2 tsp. dried thyme
- salt and pepper to taste

Directions

- Bring to boil vegetable broth in a pot, add pasta and then let to cook until al dente or for about 8 to 10 minutes.
- In the meantime, over medium heat, heat oil in a skillet, add garlic and onions and sauté until translucent. Mix into the pasta and then pour in basil, pepper, garbanzo beans, salt, tomatoes and thyme and heat through before serving.

Nutrition Information

- Nutritionist's Calories: 276 kcal 14%
- Total Fat: 5.7 g 9%
- Carbohydrates: 48.8g 16%
- Protein: 9.6 g 19%
- Cholesterol: 0 mg 0%
- Sodium: 1699 mg 68%

133. Garlic Chicken And Grapes

"This unique recipe is made of sesame seeds and grapes baked together with chicken. You can served together with a mustard sauce."

Servings: 6 | Prep: 5 m | Ready In: 45 m

Ingredients

- 3 tbsps. Dijon-style prepared mustard
- 3 tbsps. soy sauce
- 2 tbsps. honey
- 2 tbsps. white wine vinegar
- 2 cloves garlic, minced
- 2 tbsps. vegetable oil
- 3 pounds skinless, boneless chicken breast halves
- 1 tbsp. sesame seeds
- 2 c seedless green grapes

Directions

- Mix vinegar, honey, mustard and soy sauce. Reserve the sauce.
- Mix oil and garlic in a pan of 9 x 13 inch. Transfer chicken to pan with the skin side facing down.
- Bake while covered for 25 minutes at 205 degrees C (400 degrees F) if using thighs. Bake while covered for 10 minutes at 250 degrees C (400 degrees F) if using breasts. Remove cover and flip over the chicken pieces. Drizzle sesame seeds on top. Bake for about 15 to 20 minutes until no pink color remains at the center. Drizzle grapes on top of chicken and then bake for five minutes. Take out from the oven and spread the grapes and chicken onto a platter. Bring the sauce when serving.

Nutrition Information

- Nutritionist's Calories: 373 kcal 19%
- Total Fat: 11.1 g 17%
- Carbohydrates: 18.1g 6%
- Protein: 48.4 g 97%
- Cholesterol: 129 mg 43%
- Sodium: 753 mg 30%

---

134. Garlic Chicken with Orzo Noodles

"If you love garlic, this easy recipe is for you and has a spicy kick. I love combining my favorite clam sauce and linguine dish with this recent addition of orzo pasta. This recipe has a few variations. For more spice, pour in extra red pepper. Replace chicken with shrimp or clams. Replace spinach leaves with diced tomatoes. For an Italian flavor, add spices like oregano, basil and rosemary."

Servings: 4 | Prep: 15 m | Ready In: 30 m

Ingredients

- 1 c uncooked orzo pasta
- 2 tbsps. olive oil
- 2 cloves garlic
- 1/4 tsp. crushed red pepper
- 2 skinless, boneless chicken breast halves - cut into bite-size pieces
- salt to taste
- 1 tbsp. chopped fresh parsley
- 2 c fresh spinach leaves
- grated Parmesan cheese for topping

Directions

- Bring to boil lightly salted water in a pot and add orzo pasta. Cook until al dente or for about 8 to 10 minutes. Drain.
- Over medium-high heat, heat oil in a skillet, add red pepper and garlic and then cook for 1 minute until the garlic turns golden brown. Add in salt and chicken, stir and then cook for about 2 to 5 minutes until and the juice runs clear and browned lightly. Decrease the heat to medium, add in cooked orzo and parsley and mix. Put spinach into skillet and continue to cook while stirring frequently for 5 minutes until the spinach becomes wilted. Top with Parmesan cheese and serve.

Nutrition Information

- Nutritionist's Calories: 351 kcal 18%
- Total Fat: 10.6 g 16%
- Carbohydrates: 40.4g 13%
- Protein: 22.3 g 45%
- Cholesterol: 38 mg 13%
- Sodium: 164 mg 7%

---

135. Garlic Penne Pasta

"Delicious pasta recipe that is super simple to prepare and

often hit at dinner. Also great as leftovers! The ingredients are readily available and feel free to substitute penne with pasta you love."

Servings: 8 | Prep: 5 m | Ready In: 20 m

Ingredients

- 1 (16 ounce) package penne pasta
- 1/4 c olive oil, divided
- 3 cloves garlic, chopped
- 2 sun-dried tomatoes, chopped (optional)
- 1 tbsp. dried parsley
- 1 tsp. crushed red pepper flakes
- 1/2 tsp. black pepper
- 1/4 c grated Parmesan cheese

Directions

- Bring to boil lightly salted water in a pot and add pasta. Cook until al dente or for about 8 to 10 minutes. Drain pasta and take back to the pot.
- Over medium heat, heat one tbsp. of olive oil in a skillet, add parsley, sun-dried tomatoes and garlic and then sauté for approximately one minute. Add black pepper and red pepper flakes to taste. Mix into the cooked pasta and pour in the olive oil remaining. Serve topped with Parmesan.

Nutrition Information

- Nutritionist's Calories: 276 kcal 14%
- Total Fat: 8.9 g 14%
- Carbohydrates: 41.9g 14%
- Protein: 8.6 g 17%
- Cholesterol: 2 mg < 1%
- Sodium: 53 mg 2%

136. Garlic Ranch Chicken

"Chicken recipe that is super simple and quick. Keep the calories down by adding fat free dressing and also keep chicken from burning."

Servings: 4 | Prep: 20 m | Ready In: 1 h 5 m

Ingredients

- 4 skinless, boneless chicken breasts
- 1 c fat free ranch dressing
- 2 tbsps. chopped garlic
- 1 tbsp. chopped fresh basil

Directions

- In a plastic bag that is sealable, mix basil, garlic and dressing. Pour in pieces of chicken and turn to coat. Remove air by squeezing and then seal the bag. Refrigerate for 30 minutes.
- Preheat the grill over medium heat.
- Let the chicken breasts grill while flipping occasionally for about 6 to 8 minutes per side until the juice is clear when poked with a fork.

Nutrition Information

- Nutritionist's Calories: 232 kcal 12%
- Total Fat: 2.2 g 3%
- Carbohydrates: 22.6g 7%
- Protein: 28 g 56%
- Cholesterol: 69 mg 23%
- Sodium: 779 mg 31%

137. Garlic Shrimp Linguine

"This recipe is so easy and tasty. It makes a classy dish to serve dinner guests."

Servings: 8 | Prep: 10 m | Ready In: 30 m

Ingredients

- 1 pound uncooked linguine
- 1 tbsp. butter
- 3 tbsps. white wine
- 2 tsps. grated Parmesan cheese
- 3 cloves garlic, minced
- 1 tsp. chopped fresh parsley
- 1 pinch salt and pepper to taste
- 1 pound medium shrimp, peeled and deveined

Directions

- Bring to boil lightly salted water in a pot and add pasta. Cook until al dente or for about 8 to 10 minutes and then drain.
- Over medium low heat, melt butter in a medium saucepan and then pour in parsley, wine, garlic, pepper, salt and cheese. Over low heat, let to simmer while stirring occasionally for about 3 to 5 minutes.
- Raise the heat to medium high and then pour in shrimp into the saucepan. Let to cook for approximately 3 to 4 minutes or until the shrimp starts become pink. Avoid overcooking.
- Subdivide the pasta into portions and then spread the sauce at the top. If desired, sprinkle fresh parsley and Parmesan cheese on top.

Nutrition Information

- Nutritionist's Calories: 287 kcal 14%
- Total Fat: 4.9 g 8%
- Carbohydrates: 42.3g 14%
- Protein: 17.6 g 35%
- Cholesterol: 77 mg 26%
- Sodium: 126 mg 5%

138. Garlic Shrimp Pasta

"The key to fast and quick dish is preparing garlic butter in the microwave. A great recipe for dinner with friends or family."

Servings: 8

Ingredients

- 1 pound vermicelli pasta
- 1 tbsp. vegetable oil
- 1 pound medium shrimp - peeled and deveined
- 3 tbsps. minced garlic
- 2 tbsps. butter
- 2 tbsps. grated Parmesan cheese

Directions

- In a pot containing boiling water and vegetable oil, cook pasta until al dente.
- In the meantime, add shrimp into the hot salty water and let cook for about 3 to 5 minutes until they become pink. The cooking time depends on the shrimp's size. Take out the tails and transfer to warm water in a bowl.
- Combine minced garlic and margarine or butter in a microwave safe bowl. Heat for 45 seconds in microwave on high or until melted and then mix.
- Drain the pasta and then place onto serving dish. Mix with shrimp and garlic butter. Add grated Parmesan cheese on top and then serve while still warm.

Nutrition Information

- Nutritionist's Calories: 314 kcal 16%
- Total Fat: 7.3 g 11%
- Carbohydrates: 42.9g 14%
- Protein: 19.8 g 40%
- Cholesterol: 95 mg 32%
- Sodium: 127 mg 5%

139. German Chicken

"These are boneless chicken breasts that are cooked on sauerkraut and then covered with barbecue sauce. It's delicious and may sound strange. My family favorite. It's a bit sweet due to the BBQ sauce. I usually serve it together with mashed potatoes."

Servings: 4

Ingredients

- 4 skinless, boneless chicken breast halves
- 1 c barbecue sauce
- 22 ounces sauerkraut

Directions

- Preheat an oven to 175 degrees C (350 degrees F).
- Spread a single layer of sauerkraut in a baking dish of 9x13 inch. Add chicken breasts over sauerkraut. Spread on top of chicken, the barbecue sauce. Cover the dish and then bake for about 30 minutes or until juice runs clear and chicken is done.

Nutrition Information

- Nutritionist's Calories: 253 kcal 13%
- Total Fat: 1.9 g 3%
- Carbohydrates: 29.2g 9%
- Protein: 28.6 g 57%
- Cholesterol: 68 mg 23%
- Sodium: 1794 mg 72%

140. Gina's Lemon Pepper Chicken

"This dish is fast and super simple. I found this recipe sometime back by experimenting. You like it just like me! Good alongside a tossed salad or together with a vegetable and tater tots."

Servings: 6

Ingredients

- 6 skinless, boneless chicken breast halves
- 1 tsp. lemon pepper
- 1 pinch garlic powder
- 1 tsp. onion powder

Directions

- Preheat an oven to 175 degrees C (350 degrees F).
- Into a baking dish of 9x13 inch that is greased lightly, put chicken. Add to taste onion powder, lemon pepper and garlic powder. Bake for about 15 minutes in oven.
- Flip the chicken pieces over and then season again to suit your taste. Bake for about 15 more minutes or until the juice runs clear and the chicken is done.

Nutrition Information

- Nutritionist's Calories: 133 kcal 7%
- Total Fat: 2.8 g 4%
- Carbohydrates: 0.5g < 1%
- Protein: 24.6 g 49%
- Cholesterol: 67 mg 22%
- Sodium: 136 mg 5%

141. Ginger Glazed Mahi Mahi

"This is a sweet, sour ginger Glazed Mahi Mahi with a

rich flavor. Needs 30 minutes to prepare and includes 20 minutes for marinating. The recipe is very tasty and you will like it!"

Servings: 4 | Prep: 5 m | Ready In: 37 m

Ingredients

- 3 tbsps. honey
- 3 tbsps. soy sauce
- 3 tbsps. balsamic vinegar
- 1 tsp. grated fresh ginger root
- 1 clove garlic, crushed or to taste
- 2 tsps. olive oil
- 4 (6 ounce) mahi mahi fillets
- salt and pepper to taste
- 1 tbsp. vegetable oil

Directions

- Combine together olive oil, garlic, ginger, honey, soy sauce and balsamic vinegar in a shallow glass dish. Add pepper and salt to fish fillets and then transfer to the dish. Place with the skin side facing downwards in case fillets have skin. Cover the dish and marinate for 20 minutes in a fridge.
- Over medium-high heat, heat vegetable oil in a skillet. Take out the fish from dish and set the marinade aside. Let the fish fry for about 4 to 6 minutes per side, flip once, until the fish easily flakes using a fork. Transfer the fillets onto a serving platter and then maintain them warm.
- Into the skillet, add the marinade reserved and then heat at a medium heat until mixture decreases to a glaze constantly. On top of fish, pour the glaze and then serve right away.

Nutrition Information

- Nutritionist's Calories: 259 kcal 13%
- Total Fat: 7 g 11%
- Carbohydrates: 16g 5%
- Protein: 32.4 g 65%

- Cholesterol: 124 mg 41%
- Sodium: 830 mg 33%

142. Grandma's Chicken Noodle Soup

"My grandma gave me this recipe. The soup is spicy and delicious and I hope you'll love it. You can add smoked chicken in case you want more flavor!!"

Servings: 12 | Prep: 20 m | Ready In: 45 m

Ingredients

- 2 1/2 c wide egg noodles
- 1 tsp. vegetable oil
- 12 c chicken broth
- 1 1/2 tbsps. salt
- 1 tsp. poultry seasoning
- 1 c chopped celery
- 1 c chopped onion
- 1/3 c cornstarch
- 1/4 c water
- 3 c diced, cooked chicken meat

Directions

- Bring to boil lightly salted water in a pot and add oil and egg noodles. Let to boil for about 8 minutes or until tender. Then drain and use cold running water to rinse.
- Mix poultry seasoning, broth and salt in a Dutch oven or saucepan. Heat to boil. Add in onion and celery and stir. Decrease the heat, cover the pan and allow to simmer about 15 minutes.
- Combine together water and cornstarch in a small bowl until the cornstarch dissolves completely. Slowly add while stirring continuously to soup. Add in chicken and noodles, stir and then heat through.

Nutrition Information

- Nutritionist's Calories: 147 kcal 7%
- Total Fat: 3.6 g 5%
- Carbohydrates: 11.4g 4%
- Protein: 15.7 g 31%
- Cholesterol: 33 mg 11%
- Sodium: 1664 mg 67%

143. Grandma's Slow Cooker Vegetarian Chili

"A simple slow cooked recipe that can please a crowd and can sit the slow cooker until serving."

Servings: 8 | Prep: 10 m | Ready In: 2 h 10 m

Ingredients

- 1 (19 ounce) can black bean soup
- 1 (15 ounce) can kidney beans, rinsed and drained
- 1 (15 ounce) can garbanzo beans, rinsed and drained
- 1 (16 ounce) can vegetarian baked beans
- 1 (14.5 ounce) can chopped tomatoes in puree
- 1 (15 ounce) can whole kernel corn, drained
- 1 onion, chopped
- 1 green bell pepper, chopped
- 2 stalks celery, chopped
- 2 cloves garlic, chopped
- 1 tbsp. chili powder, or to taste
- 1 tbsp. dried parsley
- 1 tbsp. dried oregano
- 1 tbsp. dried basil

Directions

- Mix black bean soup, baked beans, kidney beans, celery, garbanzo beans, bell pepper,

tomatoes, onion and corn in a slow cooker. Season with basil, oregano, garlic, parsley and chili powder. Let to cook for a minimum of 2 hours on High.

Nutrition Information

- Nutritionist's Calories: 260 kcal 13%
- Total Fat: 2 g 3%
- Carbohydrates: 52.6g 17%
- Protein: 12.4 g 25%
- Cholesterol: < 1 mg < 1%
- Sodium: 966 mg 39%

144. Great Garlic Knots

"These tasty knots of herb-seasoned bread are easy and fast to prepare goes well any meal. You can enjoy them as a delicious snack in between meals along with spread slathered on! The knots are fragrant when you add fresh rosemary."

Servings: 4 | Prep: 5 m | Ready In: 15 m

Ingredients

- 1 (11 ounce) container refrigerated breadstick dough
- 1 egg, lightly beaten
- 1 tsp. garlic powder
- 1 tbsp. chopped fresh rosemary

Directions

- Preheat an oven to 190 degrees C (375 degrees F).
- Twist dough to form 12 knots and then transfer to a cookie sheet. Use egg to polish the knots and then drizzle garlic and rosemary on top of knots. Follow the package instructions on how to bake the knots.

Nutrition Information

- Nutritionist's Calories: 242 kcal 12%
- Total Fat: 5.4 g 8%
- Carbohydrates: 38.7g 12%
- Protein: 7.7 g 15%
- Cholesterol: 53 mg 18%
- Sodium: 596 mg 24%

145. Greek Chicken Pasta

"A pasta recipe with flavors of Greece. The recipe makes a nice and filling meal. Mix in some kalamata olives for more flavor. Add pasta you love."

Servings: 6 | Prep: 15 m | Ready In: 30 m

Ingredients

- 1 (16 ounce) package linguine pasta
- 1/2 c chopped red onion
- 1 tbsp. olive oil
- 2 cloves garlic, crushed
- 1 pound skinless, boneless chicken breast meat - cut into bite-size pieces
- 1 (14 ounce) can marinated artichoke hearts, drained and chopped
- 1 large tomato, chopped
- 1/2 c crumbled feta cheese
- 3 tbsps. chopped fresh parsley
- 2 tbsps. lemon juice
- 2 tsps. dried oregano
- salt and pepper to taste
- 2 lemons, wedged, for garnish

Directions

- Bring to boil lightly salted water in a pot and add pasta. Cook for about 8 to 10 minutes until the pasta becomes tender but firm when bitten. Drain.
- Over medium-high heat, heat olive oil in a skillet, add garlic and onion and then sauté for two minutes until fragrant. Add in chicken, stir and then cook while stirring frequently for about 5 to 6 minutes until the juice runs clear and the no pink color of chicken remains at the center.
- Decrease the heat to medium-low and then pour in the cooked pasta, oregano, artichoke hearts, lemon juice, tomato, parsley and feta cheese. Cook while stirring for 2 to 3 minutes until heated through. Take out from the heat source, add pepper and salt to taste and then add lemon wedges on top.

Nutrition Information

- Nutritionist's Calories: 488 kcal 24%
- Total Fat: 11.4 g 18%
- Carbohydrates: 70g 23%
- Protein: 32.6 g 65%
- Cholesterol: 55 mg 18%
- Sodium: 444 mg 18%

146. Greek Pasta with Tomatoes and White Beans

"This recipe is simple, fast and delicious. The different flavors blend and meld together nicely."

Servings: 4 | Prep: 10 m | Ready In: 25 m

Ingredients

- 2 (14.5 ounce) cans Italian-style diced tomatoes
- 1 (19 ounce) can cannellini beans, drained and rinsed
- 10 ounces fresh spinach, washed and chopped
- 8 ounces penne pasta
- 1/2 c crumbled feta cheese

Directions

- In a pot containing boiling salted water, cook pasta until al dente.
- In the meantime, mix beans and tomatoes in a non-stick skillet. Over medium high heat, heat to boil, low the heat and let to simmer for about 10 minutes.
- Pour into the sauce, spinach and then let to cook while stirring continuously for about two minutes or until the spinach has wilted.
- You can serve the sauce on top of pasta and top with feta.

Nutrition Information

- Nutritionist's Calories: 460 kcal 23%
- Total Fat: 5.9 g 9%
- Carbohydrates: 79g 25%
- Protein: 23.4 g 47%
- Cholesterol: 17 mg 6%
- Sodium: 593 mg 24%

147. Greek Penne and Chicken

"I love this 'stand by' recipe. I usually have the ingredients to prepare a fast, tasty and filling meal."

Servings: *4* | **Prep:** *20 m* | **Ready In:** *50 m*

Ingredients

- 1 (16 ounce) package penne pasta
- 1 1/2 tbsps. butter
- 1/2 c chopped red onion
- 2 cloves garlic, minced
- 1 pound skinless, boneless chicken breast halves - cut into bite-size pieces
- 1 (14 ounce) can artichoke hearts in water
- 1 tomato, chopped

- 1/2 c crumbled feta cheese
- 3 tbsps. chopped fresh parsley
- 2 tbsps. lemon juice
- 1 tsp. dried oregano
- salt to taste
- ground black pepper to taste

Directions

- Cook penne pasta in a pot containing boiling salted water until al dente and then drain pasta.
- In the meantime, over medium-high heat, heat butter in a skillet, pour in garlic and onion and let to cook for two minutes. Pour in sliced chicken and continue to cook stirring frequently for 5 to 6 minutes until golden brown.
- Decrease the heat to medium- low. Then drain and slice the artichoke hearts. Transfer the chopped hearts, dried oregano, chopped tomato, drained penne pasta, feta cheese, lemon juice and fresh parsley to the skillet. Let to cook for 2 to 3 minutes until heated through.
- Add ground black pepper and salt to taste. Serve while still warm.

Nutrition Information

- Nutritionist's Calories: 685 kcal 34%
- Total Fat: 13.2 g 20%
- Carbohydrates: 96.2g 31%
- Protein: 47 g 94%
- Cholesterol: 94 mg 31%
- Sodium: 826 mg 33%

148. Green Salsa

"This delicious and tangy salsa can be used for cooking or over Mexican foods! Alter the amount of jalapeno to suit your taste."

Servings: 16 | Prep: 20 m | Ready In: 20 m

Ingredients

- 8 tomatillos, husked
- 3 shallots
- 2 cloves garlic, peeled
- 1 (4 ounce) can chopped green chile peppers
- 1/4 c chopped fresh cilantro
- 1 fresh jalapeno pepper, seeded
- salt to taste

Directions

- Put jalapeno pepper, tomatillos, salt, shallots, garlic, cilantro and green chile peppers in a food processor. Chop coarsely with the pulse setting. Cover and then refrigerate until when serving.

Nutrition Information

- Nutritionist's Calories: 15 kcal < 1%
- Total Fat: 0.2 g < 1%
- Carbohydrates: 3.1g 1%
- Protein: 0.5 g 1%
- Cholesterol: 0 mg 0%
- Sodium: 84 mg 3%

149. Grilled Asparagus

"The main advantage of this dish is the simplicity in it. Over high heat, fresh asparagus along with pepper, salt and some oil is cooked fast on the grill. The dish has natural flavor of vegetables."

Servings: 4 | Prep: 15 m | Ready In: 18 m

Ingredients

- 1 pound fresh asparagus spears, trimmed
- 1 tbsp. olive oil
- salt and pepper to taste

Directions

- Preheat the grill over high heat.
- Use olive oil to coat asparagus spears lightly. Add to taste, pepper and salt.
- Over high heat, grill for about 2 to 3 minutes or to the doneness desired.

Nutrition Information

- Nutritionist's Calories: 53 kcal 3%
- Total Fat: 3.5 g 5%
- Carbohydrates: 4.4g 1%
- Protein: 2.5 g 5%
- Cholesterol: 0 mg 0%
- Sodium: 2 mg < 1%

150. Grilled Chicken Adobo

"A Filipino chicken dish recipe that is delicious and simple. It's prepared with vinegar, soy sauce and garlic. You can easily increase this chicken recipe to feed guests at a party. You can serve on top of rice along with some of the sauce and not too much."

Servings: 8 | Prep: 15 m | Ready In: 50 m

Ingredients

- 1 1/2 c soy sauce
- 1 1/2 c water
- 3/4 c vinegar
- 3 tbsps. honey
- 1 1/2 tbsps. minced garlic
- 3 bay leaves

- 1/2 tsp. black pepper
- 3 pounds skinless, boneless chicken thighs

Directions

- Preheat the outdoor grill over high heat and polish the grate lightly with oil.
- Combine soy sauce, bay leaves, water, vinegar, pepper, honey and garlic in a large pot. Heat to boil the mixture and transfer chicken to pot. Low the heat, cover and let to cook for about 35 to 40 minutes.
- Take out the chicken, use paper towels to drain and reserve. Get rid of bay leaves. Heat the mixture to boil again and then let to cook until decreased to around 1 1/2 c.
- Onto the grill prepared, put the chicken and then grill for about 5 minutes per side until crisp and browned. You can serve together with the soy sauce mixture remaining.

Nutrition Information

- Nutritionist's Calories: 255 kcal 13%
- Total Fat: 6.7 g 10%
- Carbohydrates: 10.8g 3%
- Protein: 36.6 g 73%
- Cholesterol: 141 mg 47%
- Sodium: 2854 mg 114%

151. Grilled Cilantro Salmon

"Grilled salmon for summer! This salmon marinade blends cilantro, lime, garlic and honey."

Servings: 6 | Prep: 15 m | Ready In: 45 m

Ingredients

- 1 bunch cilantro leaves, chopped
- 2 cloves garlic, chopped
- 2 c honey
- juice from one lime
- 4 salmon steaks
- salt and pepper to taste

Directions

- Over medium-low heat, combine together lime juice, honey, cilantro and garlic in a small saucepan. Heat for 5 minutes until honey becomes stirred easily. Take out from the heat source and cool a bit.
- In a baking dish, put salmon steaks and add pepper and salt. Spread the marinade on top of salmon, cover and chill for ten 10 minutes.
- Preheat the outdoor grill over high heat.
- Polish grill grate lightly with oil. Onto the grill, put salmon steaks and let to cook for five minutes per side or until the fish flakes easily with a fork.

Nutrition Information

- Nutritionist's Calories: 459 kcal 23%
- Total Fat: 4.5 g 7%
- Carbohydrates: 94.3g 30%
- Protein: 17 g 34%
- Cholesterol: 34 mg 11%
- Sodium: 41 mg 2%

152. Grilled Peanut Chicken

"A great dish when expecting guests and don't' know what to prepare and want to please them at dinner."

Servings: 4 | Prep: 15 m | Ready In: 30 m

Ingredients

- 2 tbsps. reduced fat peanut butter
- 1 tbsp. fresh lime juice
- 2 tsps. soy sauce
- 1 clove garlic, chopped
- 1/3 tsp. curry powder
- 1 dash ground cayenne pepper
- 4 skinless, boneless chicken breast halves

Directions

- Preheat the grill over high heat.
- Combine cayenne pepper, curry powder, peanut butter, soy sauce, lime juice and garlic in a bowl.
- Polish grill grate lightly with oil. Onto the grate, put chicken and then use half of the sauce to brush chicken. Let to grill for about 6 to 8 minutes. Flip chicken and use the sauce remaining to brush it. Continue to grill for about 6 to 8 minutes until the juice of chicken runs clear.

Nutrition Information

- Nutritionist's Calories: 176 kcal 9%
- Total Fat: 5.6 g 9%
- Carbohydrates: 3.6g 1%
- Protein: 27 g 54%
- Cholesterol: 67 mg 22%
- Sodium: 253 mg 10%

153. Grilled Portobello Mushrooms

"The steaks of mushroom family are Portobello mushrooms. They are first marinated and then grilled!"

Servings: 3 | Prep: 10 m | Ready In: 1 h 20 m

Ingredients

- 3 portobello mushrooms
- 1/4 c canola oil
- 3 tbsps. chopped onion
- 4 cloves garlic, minced
- 4 tbsps. balsamic vinegar

Directions

- Wash mushrooms, take out the stems and set aside for other use. Transfer the caps with gills facing upwards onto a plate.
- Mix vinegar, garlic, oil and onion in a small bowl. Onto the mushroom caps, spread the mixture evenly and allow to stand for one hour.
- Let to cook over a hot grill for about 10 minutes. Serve right away.

Nutrition Information

- Nutritionist's Calories: 217 kcal 11%
- Total Fat: 19 g 29%
- Carbohydrates: 11g 4%
- Protein: 3.2 g 6%
- Cholesterol: 0 mg 0%
- Sodium: 13 mg < 1%

154. Halibut with Rice Wine

"A nice way to make salmon, cod, sea bass or halibut. You can serve it together with rice or couscous."

Servings: 6 | Prep: 20 m | Ready In: 1 h

Ingredients

- 1 tsp. vegetable oil
- 1 shallots, finely chopped
- 2 cloves garlic, finely chopped

- 1 tbsp. black bean sauce
- 1/2 c mirin (Japanese sweet wine)
- 1 tbsp. soy sauce
- 1 tbsp. rice vinegar
- 6 (4 ounce) fillets halibut, skin removed
- 1 tsp. sesame oil
- 1/4 tsp. pepper
- 2 tbsps. chopped fresh cilantro

Directions

- Over medium heat, heat oil in non-stick saucepan, add garlic and shallots and then cook gently until they are fragrant and not brown. Add in soy sauce, black bean sauce and rice wine and stir. Heat to boil and let to cook until decreased by half. Take out from the heat source, add vinegar, stir and reserve.
- Pat dry the fish. Use sesame oil to rub fish and drizzle pepper. Preheat the outdoor grill over high heat and polish grate lightly with oil.
- Let the fish grill for 5 minutes on each side or until cooked through. Drizzle cilantro on top. Spread the sauce on top and serve.

Nutrition Information

- Nutritionist's Calories: 194 kcal 10%
- Total Fat: 4.3 g 7%
- Carbohydrates: 8.6g 3%
- Protein: 23.9 g 48%
- Cholesterol: 36 mg 12%
- Sodium: 231 mg 9%

---

155. Ham and Beans

"This recipe was developed by my mother and loved it when I was a kid. I adjusted the recipe to suit my taste and kicked it up a little. It's fantastic and has few ingredients! You can make with leftover ham and will be liked by everyone."

Servings: 7 | Prep: 15 m | Ready In: 10 h 15 m

Ingredients

- 1 pound dry great Northern beans
- 1/2 pound cooked ham, diced
- 1 small onion, diced
- 1/2 c brown sugar
- salt and pepper to taste
- 1/4 tsp. cayenne pepper
- 1 tbsp. dried parsley

Directions

- In a large pot, rinse beans. Get rid of the shriveled beans and small stones present. Pour in 8 c cold water. Allow to rest for a minimum of 8 hours or overnight. Drain beans and then rinse.
- Take back the beans to the pot and pour in cayenne, brown sugar, ham, onion, parsley, pepper and salt. Cover with water. Heat to boil, low the heat and allow to simmer for about 1 1/2 to 2 hours until the beans become tender. If need be, pour in extra water while cooking.

Nutrition Information

- Nutritionist's Calories: 300 kcal 15%
- Total Fat: 6.7 g 10%
- Carbohydrates: 42.8g 14%
- Protein: 18.6 g 37%
- Cholesterol: 18 mg 6%
- Sodium: 423 mg 17%

---

156. Hawaiian Chicken Kabobs

"Delicious kabobs that are tender and sweet. They are simple to prepare and need a few ingredients."

Ingredients

- 3 tbsps. soy sauce
- 3 tbsps. brown sugar
- 2 tbsps. sherry
- 1 tbsp. sesame oil
- 1/4 tsp. ground ginger
- 1/4 tsp. garlic powder
- 8 skinless, boneless chicken breast halves - cut into 2 inch pieces
- 1 (20 ounce) can pineapple chunks, drained
- skewers

Directions

- Combine ginger, sherry, soy sauce, garlic powder, brown sugar and sesame oil in a shallow glass dish. Mix pineapple and pieces of chicken into the marinade until coated well. Cover and then refrigerate for at least two hours to marinate.
- Preheat the grill over medium-high heat.
- Polish grill grate lightly with oil. Onto skewers, thread pineapple and chicken alternately. Let to grill while turning frequently for about 15 to 20 minutes or until the juice of chicken runs clear.

Nutrition Information

- Nutritionist's Calories: 203 kcal 10%
- Total Fat: 4.2 g 6%
- Carbohydrates: 17.1g 6%
- Protein: 23.6 g 47%
- Cholesterol: 61 mg 20%
- Sodium: 413 mg 17%

157. Herb and Chicken Pasta

"Adjust the spices and herbs to suit your taste. Decorate with green onions and then serve together with biscuits made at home if desired."

Servings: 4 | Prep: 15 m | Ready In: 30 m

Ingredients

- 1 (16 ounce) package angel hair pasta
- 4 skinless, boneless chicken breast halves
- salt and pepper to taste
- 1/2 tsp. dried basil
- 1/2 tsp. dried rosemary
- 1/2 tsp. Cajun seasoning (optional)
- 1/2 tsp. crushed red pepper flakes (optional)
- 1/4 c olive oil
- 3 cloves garlic, chopped
- 1 onion, chopped
- 1 c chicken broth

Directions

- Bring to boil lightly salted water in a pot and add pasta. Cook until al dente or for about 8 to 10 minutes. Drain and then set aside.
- In the meantime, season the chicken with red pepper flakes, salt, Cajun seasoning, pepper, rosemary and basil. Over medium heat, heat oil in a skillet, add the chicken and then let to cook until browned. Take out the chicken from the skillet, add in onions, garlic and stir. Cook while stirring until clear.
- Place chicken onto the onion mixture in skillet and pour in broth. Let to simmer until no pink color remains and the chicken is done. Pour the mixture on top of pasta and then serve.

Nutrition Information

- Nutritionist's Calories: 597 kcal 30%
- Total Fat: 18.5 g 28%
- Carbohydrates: 66.2g 21%

- Protein: 41 g 82%
- Cholesterol: 68 mg 23%
- Sodium: 559 mg 22%

158. Herbed Chicken Nuggets

"These are tender and tasty chicken nuggets! They are a favorite for my hubby and friends have requested for the recipe!"

Servings: 4 | Prep: 25 m | Ready In: 40 m

Ingredients

- 4 skinless, boneless chicken breasts
- 2 eggs, beaten
- 1 tbsp. water
- 1 tsp. chopped fresh parsley
- 1/2 tsp. dried thyme
- 1 pinch crushed red pepper flakes
- 1/2 c dried bread crumbs, seasoned
- 1/2 c wheat germ
- 1 tsp. dried basil
- 1 tsp. ground black pepper
- 1 tbsp. vegetable oil

Directions

- Preheat an oven to 220 degrees C (425 degrees F). Use a non-stick cooking spray to coat a baking sheet.
- Trim fat present from the chicken and then chop into one-inch cubes.
- Beat eggs and water in a bowl and then pour in chicken.
- Mix basil, bread crumbs, parsley, wheat germ, thyme, pepper and red pepper. Use a fork to mix oil and combine well to distribute evenly. Transfer the seasoning mixture to a plastic bag that is resealable and mix the pieces of chicken to coat.

- Into the baking sheet prepared, put the coated pieces of chicken and then bake for 10 minutes at 220 degrees C (425 degrees F), flip the pieces, and then bake for five more minutes.

Nutrition Information

- Nutritionist's Calories: 309 kcal 15%
- Total Fat: 9.7 g 15%
- Carbohydrates: 18.7g 6%
- Protein: 36 g 72%
- Cholesterol: 162 mg 54%
- Sodium: 378 mg 15%

159. Herbed Chicken Pasta

"A dish that is delicious and super easy to prepare. Chicken is sautéed in a mixture of basil, vegetables and garlic and then served over pasta."

Servings: 4

Ingredients

- 1 pound uncooked linguine
- 2 tsps. vegetable oil
- 1 1/2 c fresh sliced mushrooms
- 1/2 c chopped onion
- 1 clove garlic, minced
- 1 pound skinless, boneless chicken breast halves - cut into 1 inch pieces
- 1/2 tsp. salt
- 1/2 tsp. dried basil
- 1/4 tsp. ground black pepper
- 2 c chopped tomatoes
- 1/4 c grated Parmesan cheese

Directions

- In around four quarts of boiling salty water, cook pasta until al dente and then drain.

- In the meantime, over medium high heat, heat oil in a nonstick skillet until it's hot. Pour in garlic, onions and mushrooms and then sauté for two minutes. Pour in pepper, chicken, basil and salt. Sauté for five minutes or until the chicken is cooked. Pour in sliced tomato and then sauté for two more minutes.
- Spread the chicken herb sauce on top of pasta and serve. Top with Parmesan cheese.

Nutrition Information

- Nutritionist's Calories: 605 kcal 30%
- Total Fat: 8 g 12%
- Carbohydrates: 89.5g 29%
- Protein: 45.2 g 90%
- Cholesterol: 70 mg 23%
- Sodium: 454 mg 18%

160. Homemade Black Bean Veggie Burgers

"This dish will make you to dislike frozen vegetable burgers. The dish is super simple and you will love this vegan delight."

Servings: 4 | Prep: 15 m | Ready In: 35 m

Ingredients

- 1 (16 ounce) can black beans, drained and rinsed
- 1/2 green bell pepper, cut into 2 inch pieces
- 1/2 onion, cut into wedges
- 3 cloves garlic, peeled
- 1 egg
- 1 tbsp. chili powder
- 1 tbsp. cumin
- 1 tsp. Thai chili sauce or hot sauce
- 1/2 c bread crumbs

Directions

- Preheat the outdoor grill over high heat if you're grilling and then coat a sheet of aluminum foil lightly with oil. Preheat an oven to 190 degrees C (375 degrees F) if you're baking and coat a baking sheet lightly with oil.
- Use a fork to mash black beans in a medium bowl until pasty and thick.
- Chop finely bell pepper, garlic and onion in a food processor. Mix into the mashed beans.
- Combine together chili sauce, egg, cumin and chili powder in a small bowl.
- Mix egg mixture into mashed beans. Add in bread crumbs and stir until mixture holds together and is sticky. Subdivide the mixture into 4 patties.
- In case you're grilling, transfer the patties to the foil and let to grill for 8 minutes per side. In case you're baking, transfer the patties to the baking sheet and then bake for approximately 10 minutes per side.

Nutrition Information

- Nutritionist's Calories: 198 kcal 10%
- Total Fat: 3 g 5%
- Carbohydrates: 33.1g 11%
- Protein: 11.2 g 22%
- Cholesterol: 46 mg 16%
- Sodium: 607 mg 24%

161. Honey Lime Tilapia

"This tilapia is sweet and tangy along with fresh vegetables covered with mozzarella cheese."

Servings: 4 | Prep: 15 m | Ready In: 1 h 35 m

Ingredients

- 1/4 c honey

- 3 tbsps. lime juice
- 2 cloves garlic, minced
- 1 pound tilapia fillets
- salt and pepper to taste
- 1 butternut squash - peeled, seeded and sliced
- 1 bunch fresh asparagus spears, trimmed and chopped
- poultry seasoning
- 1/2 c mozzarella cheese

Directions

- Combine garlic, honey and lime juice in a bowl. Season tilapia with pepper and salt and then put in the bowl. Refrigerate for 1 hour to marinate.
- Preheat an oven to 175 degrees C (350 degrees F). Coat a medium baking dish lightly with grease.
- Into the baking dish, spread asparagus and squash. Put the tilapia over the veggies and then season using poultry seasoning. Get rid of the marinade remaining.
- Bake for about 20 minutes until the fish flakes easily and the veggies become tender. Drizzle mozzarella on top and continue to bake for about five minutes or until the cheese becomes browned lightly.

Nutrition Information

- Nutritionist's Calories: 383 kcal 19%
- Total Fat: 4.3 g 7%
- Carbohydrates: 60.4g 19%
- Protein: 32.6 g 65%
- Cholesterol: 51 mg 17%
- Sodium: 154 mg 6%

---

162. Imitation Meatloaf

"This recipe is made of tomatoes, onions, bread crumbs, brown rice and lentils mixed with herbs and eggs and then baked into a vegan style favorite. Drizzle shredded cheese onto loaf and then bake for five more minutes if desired."

Servings: 6 | Prep: 10 m | Ready In: 1 h 55 m

Ingredients

- 3/4 c dry brown lentils
- 1/2 c uncooked brown rice
- 1/2 c wheat germ
- 1 1/2 c dry bread crumbs
- 2 eggs
- 1 large onion, chopped
- 1 tsp. dried thyme
- 1/3 c crushed tomatoes
- 2 tsps. hot sauce
- 2 tbsps. ketchup
- 1 tbsp. soy sauce
- 1/3 c shredded mozzarella cheese

Directions

- Preheat an oven to 165 degrees C (325 degrees F). Cook brown rice and lentils by following the package instructions.
- Mash lentils in a large bowl. Add onion, eggs, wheat germ, bread crumbs, soy sauce, brown rice, cheese, thyme, tomatoes and ketchup to the lentils. Transfer to loaf pan.
- Bake while covered for one hour.

Nutrition Information

- Nutritionist's Calories: 331 kcal 17%
- Total Fat: 5.7 g 9%
- Carbohydrates: 53.2g 17%
- Protein: 17.4 g 35%
- Cholesterol: 66 mg 22%
- Sodium: 498 mg 20%

163. Italian Style Flounder

"My mom's dish that is delicious and super simple. You can use any other fish besides flounder. You can top with American cheese prior to baking just like my mom did and its soo good."

Servings: 4 | Prep: 15 m | Ready In: 45 m

Ingredients

- 2 pounds flounder fillets
- 1/2 tbsp. butter
- salt and pepper to taste
- 1 tbsp. lemon juice
- 1/2 c diced fresh tomato
- 2 tsps. dried basil
- 1 tsp. garlic powder

Directions

- Preheat an oven to 175 degrees C (350 degrees F).
- In a medium baking dish, spread flounder and then use butter to dot. Season with pepper and salt and then drizzle lemon juice on top. Add garlic powder, tomato and basil on top.
- Cover and then bake for about 30 minutes or until the fish flakes easily with a fork.

Nutrition Information

- Nutritionist's Calories: 228 kcal 11%
- Total Fat: 4.2 g 6%
- Carbohydrates: 1.9g < 1%
- Protein: 43.2 g 86%
- Cholesterol: 113 mg 38%
- Sodium: 196 mg 8%

164. Jamaican Jerk Chicken

"A tropical treat of Jamaican Jerk Chicken that is hot and succulent. This marinade has a nice flavor and will love the heat."

Servings: 6 | Prep: 20 m | Ready In: 3 h 20 m

Ingredients

- 6 skinless, boneless chicken breast halves - cut into chunks
- 4 limes, juiced
- 1 c water
- 2 tsps. ground allspice
- 1/2 tsp. ground nutmeg
- 1 tsp. salt
- 1 tsp. brown sugar
- 2 tsps. dried thyme
- 1 tsp. ground ginger
- 1 1/2 tsps. ground black pepper
- 2 tbsps. vegetable oil
- 2 onions, chopped
- 1 1/2 c chopped green onions
- 6 cloves garlic, chopped
- 2 habanero peppers, chopped

Directions

- In a medium bowl, put chicken. Add water and lime juice to cover. Reserve.
- Put thyme, allspice, nutmeg, black pepper, salt, vegetable oil, brown sugar, ginger and thyme in a food processor or blender. Combine well and stir in habanero peppers, garlic, onions and green onions until almost smooth.
- Transfer most of the marinade mixture to the bowl containing chicken and set aside a little amount for basting as you cook. Cover the bowl and refrigerate for at least two hours to marinate.
- Preheat the outdoor grill over medium heat.
- Use oil to polish grill grate. Let the chicken cook slowly on the grill, flip occasionally and baste

often with the marinade mixture remaining. Let to cook to the doneness desired.

Nutrition Information

- Nutritionist's Calories: 221 kcal 11%
- Total Fat: 6.4 g 10%
- Carbohydrates: 13.3g 4%
- Protein: 28.8 g 58%
- Cholesterol: 68 mg 23%
- Sodium: 474 mg 19%

165. Japanese-Style Sesame Green Beans

"I found this dish at the house of my mother-in-law on a family holiday. She's from Japan and had lots of friends who came with lovely Japanese dishes. Since then, this dish has remained my favorite. It is fresh and light throughout the year."

Servings: 4 | Prep: 5 m | Ready In: 20 m

Ingredients

- 1 tbsp. canola oil
- 1 1/2 tsps. sesame oil
- 1 pound fresh green beans, washed
- 1 tbsp. soy sauce
- 1 tbsp. toasted sesame seeds

Directions

- Over medium heat, warm a wok or skillet. Once the skillet becomes hot, add sesame and canola oils. Add whole green beans to skillet. Mix beans so as to coat with the oils. Let to cook for about 10 minutes until beans are browned slightly in spots and become bright green. Take out from the heat source, add in soy sauce, stir and cover. Allow to stand for about

five minutes. Place onto a serving platter and drizzle toasted sesame seeds on top.

Nutrition Information

- Nutritionist's Calories: 97 kcal 5%
- Total Fat: 6.6 g 10%
- Carbohydrates: 8.9g 3%
- Protein: 2.7 g 5%
- Cholesterol: 0 mg 0%
- Sodium: 233 mg 9%

166. Javi's Really Real Mexican Ceviche

"My family loves this recipe. Serve it together with corn chips or corn tostadas as an appetizer or meal just like in the majority of classic Mexican restaurants. Works well with cold beer! Do not omit the hot sauce."

Servings: 12 | Prep: 15 m | Ready In: 1 h 15 m

Ingredients

- 4 pounds shrimp
- 1 pound scallops
- 6 large limes, juiced
- 1 large lemon, juiced
- 1 small white onion, chopped
- 1 cucumber, peeled and chopped
- 1 large tomato, coarsely chopped
- 1 jalapeno pepper, chopped
- 1 serrano pepper, chopped
- 1 bunch cilantro
- 1 tbsp. olive oil
- 1 tbsp. kosher salt
- ground black pepper to taste

Directions

- Mix gently scallops and shrimp together with lemon juice and lime juice in a large glass or ceramic bowl. Stir in Serrano, onion, cucumber, tomato, olive oil, jalapeno, cilantro, pepper and salt. Cover the bowl and refrigerate the ceviche for one hour until the scallops and shrimp become opaque.

Nutrition Information

- Nutritionist's Calories: 204 kcal 10%
- Total Fat: 3 g 5%
- Carbohydrates: 10.6g 3%
- Protein: 35.1 g 70%
- Cholesterol: 253 mg 84%
- Sodium: 859 mg 34%

167. Jenny's Grilled Chicken Breasts

"My family and friends often request for this recipe once the grill is taken out. It is versatile and simple and you can try on a few different meats. I usually love it together with rice pilaf, scalloped potatoes or baked potatoes. Can replace parsley with oregano or cilantro. Store the leftovers for making salad the following day."

Servings: 4 | Prep: 15 m | Ready In: 45 m

Ingredients

- 4 skinless, boneless chicken breast halves
- 1/2 c lemon juice
- 1/2 tsp. onion powder
- ground black pepper to taste
- seasoning salt to taste
- 2 tsps. dried parsley

Directions

- Preheat the outdoor grill over medium-high heat and polish grate lightly with oil.
- Dunk chicken into lemon juice and then drizzle parsley, onion powder, seasoning salt and ground black pepper. Get rid of the remaining lemon juice.
- Let to cook on grill for about 10 to 15 minutes on each side or until the juice runs clear and no pink remains.

Nutrition Information

- Nutritionist's Calories: 139 kcal 7%
- Total Fat: 1.5 g 2%
- Carbohydrates: 3g < 1%
- Protein: 27.4 g 55%
- Cholesterol: 68 mg 23%
- Sodium: 78 mg 3%

168. Jen's Fresh and Spicy Salsa

"This is a flavorful recipe! It's spicy, fresh and simple. It resembles a restaurant style salsa. The freshness is added by green onions, cilantro and lime juice while spice is added by jalapenos and hot pepper sauce like Tabasco."

Servings: 16 | Prep: 15 m | Ready In: 15 m

Ingredients

- 5 roma (plum) tomatoes, seeded and chopped
- 10 green onions
- 2 fresh jalapeno peppers, seeded
- 1/4 c chopped fresh cilantro
- 2 tbsps. fresh lime juice
- 2 tbsps. hot pepper sauce
- 1 tsp. ground black pepper
- 1 tsp. garlic powder
- 1 tsp. salt

Directions

- Pulse cilantro, tomatoes, jalapeno peppers and green onions in a food processor or blender to the consistency desired. Place into a bowl, add in garlic powder, salt, lime juice, black pepper and hot pepper sauce and stir.

Nutrition Information

- Nutritionist's Calories: 9 kcal < 1%
- Total Fat: 0.1 g < 1%
- Carbohydrates: 2g < 1%
- Protein: 0.5 g < 1%
- Cholesterol: 0 mg 0%
- Sodium: 159 mg 6%

169. Jo-Ann's Power Bars

"Tasty and nutritious power bars compared to most granola bars. They're soo satisfying. You can use dried fruits you love if you don't like dried mixed fruit. Also, use nuts you like."

Servings: 12 | Prep: 10 m | Ready In: 40 m

Ingredients

- 1 c quick-cooking rolled oats
- 1/2 c whole wheat flour
- 1/2 c wheat and barley nugget cereal (e.g. Grape-Nuts™)
- 1/2 tsp. ground cinnamon
- 1 beaten egg
- 1/4 c applesauce
- 1/4 c honey
- 3 tbsps. brown sugar
- 2 tbsps. vegetable oil
- 1/4 c unsalted sunflower seeds
- 1/4 c chopped walnuts
- 1 (7 ounce) bag chopped dried mixed fruit

Directions

- Preheat an oven to 165 degrees C (325 degrees F). Line aluminum foil onto a square baking pan of 9 inch. Use cooking spray to cook the foil.
- Combine together cinnamon, oats, cereal and flour in a large bowl. Pour in oil, honey, egg, applesauce, and brown sugar. Combine thoroughly. Add dried fruit, sunflower seeds and walnuts and stir. Into the pan prepared, pour the mixture evenly.
- Bake for about 30 minutes or until the final product is firm and browned lightly on the edges. Allow to cool. Lift from pan with foil. Chop into squares or bars and refrigerate.

Nutrition Information

- Nutritionist's Calories: 197 kcal 10%
- Total Fat: 6.6 g 10%
- Carbohydrates: 33.4g 11%
- Protein: 4.1 g 8%
- Cholesterol: 16 mg 5%
- Sodium: 40 mg 2%

170. Justin's Hoosier Daddy Chili

"In Indiana, I've won chili cook-offs with this lovely chili recipe. It's refreshing and the best chili for a cold night on winter. The secret is adding name brand tomato soup because it has great results. Friends will never know your secret ingredient."

Servings: 6 | Prep: 5 m | Ready In: 1 h 10 m

Ingredients

- 1 pound ground beef
- 1 medium onion, chopped
- 1 tsp. red pepper flakes

- 1 tbsp. ground cumin
- 2 (10.75 ounce) cans condensed tomato soup
- 2 (14.5 ounce) cans chicken broth
- 1 (14.5 ounce) can crushed tomatoes
- 5 tbsps. chili powder
- 1 tsp. ground black pepper
- 1 tsp. salt
- 2 (15.5 ounce) cans pinto beans, drained (optional)
- cayenne pepper to taste

Directions

- Over medium-high heat, crumble ground beef into a soup pot. Then cook while stirring until browned evenly. Drain most grease off. Pour in half of cumin, onion and red pepper flakes. Cook while stirring until the onion becomes tender.
- Add crushed tomatoes, tomato soup and chicken broth. Season with pepper, salt and chili powder. Let to simmer for about 30 minutes. Add beans and then season with cayenne pepper and the cumin remaining. Let to simmer for 30 minutes and serve.

Nutrition Information

- Nutritionist's Calories: 385 kcal 19%
- Total Fat: 13.3 g 20%
- Carbohydrates: 46.9g 15%
- Protein: 23.9 g 48%
- Cholesterol: 46 mg 15%
- Sodium: 1585 mg 63%

171. Key West Chicken

"Almost everyone I know of has got this recipe from Florida Keys. A fantastic chicken marinade and needs just 30 minutes from preparation time to grill! Has a perfect combo of flavors with lime juice, honey and soy sauce. For the best flavor, marinate overnight if you have time."

Servings: 4 | Prep: 15 m | Ready In: 1 h

Ingredients

- 3 tbsps. soy sauce
- 1 tbsp. honey
- 1 tbsp. vegetable oil
- 1 tsp. lime juice
- 1 tsp. chopped garlic
- 4 skinless, boneless chicken breast halves

Directions

- Blend garlic, lime juice, soy sauce, vegetable oil and honey in a shallow container. Into the mixture, put chicken breast halves and then flip to coat. Cover and then refrigerate at least 30 minutes to marinate.
- Preheat the outdoor grill over high heat.
- Polish grill grate lightly with oil. Get rid of the marinade and let the chicken grill for about 6 to 8 minutes per side until the juice runs clear.

Nutrition Information

- Nutritionist's Calories: 184 kcal 9%
- Total Fat: 6.2 g 10%
- Carbohydrates: 5.6g 2%
- Protein: 25.3 g 51%
- Cholesterol: 67 mg 22%
- Sodium: 735 mg 29%

172. Kiki's Borracho (Drunken) Beans

"My grandma from Mexico often had a pot containing beans cooking on a stove when I was kid. I usually cook these beans for my loved ones and the aroma brings her memories closer to my soul. Your family will definitely love them."

Servings: 12 | Prep: 30 m | Ready In: 3 h 30 m

Ingredients

- 1 pound dried pinto beans, washed
- 2 quarts chicken stock
- 1 tbsp. salt
- 1/2 tbsp. ground black pepper
- 1 (12 fluid ounce) can or bottle dark beer
- 2 (14.5 ounce) cans chopped stewed tomatoes
- 1 white onion, diced
- 1/4 c pickled jalapeno peppers
- 6 cloves garlic, chopped
- 3 bay leaves
- 1 1/2 tbsps. dried oregano
- 1 1/2 c chopped fresh cilantro

Directions

- In a pot containing water, soak beans overnight.
- Drain the beans and then add to pot some water and chicken stock to cover beans with two inches of liquid. Add pepper and salt to taste. Cover and heat to boil. Decrease the heat to medium-low, cover and then let to cook for about 1 1/2 hours. Mix beans frequently while cooking to prevent them from burning and sticking at the pot's bottom.
- Mix into the beans, beer, cilantro, tomatoes, garlic, onion, oregano, jalapeno peppers and bay leaves. Continue cooking without covering for one hour or until the beans become tender.
- Crush the beans a little using a potato masher to thicken bean liquid. Add pepper and salt to taste.

Nutrition Information

- Nutritionist's Calories: 181 kcal 9%
- Total Fat: 1 g 2%
- Carbohydrates: 31.8g 10%
- Protein: 9.6 g 19%

- Cholesterol: < 1 mg < 1%
- Sodium: 1074 mg 43%

173. Laura's Quick Slow Cooker Turkey Chili

"A simple chili recipe cooked in the slow cooker all day. Perfect when topped with a dollop of sour cream, Cheddar cheese and crushed corn chips."

Servings: 8 | Prep: 15 m | Ready In: 4 h 15 m

Ingredients

- 1 tbsp. vegetable oil
- 1 pound ground turkey
- 2 (10.75 ounce) cans low sodium tomato soup
- 2 (15 ounce) cans kidney beans, drained
- 1 (15 ounce) can black beans, drained
- 1/2 medium onion, chopped
- 2 tbsps. chili powder
- 1 tsp. red pepper flakes
- 1/2 tbsp. garlic powder
- 1/2 tbsp. ground cumin
- 1 pinch ground black pepper
- 1 pinch ground allspice
- salt to taste

Directions

- Over medium heat, heat oil in a skillet and add turkey. Cook until browned evenly and then drain.
- Use cooking spray to coat the inside of the slow cooker and then stir in onion, turkey, tomato soup, black beans and kidney beans. Season with cumin, chili powder, black pepper, allspice, salt, red pepper flakes and garlic powder.
- Cover and then let to cook on High for 4 hours or for 8 hours on Low.

Nutrition Information

- Nutritionist's Calories: 276 kcal 14%
- Total Fat: 7.6 g 12%
- Carbohydrates: 32.8g 11%
- Protein: 21.2 g 42%
- Cholesterol: 42 mg 14%
- Sodium: 547 mg 22%

174. Leftover Chicken Croquettes

"These croquettes are made by combining chicken, light seasoning, eggs, bread crumbs, parsley and sautéed onion. Grandma would prepare salmon cakes and I adjusted that recipe to make use cooked chicken leftovers."

Servings: 6 | Prep: 15 m | Ready In: 45 m

Ingredients

- 3 c cooked, finely chopped chicken meat
- 1 1/2 c seasoned dry bread crumbs
- 2 eggs, lightly beaten
- 2 c sautéed chopped onion
- 1 tbsp. chopped fresh parsley
- 1 tsp. salt
- 1/2 tsp. ground black pepper

Directions

- Mix onion, chicken, two eggs and bread crumbs in a bowl and combine well. You can stir in one lightly beaten egg in case the mixture becomes too dry to form patties. Pour in pepper, parsley and salt. Combine well and shape into small patties.
- Over medium heat, heat oil in a skillet and then fry the patties until they become golden brown.

Nutrition Information

- Nutritionist's Calories: 276 kcal 14%
- Total Fat: 7.8 g 12%
- Carbohydrates: 24.7g 8%
- Protein: 25.4 g 51%
- Cholesterol: 120 mg 40%
- Sodium: 660 mg 26%

175. Lemon Pepper Pasta

"This recipe is quick and simple to make prepare in advance and anytime."

Servings: 8 | Prep: 5 m | Ready In: 20 m

Ingredients

- 1 pound spaghetti
- 2 tbsps. olive oil
- 3 tbsps. lemon juice, to taste
- 1 tbsp. dried basil
- ground black pepper to taste

Directions

- Bring to boil lightly salted water in a pot and add pasta. Cook until al dente or for about 8 to 10 minutes. Drain.
- Mix black pepper, basil, olive oil and lemon juice in a small bowl. Combine well and mix with pasta. Serve while still hot or cold.

Nutrition Information

- Nutritionist's Calories: 243 kcal 12%
- Total Fat: 4.2 g 7%
- Carbohydrates: 43g 14%
- Protein: 7.5 g 15%
- Cholesterol: 0 mg 0%
- Sodium: 4 mg < 1%

176. Lemon-Orange Orange Roughy

"These orange fillets have a citrus twist. Super simple to make."

Servings: 4 | Prep: 15 m | Ready In: 20 m

Ingredients

- 1 tbsp. olive oil
- 4 (4 ounce) fillets orange roughy
- 1 orange, juiced
- 1 lemon, juiced
- 1/2 tsp. lemon pepper

Directions

- Over medium-high heat, heat oil in a skillet and spread fillets into skillet. Sprinkle lemon juice and orange juice on top. Drizzle lemon pepper on top. Let to cook for five minutes or until the fish flakes easily with a fork.

Nutrition Information

- Nutritionist's Calories: 140 kcal 7%
- Total Fat: 4.3 g 7%
- Carbohydrates: 7.9g 3%
- Protein: 19.1 g 38%
- Cholesterol: 67 mg 22%
- Sodium: 139 mg 6%

177. Lemony Steamed Fish

"These flaky fish fillets are mild flavored. You can add any amount of different types of fish you like to increase the recipe. Experiment with trout, red snapper, salmon, halibut, cod, etc. Can serve alongside a white and wild rice blend."

Servings: 6 | Prep: 15 m | Ready In: 45 m

Ingredients

- 6 (6 ounce) halibut fillets
- 1 tbsp. dried dill weed
- 1 tbsp. onion powder
- 2 tsps. dried parsley
- 1/4 tsp. paprika
- 1 pinch seasoned salt, or more to taste
- 1 pinch lemon pepper
- 1 pinch garlic powder
- 2 tbsps. lemon juice

Directions

- Preheat an oven to 190 degrees C (375 degrees F).
- Chop six foil squares that are big enough for every fillet.
- Place the fillets at the center of the foil squares and then drizzle onto each with garlic powder, dill weed, seasoned salt, onion powder, lemon pepper, parsley and paprika. Drizzle lemon juice on top of each fillet. Roll the foil over the fillets to form a pocket and seal the edges by folding. Transfer the sealed packets to a baking sheet.
- Bake for about 30 minutes until the fish easily flakes with a fork.

Nutrition Information

- Nutritionist's Calories: 142 kcal 7%
- Total Fat: 1.1 g 2%
- Carbohydrates: 1.9g < 1%
- Protein: 29.7 g 59%
- Cholesterol: 61 mg 20%
- Sodium: 184 mg 7%

178. Lentil and Smoked Sausage Soup

"This is a nutritious soup made with cabbage, onion, tomatoes, lentils and smoked vegetarian sausage."

Servings: 4 | Prep: 10 m | Ready In: 50 m

Ingredients

- 2 tbsps. olive oil
- 7 ounces dry lentils
- 1 small onion, chopped
- 3/4 c finely shredded green cabbage
- 1 clove garlic, crushed
- 2 vegetarian smoked sausages, diced
- 1 (16 ounce) can diced tomatoes
- 2 cubes vegetable bouillon
- 4 c water
- 1 bay leaf
- 1 tsp. thyme leaves
- 1/2 tsp. cayenne pepper
- salt and pepper to taste

Directions

- Over medium heat, heat oil in a saucepan. Add in garlic, lentils, cabbage and onion and stir. Let to cook until tender. Add in tomatoes and sausage and stir. Then crumble the vegetable cubes on top of the mixture and add water. Add in cayenne pepper, bay leaf and thyme and stir. Heat to boil, cover and let to simmer for about 30 minutes until the lentils become tender. Add pepper and salt to taste.

Nutrition Information

- Nutritionist's Calories: 320 kcal 16%
- Total Fat: 10.8 g 17%
- Carbohydrates: 38.4g 12%
- Protein: 17.7 g 35%
- Cholesterol: 0 mg 0%
- Sodium: 443 mg 18%

179. Lentil Soup III

"I hardly get time to eat or cook because am always busy in college. My mom made this soup when I was a kid and have been preparing it when in college. The soup is super simple and surprisingly good. When soup is almost done, feel free to add chopped, diced or shredded cooked chicken. The soup is tasty and may be incredibly dull in color. Garnish with a thin lemon slice on top and some chopped chives or parsley."

Servings: 8 | Prep: 5 m | Ready In: 35 m

Ingredients

- 2 c dry lentils
- 2 quarts chicken broth
- 1 onion, diced
- 1/4 c tomato paste
- 2 cloves garlic, minced
- 1 tbsp. ground cumin

Directions

- Mix garlic, cumin, onion, lentils, broth and tomato paste in a large saucepan. Heat to boil, low the heat, cover the pan and let to simmer for about 30 to 45 minutes until the lentils become soft. You can serve along with a squeeze of lemon.

Nutrition Information

- Nutritionist's Calories: 156 kcal 8%
- Total Fat: 0.7 g 1%
- Carbohydrates: 27.7g 9%
- Protein: 11.5 g 23%
- Cholesterol: 0 mg 0%

- Sodium: 69 mg 3%

180. Lentils And Spinach

"An Indian recipe I adapted. May look simple but it's surprisingly delicious. You can serve on top a diced baked potato or hot rice. For a full meal, serve with a fresh chopped tomato, carrots and cauliflower."

Servings: 4 | Prep: 10 m | Ready In: 1 h 5 m

Ingredients

- 1 tbsp. vegetable oil
- 2 white onions, halved and sliced into 1/2 rings
- 3 cloves garlic, minced
- 1/2 c lentils
- 2 c water
- 1 (10 ounce) package frozen spinach
- 1 tsp. salt
- 1 tsp. ground cumin
- freshly ground black pepper to taste
- 2 cloves garlic, crushed

Directions

- Over medium heat, heat oil in a heavy pan, add onion and sauté for about 10 minutes or until it starts to become golden. Pour in minced garlic and then sauté for about 1 minute.
- Into the saucepan, pour in water and lentils. Heat to boil. Cover the pan, decrease the heat and let to simmer for approximately 35 minutes until the lentils become soft (the time varies depending on the lentils and water).
- In the meantime, let the spinach cook in microwave by following the package instructions. Into the saucepan, pour in cumin, spinach and salt. Cover the pan and allow to simmer for about 10 minutes until heated through. Push in some pepper and more garlic to suit your taste.

Nutrition Information

- Nutritionist's Calories: 165 kcal 8%
- Total Fat: 4.3 g 7%
- Carbohydrates: 24g 8%
- Protein: 9.7 g 19%
- Cholesterol: 0 mg 0%
- Sodium: 639 mg 26%

181. Light and Spicy Fish

"A simple recipe and it's nutritious. Feel free to replace with firm fleshed fish like ocean perch or grouper."

Servings: 2 | Prep: 5 m | Ready In: 25 m

Ingredients

- 2 (6 ounce) fillets red snapper
- 1/4 tsp. garlic powder
- salt and ground black pepper to taste
- 1/4 c picante sauce
- 1/2 lime, juiced

Directions

- Preheat an oven to 175 degrees C (350 degrees F). Line a baking sheet with a sheet of aluminum foil and then lightly grease.
- Onto the foil, put fillets and drizzle with pepper, salt and garlic powder. Pour picante sauce on top of fillets and then squeeze lime juice on top of all. Bring together foil sides and seal in fish by folding the seam.
- Bake for about 15 to 20 minutes or until the fish easily flakes with a fork.

Nutrition Information

- Nutritionist's Calories: 183 kcal 9%
- Total Fat: 2.3 g 4%
- Carbohydrates: 4.1g 1%
- Protein: 34.7 g 69%
- Cholesterol: 62 mg 21%
- Sodium: 341 mg 14%

---

182. Linguine with White Clam Sauce I

"Fast and simple! You can use it if you forget to remove something else from the freezer. Can replace clam juice with water if desired."

Servings: 5

Ingredients

- 1 (16 ounce) package linguini pasta
- 1 tbsp. olive oil
- 3 cloves garlic, minced
- 2 (6.5 ounce) cans minced clams, with juice
- 1/4 c clam juice
- 1 tbsp. chopped fresh parsley
- salt to taste
- ground black pepper to taste

Directions

- Cook linguini pasta in a pot containing boiling salted water until al dente.
- In the meantime, over medium heat, cook minced garlic in olive oil in a medium sized saucepan until the garlic becomes translucent. Pour in chopped parsley, sliced clams and clam juice or water. Season with ground black pepper and salt. Heat to boil. Reduce the heat and allow to simmer for three minutes.
- Combine the pasta with the clam sauce and then serve while still warm.

Nutrition Information

- Nutritionist's Calories: 457 kcal 23%
- Total Fat: 6.2 g 10%
- Carbohydrates: 69.7g 22%
- Protein: 31 g 62%
- Cholesterol: 50 mg 17%
- Sodium: 114 mg 5%

---

183. Linguine with White Clam Sauce II

"This clam sauce is light and can be served on top of linguini noodles. Very nutritious!"

Servings: 5

Ingredients

- 1 (12 ounce) package linguini pasta
- 3 (8 ounce) cans minced clams, with juice
- 1/4 c olive oil
- 1 clove garlic, minced
- 3/4 c chopped parsley
- 2 tbsps. white wine
- 1 tsp. dried basil
- 1/2 tsp. salt

Directions

- Cook linguini pasta in a pot containing boiling salted water until al dente and then drain.
- Sauté garlic in olive oil in a skillet. Pour in basil, white wine, parsley, salt and liquid from the clams. Mix well. Let to cook for ten minutes. Add in clams and stir until heated through.
- Nix the clam sauce with the cooked and drained linguini pasta and then serve while warm.

Nutrition Information

- Nutritionist's Calories: 545 kcal 27%
- Total Fat: 15.1 g 23%
- Carbohydrates: 56.9g 18%
- Protein: 43.6 g 87%
- Cholesterol: 90 mg 30%
- Sodium: 392 mg 16%

184. Linguini with Broccoli and Red Peppers

"A lovely side dish but often use it as a whole meal together with bread and a salad!"

Servings: 6 | Prep: 5 m | Ready In: 20 m

Ingredients

- 1 pound linguini pasta
- 1 pound fresh broccoli, chopped
- 3 tbsps. extra virgin olive oil
- 1 tbsp. butter
- 3 cloves garlic, minced
- 1 red bell pepper, thinly sliced
- 1 pinch garlic salt
- 1/4 c grated Parmesan cheese

Directions

- Bring to boil lightly salted water in a pot and add pasta. Cook until al dente or for about 8 to 10 minutes and then drain.
- In the microwave, steam broccoli along with two tbsps. of water for about 6-7 minutes.
- Over low heat, heat butter and olive oil in a 10-inch skillet. Add in slices of red pepper, garlic (more or less as desired), and stir and then sauté gently.
- Drain the steamed broccoli and transfer to skillet. Drizzle lightly using garlic salt and then sauté the peppers and broccoli until soft.

- Mix the hot pasta with the vegetable mixture. Top with Parmesan cheese.

Nutrition Information

- Nutritionist's Calories: 393 kcal 20%
- Total Fat: 11.2 g 17%
- Carbohydrates: 60.5g 20%
- Protein: 12.8 g 26%
- Cholesterol: 8 mg 3%
- Sodium: 147 mg 6%

185. Mahi Mahi with Onions and Mushrooms

"These mahi mahi filets that are simple and very good and they're steamed on top of garlic, yellow onions and button mushrooms."

Servings: 4 | Prep: 10 m | Ready In: 30 m

Ingredients

- 2 tbsps. olive oil
- 3 small onions, chopped
- 4 cloves garlic, minced
- 5 button mushrooms, sliced
- 1 1/2 pounds mahi mahi
- salt and pepper to taste
- 1/4 c white cooking wine
- 1 tbsp. fresh lemon juice
- 1 tsp. cornstarch
- 2 tbsps. water

Directions

- Over medium heat, heat olive oil and then cook garlic, mushrooms and onions in a large skillet until the onions become transparent.

- Chop mahi mahi into three inch long filets. Transfer Mahi Mahi fillets on top of the garlic, mushrooms and onions. Drizzle pepper and salt onto the first side of filets. Pour in lemon juice and white cooking wine.
- Cover the skillet and let to cook for about 4 to 5 minutes. Flip over the filets and drizzle pepper and salt onto the second side. Let to cook for about 4 to 5 minutes or until the fish easily flakes.
- Transfer the fish only to a heated plate to maintain it warm until when the sauce is ready.
- Increase the heat to medium/high in the skillet containing all the garlic, mushrooms, cooking wine and onions. Heat to boil. In two tbsps. water, dissolve cornstarch and mix into the skillet. Mix sauce constantly until it becomes thick to the consistency desired.
- Spread the sauce on top of mahi mahi filets. Serve right away.

Nutrition Information

- Nutritionist's Calories: 251 kcal 13%
- Total Fat: 8.1 g 12%
- Carbohydrates: 8g 3%
- Protein: 33 g 66%
- Cholesterol: 124 mg 41%
- Sodium: 155 mg 6%

186. Mango Salsa

"A very delicious mango salsa and perfect when served on top of fish. I love fish that is blackened with Cajun seasoning and then salsa added on top. Perfect also for dipping chips."

Servings: 8 | Prep: 15 m | Ready In: 45 m

Ingredients

- 1 mango - peeled, seeded, and chopped
- 1/4 c finely chopped red bell pepper
- 1 green onion, chopped
- 2 tbsps. chopped cilantro
- 1 fresh jalapeno chile pepper, finely chopped
- 2 tbsps. lime juice
- 1 tbsp. lemon juice

Directions

- Combine lime juice, cilantro, jalapeno, mango, lemon juice, red bell pepper and green onion in a medium bowl. Cover the bowl and let to stand for at least 30 minutes prior to serving.

Nutrition Information

- Nutritionist's Calories: 21 kcal 1%
- Total Fat: 0.1 g < 1%
- Carbohydrates: 5.4g 2%
- Protein: 0.3 g < 1%
- Cholesterol: 0 mg 0%
- Sodium: 1 mg < 1%

187. Maple-Garlic Marinated Pork Tenderloin

"This marinade is tasty and made with real maple syrup. Perfect of pork tenderloin or chicken."

Servings: 6 | Prep: 5 m | Ready In: 8 h 30 m

Ingredients

- 2 tbsps. Dijon mustard
- 1 tsp. sesame oil
- 3 cloves garlic, minced
- fresh ground black pepper to taste
- 1 c maple syrup

- 1 1/2 pounds pork tenderloin

Directions

- Mix maple syrup, garlic, mustard, pepper and sesame oil. In a shallow dish, put pork and then use the marinade to coat it thoroughly. Cover and refrigerate for a minimum of 8 hours or overnight.
- Preheat the grill over medium-low heat.
- Take out pork from the marinade and reserve. Place the marinade remaining into a small saucepan and let to cook on a stove for 5 minutes at a medium-low heat.
- Use oil to polish the grate and then transfer the meat onto the grate. Let pork to grill for about 15 to 25 minutes while basting with the marinade reserved, or until no pink in the interior remains. Don't sue high temperatures because the marinade will burn.

Nutrition Information

- Nutritionist's Calories: 288 kcal 14%
- Total Fat: 4.9 g 8%
- Carbohydrates: 36.8g 12%
- Protein: 23.5 g 47%
- Cholesterol: 74 mg 25%
- Sodium: 189 mg 8%

188. Margarita Chicken II

"The sauce of this dish is flavored by honey, lime zest, gold tequila and lime juice. This recipe resembles that of a popular restaurant chain."

Servings: 4 | Prep: 15 m | Ready In: 30 m

Ingredients

- 1/2 tsp. lime zest
- 1/4 c lime juice
- 2 tbsps. gold tequila
- 2 tbsps. honey
- 1 tbsp. vegetable oil
- 2 tsps. cornstarch
- 1/4 tsp. garlic salt
- 1/4 tsp. ground black pepper
- 4 skinless, boneless chicken breast halves
- 4 (10 inch) flour tortillas, warmed
- 1 tomato, cut into 8 wedges
- 1 avocado - pitted, peeled, and cubed
- 1 lime, cut into 8 wedges

Directions

- Preheat an oven so that it can broil.
- Over medium heat, mix garlic salt, lime zest, cornstarch, lime juice, pepper, tequila, oil and honey in a small saucepan. Heat to boil while stirring to make sauce thick.
- Broil the chicken breasts for about 10 to 15 minutes or until they are cooked through (no pink remains inside). Use the sauce prepared to baste in the final five minutes of cooking.
- Spread a folded tortilla onto every of the four plates, put a chicken breast, a few avocado chunks and two tomato wedges. Sprinkle onto the chicken, the sauce remaining and decorate with two lime wedges. Serve.

Nutrition Information

- Nutritionist's Calories: 552 kcal 28%
- Total Fat: 18.7 g 29%
- Carbohydrates: 58.4g 19%
- Protein: 35.1 g 70%
- Cholesterol: 68 mg 23%
- Sodium: 793 mg 32%

189. Margarita Grilled Chicken

"The best grilled chicken ever! It also makes very good cold sandwiches!"

Servings: 8 | Prep: 15 m | Ready In: 4 h 30 m

Ingredients

- 3 pounds boneless, skinless chicken breast halves
- 2 c bottled margarita mix

Directions

- Into a large plastic bag that is sealable, put margarita mix. Place in chicken breasts and squeeze out as much air as you can before you seal. Refrigerate for about 4 to 8 hours to marinate.
- Preheat the outdoor grill over medium-high heat.
- Polish grill grate lightly with oil. Take out the chicken from the marinade and get rid of marinade. Let the chicken grill for about 8 minutes on each side or until the juice runs clear.

Nutrition Information

- Nutritionist's Calories: 238 kcal 12%
- Total Fat: 4.1 g 6%
- Carbohydrates: 12g 4%
- Protein: 35.4 g 71%
- Cholesterol: 97 mg 32%
- Sodium: 124 mg 5%

190. Marinated Rosemary Lemon Chicken

"Great for summer barbecue! Serve together with grilled corn, rice and a light pasta salad. Perfect for summer!"

Servings: 4 | Prep: 15 m | Ready In: 8 h 30 m

Ingredients

- 1/2 c lemon juice
- 1/8 c olive oil
- 2 tbsps. dried rosemary
- 4 skinless, boneless chicken breast halves
- 1 lemon, sliced

Directions

- Combine rosemary, olive oil and lemon juice in a large plastic bag that is resealable. Add lemon slices and chicken into the bag. Seal the bag and then shake to coat. Refrigerate for about 8 hours or overnight to marinate.
- Preheat a grill over high heat.
- Polish grill grate lightly with oil. Get rid of the marinade. Grill the chicken for about 8 minutes on each side or until the juice runs clear. Have no worries if rosemary sticks to the chicken because it tastes nice when grilled. Throw stems onto the coals in case you're using fresh rosemary sprigs to have a smoky rosemary flavor on the chicken.

Nutrition Information

- Nutritionist's Calories: 209 kcal 10%
- Total Fat: 9.9 g 15%
- Carbohydrates: 6.6g 2%
- Protein: 25 g 50%
- Cholesterol: 67 mg 22%
- Sodium: 61 mg 2%

191. Marinated Turkey Breast

"My mom gave me this recipe. The recipe usually turns

out tender and juicy no matter how long they are left on the grill! Simple to make but usually perfect once marinated for a minimum of four hours."

Servings: 12 | Prep: 20 m | Ready In: 5 h

Ingredients

- 2 cloves garlic, peeled and minced
- 1 tbsp. finely chopped fresh basil
- 1/2 tsp. ground black pepper
- 2 (3 pound) boneless turkey breast halves
- 6 whole cloves
- 1/4 c vegetable oil
- 1/4 c soy sauce
- 2 tbsps. lemon juice
- 1 tbsp. brown sugar

Directions

- Combine together pepper, basil and garlic in a small bowl and then brush onto turkey breasts. Into each end of turkey breast, insert one clove and then insert one at the middle.
- Combine brown sugar, soy sauce, vegetable oil and lemon juice in a large shallow dish. Transfer the breasts to the dish and then flip to coat. Cover the dish and refrigerate for a minimum of four hours to marinate.
- Preheat the grill over high heat.
- Polish grill grate lightly with oil. Get rid of the marinade and transfer the turkey breasts onto grill. Cover with lid and then grill the turkey breasts for approximately 15 minutes per side or until the internal temperature is 68 degrees C (170 degrees F).

Nutrition Information

- Nutritionist's Calories: 317 kcal 16%
- Total Fat: 6 g 9%
- Carbohydrates: 2.2g < 1%
- Protein: 59.8 g 120%
- Cholesterol: 164 mg 55%

- Sodium: 405 mg 16%

192. Mediterranean Chicken with Eggplant

"My grandma showed me this recipe and she still resides on the Mediterranean shore."

Servings: 5 | Prep: 50 m | Ready In: 1 h 20 m

Ingredients

- 3 eggplants, peeled and cut lengthwise into 1/2 inch thick slices
- 3 tbsps. olive oil
- 6 skinless, boneless chicken breast halves - diced
- 1 onion, diced
- 2 tbsps. tomato paste
- 1/2 c water
- 2 tsps. dried oregano
- salt and pepper to taste

Directions

- In a large pot containing lightly salted water, soak strips of eggplant for about 30 minutes (this improves taste and leaves behind a brown color in pot).
- Take out eggplant from the pot and use olive oil to polish lightly. Grill or sauté until browned lightly and then transfer to a baking dish of 9x13 inch. Reserve.
- Over medium heat, sauté onion and diced chicken in a skillet. Add in water and tomato paste and stir. Cover the skillet, decrease the heat to low and let to simmer for about 10 minutes.
- Preheat an oven to 200 degrees C (400 degrees F).
- Onto eggplant, spread the chicken/tomato mixture. Season with pepper, salt and oregano

and then use aluminum foil to cover. Bake for 20 minutes in oven.

Nutrition Information

- Nutritionist's Calories: 336 kcal 17%
- Total Fat: 10.6 g 16%
- Carbohydrates: 26.6g 9%
- Protein: 35.5 g 71%
- Cholesterol: 82 mg 27%
- Sodium: 147 mg 6%

193. Mexican Chicken I

"Adjust the seasoning as desired!"

Servings: 6

Ingredients

- 6 skinless, boneless chicken breast halves
- 1 (20 ounce) jar salsa
- 1 large red bell pepper, chopped
- 2 tbsps. ground cumin
- 2 tbsps. lemon juice
- 2 tbsps. chili powder
- 3 cloves crushed garlic
- 2 (15 ounce) cans black beans, rinsed and drained

Directions

- Preheat an oven to 205 degrees C (400 degrees F).
- Into a baking dish of 9x13 inch or a 3 quart casserole dish, spread pieces of chicken. Mix garlic, chili powder, salsa, lemon juice, cumin and red bell pepper. Spread the mixture on top of chicken. Add black beans over all and then cover. Bake for about 1 to 1 1/2 hours. If desired, serve along with rice.

Nutrition Information

- Nutritionist's Calories: 301 kcal 15%
- Total Fat: 3.7 g 6%
- Carbohydrates: 29.1g 9%
- Protein: 37.3 g 75%
- Cholesterol: 68 mg 23%
- Sodium: 1099 mg 44%

194. Mexican Cucumber Salad

"This is a mix of cool and crunchy veggies along with crushed red pepper and other seasonings."

Servings: 6 | Prep: 10 m | Ready In: 50 m

Ingredients

- 1 medium cucumber, chopped
- 1 (8.75 ounce) can whole kernel corn, drained
- 1 (16 ounce) can stewed tomatoes, drained and sliced
- 1 green bell pepper, chopped
- 1 red bell pepper, chopped
- 2 tbsps. red wine vinegar
- 1 tbsp. crushed red pepper flakes
- 1/2 tsp. garlic, minced
- 1/2 tsp. cumin
- 1/4 tsp. dried cilantro
- 1/4 tsp. salt
- 1/8 tsp. ground black pepper

Directions

- Mix together red bell pepper, cucumber, red wine vinegar, corn, green bell pepper and tomatoes in a large bowl. Season with cilantro, crushed red pepper flakes, black pepper, salt, garlic and cumin. Cover the bowl and refrigerate for a minimum of 30 minutes prior to serving.

Nutrition Information

- Nutritionist's Calories: 75 kcal 4%
- Total Fat: 1 g 1%
- Carbohydrates: 17g 5%
- Protein: 2.6 g 5%
- Cholesterol: 0 mg 0%
- Sodium: 387 mg 15%

195. Mexican Pasta

"This is a nice vegan meal with a kick!"

Servings: 4 | Prep: 5 m | Ready In: 20 m

Ingredients

- 1/2 pound seashell pasta
- 2 tbsps. olive oil
- 2 onions, chopped
- 1 green bell pepper, chopped
- 1/2 c sweet corn kernels
- 1 (15 ounce) can black beans, drained
- 1 (14.5 ounce) can peeled and diced tomatoes
- 1/4 c salsa
- 1/4 c sliced black olives
- 1 1/2 tbsps. taco seasoning mix
- salt and pepper to taste

Directions

- Bring to boil lightly salted water in a pot and add pasta. Cook until al dente or for about 8 to 10 minutes and drain.
- As the pasta cooks, over medium heat, heat olive oil in a skillet, add pepper and onions and then cook for 10 minutes until browned lightly. Add in corn, stir and heat through.

Mix in taco seasoning, black beans, olives, salsa, tomatoes, pepper and salt. Cook for 5 minutes until heated thoroughly.
- Mix the sauce together with the cooked pasta and then serve.

Nutrition Information

- Nutritionist's Calories: 358 kcal 18%
- Total Fat: 9.4 g 14%
- Carbohydrates: 59.5g 19%
- Protein: 10.3 g 21%
- Cholesterol: 0 mg 0%
- Sodium: 589 mg 24%

196. Michelle's Blonde Chicken Chili

"Those who have eaten this thick blend of chicken, spices and beans state that it makes someone very perky! Have always made it in Halloween chili cook-off at my workstation for the last 3 years. Seem different but it tastes very good! You can serve together with warm flour tortillas and shredded Monterey Jack cheese."

Servings: 10 | Prep: 30 m | Ready In: 1 h

Ingredients

- 1 tbsp. vegetable oil
- 3 pounds skinless, boneless chicken breast meat - cubed
- 1 c chopped onion
- 2 c chicken broth
- 2 (4 ounce) cans chopped green chile peppers
- 5 (14.5 ounce) cans great Northern beans, undrained
- 1 tbsp. garlic powder
- 1 tbsp. ground cumin
- 1 tbsp. dried oregano
- 2 tsps. chopped fresh cilantro
- 1 tsp. crushed red pepper

Directions

- Over medium-high heat, add chicken and vegetable oil in a skillet and then cook while stirring frequently until the chicken pieces are browned evenly. Add in onions and stir. Let to cook until onions are translucent. Drain the mixture and reserve.
- Over medium heat, bring to boil green chile peppers and chicken broth in a large saucepan. Mix in garlic powder three cans of great northern beans, crushed red pepper, cumin, oregano and cilantro. Add in chicken and onion mixture, stir and low the heat. Let to simmer for 30 more minutes as you add more beans from the cans remaining to have a thicker consistency as desired.

Nutrition Information

- Nutritionist's Calories: 412 kcal 21%
- Total Fat: 4.1 g 6%
- Carbohydrates: 46.6g 15%
- Protein: 47.2 g 94%
- Cholesterol: 79 mg 26%
- Sodium: 362 mg 14%

197. Microwave Corn on the Cob

"A great corn on the cob recipe. Great whenever you run out of grill or stove space. Can chill corn on cob in plastic bags and then take out an ear of chilled corn in winter to enjoy a delicious summer corn the entire year!"

Servings: 1 | Ready In: 5 m

Ingredients

- 1 ear corn, husked and cleaned

Directions

- Moisten a paper towel and then wring out. Use the moist towel to wrap the corn ear and transfer to a dinner plate. Let to cook for 5 minutes in a microwave. Remove the paper towel carefully and serve.

Nutrition Information

- Nutritionist's Calories: 123 kcal 6%
- Total Fat: 1.7 g 3%
- Carbohydrates: 27.2g 9%
- Protein: 4.6 g 9%
- Cholesterol: 0 mg 0%
- Sodium: 21 mg < 1%

198. Mimi's Giant Whole-Wheat Banana-Strawberry Muffins

"This breakfast treat is very healthy! These tasty and moist muffins have a natural sweetness due to addition of strawberries and bananas."

Servings: 12 | Prep: 15 m | Ready In: 35 m

Ingredients

- 2 eggs
- 1/2 c unsweetened applesauce
- 1/4 c vegetable oil
- 3/4 c packed brown sugar
- 1 tsp. vanilla extract
- 3 bananas, mashed
- 2 c whole wheat flour
- 1 tsp. baking soda
- 1 tbsp. ground cinnamon
- 1 c frozen sliced strawberries

Directions

- Preheat an oven to 190 degrees C (375 degrees F). Line paper liners onto 12 big muffin c or grease the c.
- Whisk together bananas, vanilla, oil, eggs, applesauce and brown sugar in a large bowl. Mix flour, cinnamon and baking soda. Mix into the mixture of banana until moistened. Add in strawberries and stir until distributed evenly. Into the muffins c, pour batter until filled completely.
- Bake in oven for about 20 minutes or until muffin tops spring back when pressed a little. Let to cool before taking out from muffin tins.

Nutrition Information

- Nutritionist's Calories: 212 kcal 11%
- Total Fat: 5.9 g 9%
- Carbohydrates: 38.1g 12%
- Protein: 4.2 g 8%
- Cholesterol: 31 mg 10%
- Sodium: 122 mg 5%

---

199. Minute Tomato Soup with Tortellini

"My friend and I wanted our grilled cheese sandwiches and tomato soup favorite and I decide to make this tasty soup on a chilly day. The soup is ready in a short while and tastes great. Tortellini is ⅓ of a nine ounce package."

Servings: 4 | Ready In: 20 m

Ingredients

- 2 (10.75 ounce) cans condensed tomato soup
- 1 tsp. dried oregano
- 1 tbsp. dried basil
- 1 tsp. dried parsley
- 3/4 tsp. ground black pepper
- 4 1/2 ounces fresh tortellini pasta

Directions

- In a medium saucepan, prepare soup by following the package instructions. Pour in ground black pepper, oregano, parsley and basil. Over medium heat, heat while stirring well. Let to simmer for five minutes, decrease the heat to low and pour in tortellini. Continue simmering for about five minutes or until the tortellini is cooked.

Nutrition Information

- Nutritionist's Calories: 178 kcal 9%
- Total Fat: 4.4 g 7%
- Carbohydrates: 31.2g 10%
- Protein: 6 g 12%
- Cholesterol: 7 mg 2%
- Sodium: 925 mg 37%

---

200. Miracle Soup

"For you reduce pounds fast, you need this potful after every 2 to 3 days!"

Servings: 20 | Prep: 15 m | Ready In: 45 m

Ingredients

- 1 tbsp. olive oil
- 1/4 c chopped fresh ginger root
- 1/4 c chopped garlic
- 2 (32 ounce) packages fat-free chicken broth
- 1/2 c cornstarch
- 1 (6 ounce) can mushrooms, drained
- 1 (8 ounce) can bamboo shoots, drained
- 1/2 c soy sauce
- 1/4 c rice wine vinegar
- 1 tbsp. fructose (fruit sugar)

- 1 tsp. crushed red pepper
- 2 (16 ounce) packages frozen mixed stir-fry vegetables
- 1 pound frozen, peeled and deveined shrimp
- 1/4 c chopped fresh cilantro
- 1 (10 ounce) package frozen chopped spinach, thawed and drained

Directions

- Over medium heat, heat oil in a big pot. Add in garlic and ginger and stir. Cook for three minutes until tender. Mix cornstarch and one c of broth together. Add the mixture of cornstarch to the pot containing crushed red pepper, mushrooms, vinegar, bamboo, the broth remaining, soy and fructose. Heat to boil and then cook until thickened.
- Mix in cilantro, frozen shrimp and frozen mixed vegetables. Let to simmer for about 10 minutes until the shrimp becomes opaque. Add in spinach and stir for 2 minutes until just wilted. Serve right away.

Nutrition Information

- Nutritionist's Calories: 91 kcal 5%
- Total Fat: 1.3 g 2%
- Carbohydrates: 12.3g 4%
- Protein: 8.8 g 18%
- Cholesterol: 35 mg 12%
- Sodium: 650 mg 26%

201. Miso Soup

"Dashi refers to a simple stock that is used in Japanese cooking and prepared by boiling dried bonito (fish) and dried kelp (seaweed). The instant dashi granules are bought in conveniently-sized packets or jars and have different strength. For a stronger stock, add extra dashi to the soup. Add red, white or yellow miso paste for the soup. The red miso is saltier and stronger while the yellow miso is creamy

and sweet."

Servings: 4 | Prep: 5 m | Ready In: 20 m

Ingredients

- 2 tsps. dashi granules
- 4 c water
- 3 tbsps. miso paste
- 1 (8 ounce) package silken tofu, diced
- 2 green onions, sliced diagonally into 1/2 inch pieces

Directions

- Over medium-high heat, mix water and dashi granules in a medium saucepan and heat to boil. Decrease the heat to medium and then whisk in miso paste. Add tofu and stir. Separate green onion layers and place them into the soup. Let to simmer slowly for about 2 to 3 minutes prior to serving.

Nutrition Information

- Nutritionist's Calories: 63 kcal 3%
- Total Fat: 2.3 g 4%
- Carbohydrates: 5.3g 2%
- Protein: 5.5 g 11%
- Cholesterol: 0 mg 0%
- Sodium: 513 mg 21%

202. Mistakenly Zesty Pork Chops

"I made this recipe by mistake when using another guide recipe. The mistake was adding cocktail sauce instead of using chili sauce. Fortunately, this is the best mistake I have ever done. Pork chops had nice zip to them! Such mistakes should occur more often!"

Servings: 4 | Prep: 15 m | Ready In: 4 h 15 m

Ingredients

- 1 c soy sauce
- 3/4 c water
- 1/2 c brown sugar
- 1 tbsp. honey
- 1 dash lemon juice
- 4 pork chops
- 1 c ketchup
- 1/2 c cocktail sauce
- 1/4 c brown sugar
- 2 tbsps. water
- 1 1/2 tsps. ground dry mustard

Directions

- Over medium heat, combine lemon juice, soy sauce, brown sugar, water and honey in a saucepan. Heat to boil, take out from the heat and let to cool.
- In a large plastic bag that is sealable, put pork chops. Add the mixture of soy sauce into bag, seal and then refrigerate for about 3 to 6 hours to marinate.
- Preheat an oven to 175 degrees C (350 degrees F).
- Drain pork chops and get rid of the marinade remaining. Onto a baking dish, spread the pork chops, cover and then bake for about 30 minutes.
- Combine mustard, brown sugar, ketchup, cocktail sauce and water in a bowl. Spread on top of the pork chops and continue to bake for about 30 minutes until the temperature at the middle is 63 degrees C (145 degrees F).

Nutrition Information

- Nutritionist's Calories: 405 kcal 20%
- Total Fat: 5.5 g 9%
- Carbohydrates: 72g 23%
- Protein: 20 g 40%
- Cholesterol: 35 mg 12%

- Sodium: 4735 mg 189%

203. Mock Tuna Salad

"A chickpea spread and tastes just like a tuna salad! It's good when served in a sandwich."

Servings: 4 | Prep: 20 m | Ready In: 20 m

Ingredients

- 1 (19 ounce) can garbanzo beans (chickpeas), drained and mashed
- 2 tbsps. mayonnaise
- 2 tsps. spicy brown mustard
- 1 tbsp. sweet pickle relish
- 2 green onions, chopped
- salt and pepper to taste

Directions

- Mix chopped green onions, garbanzo beans, mustard, relish, mayonnaise, pepper and salt in a medium bowl. Combine well.

Nutrition Information

- Nutritionist's Calories: 220 kcal 11%
- Total Fat: 7 ? g 11%
- Carbohydrates: 32.7g 11%
- Protein: 7 g 14%
- Cholesterol: 3 mg < 1%
- Sodium: 507 mg 20%

204. Molly's Chicken

"This chicken dish is loved by my daughter Molly. Super simple to make and perfect with Asian-style veggies and

rice."

Servings: 6 | Prep: 10 m | Ready In: 8 h 10 m

Ingredients

- 3 1/2 pounds chicken drumsticks, skin removed
- 1/2 c soy sauce
- 1/4 c packed brown sugar
- 2 cloves garlic, minced
- 1 (8 ounce) can tomato sauce

Directions

- In a slow cooker, put drumsticks. Combine together garlic, tomato sauce, soy sauce and brown sugar in a medium bowl. Spread the sauce on top of the chicken.
- Cover and then cook for 8 hours on Low heat.

Nutrition Information

- Nutritionist's Calories: 356 kcal 18%
- Total Fat: 10.2 g 16%
- Carbohydrates: 13g 4%
- Protein: 50.7 g 101%
- Cholesterol: 156 mg 52%
- Sodium: 1543 mg 62%

205. Mom's Mozzarella Chicken for Drew

"A different chicken Parmesan made for my son who hates the usual thing. It's made with onion, garlic, mozzarella cheese and chicken broth. It's finished quickly when served along with crusty Italian bread, hot cooked pasta and salad."

Servings: 4 | Prep: 10 m | Ready In: 30 m

Ingredients

- 1/2 tbsp. olive oil
- 4 skinless, boneless chicken breast halves
- 1/2 tsp. ground black pepper
- 1/2 tsp. minced garlic
- 1/4 c minced onion
- 1/2 c chicken broth
- 4 c spaghetti sauce
- 1 c shredded mozzarella cheese

Directions

- Over medium high heat, heat oil in a skillet, add chicken breasts and then sauté for about 4 to 5 minutes per side or until white. Pour in broth, onion, pepper and garlic. Cover the skillet and over medium heat, let to simmer for about 7 to 10 minutes until the broth cooks off.
- Add in spaghetti sauce, stir, cover and let to simmer for about 10 minutes or until no pink color of chicken remains inside and is cooked through. Top with cheese, cover and let to cook for about 2 to 3 minutes or until the cheese has melted. Serve immediately.

Nutrition Information

- Nutritionist's Calories: 362 kcal 18%
- Total Fat: 10.9 g 17%
- Carbohydrates: 25.8g 8%
- Protein: 38.3 g 77%
- Cholesterol: 87 mg 29%
- Sodium: 1377 mg 55%

206. Moroccan Lentil Salad

"This is a fast, attractive, spicy and protein-rich side dish or salad."

Servings: 5

Ingredients

- 1/2 c dry lentils
- 1 1/2 c water
- 1/2 (15 ounce) can garbanzo beans, drained
- 2 tomatoes, chopped
- 4 green onions, chopped
- 2 minced hot green chile peppers
- 1 green bell pepper, chopped
- 1/2 yellow bell pepper, chopped
- 1 red bell pepper, chopped
- 1 lime, juiced
- 2 tbsps. olive oil
- 1/4 c chopped fresh cilantro
- salt to taste

Directions

- In a pot containing water, put lentils. Heat water to boil and then decrease to simmer. Let to cook for about 30 minutes or until they are tender.
- Mix lentils, bell peppers, chickpeas, green onions, tomatoes, cilantro, green chilies, lime juice, salt and olive oil in a medium size mixing bowl. Mix well. Refrigerate for 20 minutes and then serve while chilled.

Nutrition Information

- Nutritionist's Calories: 190 kcal 10%
- Total Fat: 6.3 g 10%
- Carbohydrates: 27.6g 9%
- Protein: 8.1 g 16%
- Cholesterol: 0 mg 0%
- Sodium: 94 mg 4%

207. Mushroom Lentil Barley Stew

"A recipe that is very simple and requires little attention while cooking. It has an earthy vegan flavor as a result of the blend of flavors. You can serve together with garlic bread."

Servings: 8 | Prep: 15 m | Ready In: 12 h 15 m

Ingredients

- 2 quarts vegetable broth
- 2 c sliced fresh button mushrooms
- 1 ounce dried shiitake mushrooms, torn into pieces
- 3/4 c uncooked pearl barley
- 3/4 c dry lentils
- 1/4 c dried onion flakes
- 2 tsps. minced garlic
- 2 tsps. dried summer savory
- 3 bay leaves
- 1 tsp. dried basil
- 2 tsps. ground black pepper
- salt to taste

Directions

- Combine broth, button mushrooms, basil, savory, shiitake mushrooms, bay leaves barley, lentils, garlic, onion flakes, salt and pepper in a slow cooker.
- Cover and let to cook for about 10 to 12 hours on Low or 4 to 6 hours on High. Get rid of bay leaves before you serve.

Nutrition Information

- Nutritionist's Calories: 213 kcal 11%
- Total Fat: 1.2 g 2%
- Carbohydrates: 43.9g 14%
- Protein: 8.4 g 17%
- Cholesterol: 0 mg 0%
- Sodium: 466 mg 19%

208. Navy Bean Soup I

"This refreshing soup can warm you on cold nights."

Servings: 9 | Prep: 15 m | Ready In: 4 h 25 m

Ingredients

- 1 (16 ounce) package dried navy beans
- 6 c water
- 1 (14.5 ounce) can diced tomatoes
- 1 onion, chopped
- 2 stalks celery, chopped
- 1 clove garlic, minced
- 1/2 pound chopped ham
- 1 cube chicken bouillon
- 2 tbsps. Worcestershire sauce
- 1 tbsp. dried parsley
- 2 tsps. garlic powder
- 1 bay leaf
- 1 tsp. salt
- 1/2 tsp. ground black pepper
- 3 c water

Directions

- in a stock pot, mix beans, bouillon, water, tomatoes, Worcestershire sauce, onion, celery, garlic, bay leaf, ham, parsley and garlic. Heat to boil. Decrease the heat, cover the pot and let to simmer for 2 hours.
- Pour in more water. Add pepper and salt to taste. Let to simmer for about 2 more hours. Get rid of bay leaf.

Nutrition Information

- Nutritionist's Calories: 236 kcal 12%
- Total Fat: 3.4 g 5%
- Carbohydrates: 35.7g 12%
- Protein: 16.1 g 32%
- Cholesterol: 15 mg 5%
- Sodium: 879 mg 35%

209. New Year's Day Black-Eyed Peas

"Note that eating black-eyed peas on New Year's Day may bring good luck the whole year!"

Servings: 16 | Prep: 15 m | Ready In: 3 h 15 m

Ingredients

- 1 pound dry black-eyed peas
- 2 c chopped cooked ham
- salt and pepper to taste
- 1 pinch garlic powder
- 2 onions, diced
- 1 (14.5 ounce) can whole tomatoes

Directions

- In an 8 quart pot, put black-eyed peas. Pour in plenty of water to fill pot to 3/4 full. Mix in diced onions, ham along with garlic powder, pepper and salt to taste. Into a food processor or blender, put tomatoes and then blend until tomatoes become liquefied. Pour in tomatoes into pot. Heat the ingredients to boil. Cover and let to simmer for about 2 1/2 to 3 hours on low heat or until peas become tender.

Nutrition Information

- Nutritionist's Calories: 120 kcal 6%
- Total Fat: 3.4 g 5%
- Carbohydrates: 16.8g 5%
- Protein: 5.7 g 11%
- Cholesterol: 9 mg 3%
- Sodium: 281 mg 11%

210. Oat Applesauce Muffins

"Healthy muffins that fill you with flavor and fiber rather than fat."

Servings: 12 | Prep: 10 m | Ready In: 2 h 40 m

Ingredients

- 1 c rolled oats
- 1 c buttermilk
- 1 c whole wheat flour
- 1 tsp. baking powder
- 1/2 tsp. baking soda
- 1/2 c brown sugar
- 1/2 c applesauce
- 1 egg

Directions

- In a small bowl, put oats and then add buttermilk. Allow to stand for 2 hours at room temperature.
- Preheat the oven to 190 degrees C (375 degrees F). Use paper muffin liners to line 12 muffin c or grease the c.
- Combine together whole wheat flour, brown sugar, baking soda and baking powder in a large bowl. Mix in egg, applesauce and the oat/buttermilk mixture. Combine well. Transfer the batter to the muffin c prepared.
- Bake for about 30 minutes until a toothpick comes out clean when inserted at the middle of muffin.

Nutrition Information

- Nutritionist's Calories: 101 kcal 5%
- Total Fat: 1.2 g 2%
- Carbohydrates: 20g 6%
- Protein: 3.5 g 7%
- Cholesterol: 16 mg 5%
- Sodium: 112 mg 4%

211. Oatmeal Whole Wheat Quick Bread

"This bread has no yeast and hence great for special diets. If desired, replace regular milk with soy milk. It is a little dense but good when fresh from oven, particularly with honey and butter on a cold morning!"

Servings: 12 | Prep: 20 m | Ready In: 40 m

Ingredients

- 1 c rolled oats
- 1 c whole wheat flour
- 2 tsps. baking powder
- 1/2 tsp. salt
- 1 1/2 tbsps. honey
- 1 tbsp. vegetable oil
- 1 c milk

Directions

- Preheat an oven to 230 degrees C (450 degrees F).
- In a blender or food processor, grind oatmeal. Mix oatmeal, salt, flour and baking powder in a large bowl. In another bowl, dissolve the honey in vegetable oil and mix in milk. Blend both mixtures and mix until a soft dough forms. Shape dough into a ball and transfer to a baking sheet that is oiled lightly.
- Bake for around 20 minutes or until the loaf's bottom sounds hollow when tapped.

Nutrition Information

- Nutritionist's Calories: 88 kcal 4%
- Total Fat: 2.2 g 3%
- Carbohydrates: 15.1g 5%

- Protein: 2.9 g 6%
- Cholesterol: 2 mg < 1%
- Sodium: 166 mg 7%

212. Olive Chicken II

"These chicken breasts are allowed to simmer together with a smattering of spices and herbs, tomatoes, wine, olives and chicken broth. If desired, serve together with saffron rice."

Servings: 8 | Prep: 15 m | Ready In: 1 h

Ingredients

- 8 skinless, boneless chicken breasts
- salt to taste
- 2 tbsps. vegetable oil
- 4 cloves garlic, crushed
- 1 bay leaf
- 1/4 tsp. dried thyme
- 1/4 tsp. ground black pepper
- 4 tomatoes, peeled and quartered
- 20 pimento-stuffed green olives
- 1 1/4 c dry white wine
- 1 1/4 c chicken broth

Directions

- Drizzle salt onto chicken. Over medium high heat, heat oil in a skillet, add chicken and brown for about five minutes per side. Pour in thyme, pepper, garlic and bay leaf and combine well. Mix in broth, wine, tomatoes and olives.
- Decrease the heat to low and let to simmer without covering for about 45 minutes or until the chicken juice runs clear and is cooked through. Take out bay leaf and garlic and then serve.

Nutrition Information

- Nutritionist's Calories: 276 kcal 14%
- Total Fat: 8.4 g 13%
- Carbohydrates: 11.7g 4%
- Protein: 30.7 g 61%
- Cholesterol: 69 mg 23%
- Sodium: 1013 mg 41%

213. Onion Soup Pork Chops

"This is a tasty, fast and simple way to make pork chops and also yields a nice side dish!"

Servings: 2

Ingredients

- 2 pork chops
- 1 (1 ounce) package dry onion soup mix
- 1 (6 ounce) package uncooked wild rice
- 3 c water

Directions

- Preheat an oven to 175 degrees C (350 degrees F).
- Over medium heat, brown pork chops in a medium skillet. Mix rice and soup mix in a medium bowl. Combine together and then transfer to a baking dish of 9x13 inch. On top of rice, spread the browned chops. Add water gently on top of all. Use aluminum foil to cover the dish tightly and then bake for about one hour or until the temperature at the center of the pork is 63 degrees C (145 degrees F).

Nutrition Information

- Nutritionist's Calories: 458 kcal 23%
- Total Fat: 5 g 8%

- Carbohydrates: 71.7g 23%
- Protein: 33.7 g 67%
- Cholesterol: 65 mg 22%
- Sodium: 1309 mg 52%

214. Orzo with Mushrooms and Walnuts

"The recipe yields enough. It's loved by everyone who I've served. It's easy to half the recipe."

Servings: 8 | *Prep:* 10 m | *Ready In:* 35 m

Ingredients

- 1/3 c chopped walnuts
- 3 tbsps. olive oil
- 2 onions, chopped
- 1 pound fresh mushrooms, sliced
- 4 c chicken broth
- 2 c uncooked orzo pasta
- salt and pepper to taste

Directions

- Preheat an oven to 175 degrees C (350 degrees F). Onto a baking sheet, put walnuts. Bake in oven for about 8 to 10 minutes or until walnuts release their aroma. For even roasting, stir 1 or 2 times.
- Over medium-high heat, heat oil in a heavy saucepan, add mushrooms and onion and then sauté until golden brown and tender.
- Add broth and heat to boil. Add in orzo, stir, decrease the heat to low and then cover the pan. Let to simmer for about 15 minutes until the orzo becomes tender and the liquid has been absorbed. You can uncover in case there is still liquid after 15 minutes and let to cook until the liquid evaporates. Take put from the heat source, add walnuts and stir. Add pepper and salt to taste.

Nutrition Information

- Nutritionist's Calories: 290 kcal 15%
- Total Fat: 9.5 g 15%
- Carbohydrates: 43.2g 14%
- Protein: 9.5 g 19%
- Cholesterol: 3 mg < 1%
- Sodium: 485 mg 19%

215. Pakistani Spicy Chickpeas

"These chickpeas are often eaten as an appetizer during Ramadan at Iftar."

Servings: 5

Ingredients

- 2 tbsps. vegetable oil
- 1 tsp. cumin seeds
- 1/2 tsp. salt
- 1/2 tsp. chili powder
- 1/2 tsp. lemon pepper
- 2 tomatoes, chopped
- 2 (15 ounce) cans garbanzo beans, drained
- 1 tbsp. lemon juice
- 1 onion, chopped

Directions

- Over low heat, warm oil and cumin in a pot and then heat until the cumin changes to a darker shade of brown.
- Drizzle in lemon and pepper seasoning, salt and chili powder. Combine well. Mix in tomatoes and then pour in chickpeas when the juice starts to thicken. Combine well.
- Pour in lemon juice and combine thoroughly. Stir in onions until soft.

- Take out from the heat source and transfer to a serving bowl. Serve right away.

Nutrition Information

- Nutritionist's Calories: 205 kcal 10%
- Total Fat: 7.1 g 11%
- Carbohydrates: 30.3g 10%
- Protein: 6.4 g 13%
- Cholesterol: 0 mg 0%
- Sodium: 621 mg 25%

216. Pancho Villa Baked Tilapia

"Unseal these foil pockets at diner and you'll have scent of Old Mexico wafts all over. This recipe is great for entertainment because it's ready in no time and there are no leftovers. Serve on top of rice."

Servings: 4 | Prep: 15 m | Ready In: 35 m

Ingredients

- 1 tbsp. olive oil
- 4 (4 ounce) fillets tilapia
- 1 (10 ounce) can diced tomatoes with green chile peppers
- 1 lime, juiced
- 4 tbsps. minced fresh cilantro
- 1 lime, thinly sliced

Directions

- Preheat an oven to 175 degrees C (350 degrees F). Use olive oil to coat one side of 4 (8x10 inch) aluminum foil pieces.
- At the center of each foil square, place a fillet. On top of fish, pour a generous amount of diced tomatoes including their juices. Drizzle with cilantro and lime juice. Set two lime slices

onto each fillet. Close the foil packets and then seal. Transfer to a baking tray.
- Bake for about 20 minutes or until the fish easily flakes with a fork.

Nutrition Information

- Nutritionist's Calories: 163 kcal 8%
- Total Fat: 5 g 8%
- Carbohydrates: 6.2g 2%
- Protein: 23.7 g 47%
- Cholesterol: 41 mg 14%
- Sodium: 354 mg 14%

217. Pasta and Garlic

"This dish is easy and delicious! Use pasta you love and then add garlic on top! Add your favorite cheese."

Servings: 8 | Prep: 5 m | Ready In: 15 m

Ingredients

- 1 1/2 pounds pasta
- 1/4 c olive oil
- 1 clove crushed garlic
- salt and pepper to taste
- 1/4 c grated Parmesan cheese

Directions

- Boil pasta in a pot containing salted water until al dente and then drain thoroughly.
- Heat oil slightly in a small saucepan, add garlic and sauté until browned lightly. Take care not to burn garlic.
- Mix garlic, pasta, pepper and salt. Add Romano or Parmesan on top before serving.

Nutrition Information

- Nutritionist's Calories: 316 kcal 16%
- Total Fat: 9.4 g 14%
- Carbohydrates: 46.8g 15%
- Protein: 10.6 g 21%
- Cholesterol: 64 mg 21%
- Sodium: 61 mg 2%

218. Pasta e Fagioli I

"This soup is lovely, rich and tasty and can be served with garlic toast or as a meal itself!"

Servings: 8

Ingredients

- 2 tbsps. olive oil
- 1 c chopped onion
- 3 cloves garlic, minced
- 2 (14.5 ounce) cans stewed tomatoes
- 3 c low-sodium chicken broth
- 1 (15 ounce) can cannellini beans
- 1/4 c chopped fresh parsley
- 1 tsp. dried basil leaves
- 1/4 tsp. ground black pepper
- 1/4 pound seashell pasta

Directions

- Over medium heat, heat oil in a Dutch oven of 4-quart until hot. Pour in garlic and onion and then cook for about five minutes or until the onion becomes tender.
- Into the Dutch oven, add basil, undrained tomatoes, parsley, undrained cannellini beans, pepper and chicken broth and heat to boil at high heat as you stir frequently. Allow to boil for about one minute and then simmer while covered for 10 minutes.

- Into the Dutch oven, pour in pasta and then let to simmer for about 10 to 12 minutes or until the pasta becomes tender. Serve right away.

Nutrition Information

- Nutritionist's Calories: 185 kcal 9%
- Total Fat: 4.2 g 7%
- Carbohydrates: 30.5g 10%
- Protein: 8.2 g 16%
- Cholesterol: 2 mg < 1%
- Sodium: 272 mg 11%

219. Pasta Fagioli Soup II

"I love this fast and simple Italian dish. Add grated Romano cheese for decoration."

Servings: 8 | Prep: 15 m | Ready In: 1 h 15 m

Ingredients

- 1 (29 ounce) can diced tomatoes
- 2 (14 ounce) cans great Northern beans, undrained
- 1 (14 ounce) can chopped spinach, drained
- 2 (14.5 ounce) cans chicken broth
- 1 (8 ounce) can tomato sauce
- 3 c water
- 1 tbsp. minced garlic
- 8 slices crisp cooked bacon, crumbled
- 1 tbsp. dried parsley
- 1 tsp. garlic powder
- 1 1/2 tsps. salt
- 1/2 tsp. ground black pepper
- 1/2 tsp. dried basil
- 1/2 pound seashell pasta

Directions

- Mix diced tomatoes, basil, tomato sauce, beans, spinach, garlic powder, bacon, chicken broth, water, parsley, pepper, salt and garlic in a large stock pot. Heat to boil and simmer while covered for 40 minutes.
- Pour in pasta and then cook without covering for about 10 minutes until the pasta becomes tender. Into individual serving bowls, pour the soup, top with cheese and then serve.

Nutrition Information

- Nutritionist's Calories: 288 kcal 14%
- Total Fat: 3.6 g 6%
- Carbohydrates: 48.5g 16%
- Protein: 15.8 g 32%
- Cholesterol: 7 mg 2%
- Sodium: 1135 mg 45%

220. Pasta Fagioli

"This is an old-fashioned Italian soup. To have a meal, serve together with a hot loaf of garlic bread and a crisp salad! Top with grated Parmesan cheese and serve."

Servings: 4 | Prep: 10 m | Ready In: 50 m

Ingredients

- 1 tbsp. olive oil
- 2 stalks celery, chopped
- 1 onion, chopped
- 3 cloves garlic, minced
- 2 tsps. dried parsley
- 1 tsp. Italian seasoning
- 1/4 tsp. crushed red pepper flakes
- salt to taste
- 1 (14.5 ounce) can chicken broth
- 2 medium tomatoes, peeled and chopped
- 1 (8 ounce) can tomato sauce

- 1/2 c uncooked spinach pasta
- 1 (15 ounce) can cannellini beans, with liquid

Directions

- Over medium heat, heat olive oil in a saucepan and add celery, red pepper flakes, onion, salt, garlic, Italian seasoning and parsley. Cook for about 5 minutes until the onion becomes translucent. Mix in tomato sauce, chicken broth and tomatoes. Let to simmer for about 15 to 20 minutes on low.
- Pour in pasta and let to cook for 10 minutes until the pasta becomes tender.
- Pour in undrained beans, combine thoroughly and heat through. Top with grated Parmesan cheese and serve.

Nutrition Information

- Nutritionist's Calories: 225 kcal 11%
- Total Fat: 4.4 g 7%
- Carbohydrates: 37.3g 12%
- Protein: 11 g 22%
- Cholesterol: 2 mg < 1%
- Sodium: 758 mg 30%

221. Pasta Hot! Hot! Hot!

"This dish is made of olive oil and pasta sautéed together with crushed red pepper and garlic cloves with Parmesan on top."

Servings: 4 | Prep: 15 m | Ready In: 30 m

Ingredients

- 1 (16 ounce) package spaghetti
- 1/4 c olive oil
- 3 cloves garlic, chopped
- 1/2 tsp. crushed red pepper

- 1/4 c grated Parmesan cheese

Directions

- Bring to boil lightly salted water in a pot and add pasta. Cook until al dente or for about 8 to 10 minutes and then drain.
- Over low heat, simmer peppers, olive oil and garlic in a small saucepan. Spread the mixture of olive oil on top of the cooked pasta, add Parmesan cheese on top and then serve.

Nutrition Information

- Nutritionist's Calories: 561 kcal 28%
- Total Fat: 16.7 g 26%
- Carbohydrates: 84.8g 27%
- Protein: 16.7 g 33%
- Cholesterol: 4 mg 1%
- Sodium: 84 mg 3%

222. Pasta Shells Florentine

"This pasta shells are filled with spinach and low-fat cheeses and then smothered in a marinara sauce before baking. If desired, add two tbsps. of egg substitute instead of egg white. Make it even better by adding nonfat cottage cheese."

Servings: 4

Ingredients

- 16 jumbo pasta shells
- 1 (10 ounce) package frozen chopped spinach, thawed and drained
- 6 ounces low fat mozzarella cheese, shredded
- 1 c low-fat cottage cheese
- 1 egg white
- 1 tbsp. grated Parmesan cheese
- 1/4 tsp. ground nutmeg

- 2 tbsps. Italian seasoning
- 1 (16 ounce) jar spaghetti sauce

Directions

- Boil pasta shells in a pot containing salted water until al dente. Drain pasta thoroughly and then rinse.
- Preheat an oven to 175 degrees C (375 degrees F).
- Mix spinach, egg white, mozzarella cheese, Italian seasoning, cottage cheese, nutmeg and parmesan cheese in a medium bowl until blended.
- Heap one tbsp. of the spinach mixture into each pasta shell. Into a baking dish of 8x12 inch, spread evenly one c of spaghetti sauce. Transfer the shells to pan. Spread the spaghetti sauce remaining on top of the shells. Use aluminum foil to cover and then bake about for 30 to 40 minutes or until the shells become heated through.

Nutrition Information

- Nutritionist's Calories: 539 kcal 27%
- Total Fat: 12.2 g 19%
- Carbohydrates: 73.4g 24%
- Protein: 34.7 g 69%
- Cholesterol: 30 mg 10%
- Sodium: 1078 mg 43%

223. Pasta with Asparagus

"This pasta dish contains little amount of fat. I usually prepare it for the guests. You can serve together with French bread and a fruit salad."

Servings: 4 | Prep: 15 m | Ready In: 25 m

Ingredients

- 1 1/2 pounds fresh asparagus, trimmed and cut into 1 inch pieces
- 1/4 c chicken broth
- 1/2 pound fresh mushrooms, sliced
- 8 ounces angel hair pasta
- 1 tbsp. olive oil
- 1/2 tsp. crushed red pepper
- 1/2 c grated Parmesan cheese

Directions

- Cook pasta by following the package directions.
- In a nonstick skillet, heat olive oil. Over medium heat, sauté asparagus in pan for approximately three minutes. Pour in mushroom slices and chicken broth and let to cook for three minutes.
- Drain and then pour the pasta onto a serving dish. Mix gently the pasta together with the mixture of asparagus. Drizzle crushed red pepper and Parmesan on top.

Nutrition Information

- Nutritionist's Calories: 281 kcal 14%
- Total Fat: 8.4 g 13%
- Carbohydrates: 39.4g 13%
- Protein: 15.5 g 31%
- Cholesterol: 9 mg 3%
- Sodium: 339 mg 14%

---

224. Pasta with Fresh Tomato Sauce

"A pasta dish that is lovely when served together with a green salad. The main advantage of this recipe it that it's ready in a few minutes."

Servings: 8 | Prep: 15 m | Ready In: 25 m

Ingredients

- 1 (16 ounce) package dry penne pasta
- 8 roma (plum) tomatoes, diced
- 1/2 c Italian dressing
- 1/4 c finely chopped fresh basil
- 1/4 c diced red onion
- 1/4 c grated Parmesan cheese

Directions

- Bring to boil lightly salted water in a pot and add penne pasta. Let to cook for about 10 minutes until al dente. Drain.
- Mix cooked pasta together with red onion, tomatoes, basil, Parmesan cheese and Italian dressing in a large bowl.

Nutrition Information

- Nutritionist's Calories: 257 kcal 13%
- Total Fat: 3.1 g 5%
- Carbohydrates: 46.9g 15%
- Protein: 9.8 g 20%
- Cholesterol: 3 mg 1%
- Sodium: 248 mg 10%

---

225. Pasta with Scallops, Zucchini, and Tomatoes

"This summer meal is loved by my family!"

Servings: 8 | Prep: 15 m | Ready In: 30 m

Ingredients

- 1 pound dry fettuccine pasta
- 1/4 c olive oil
- 3 cloves garlic, minced

- 2 zucchinis, diced
- 1/2 tsp. salt
- 1/2 tsp. crushed red pepper flakes
- 1 c chopped fresh basil
- 4 roma (plum) tomatoes, chopped
- 1 pound bay scallops
- 2 tbsps. grated Parmesan cheese

Directions

- Cook pasta in a pot containing boiling salted water until al dente and then drain.
- In the meantime, heat oil in a large skillet, add garlic and then cook until it's tender. Pour in zucchini, dried basil (if using), red pepper flakes and salt. Sauté for about ten minutes. Pour in fresh basil (if using), chopped tomatoes and bay scallops. Let to simmer for about five minutes or until the scallops become opaque.
- Spread the sauce on top of the cooked pasta, top with grated Parmesan cheese and serve.

Nutrition Information

- Nutritionist's Calories: 335 kcal 17%
- Total Fat: 9.1 g 14%
- Carbohydrates: 46.1g 15%
- Protein: 18.7 g 37%
- Cholesterol: 20 mg 7%
- Sodium: 266 mg 11%

226. Pasta With Tuna Sauce

"This delicious tomato sauce is made with canned tuna. Feel free to add your favorite pasta."

Servings: 6 | Prep: 15 m | Ready In: 40 m

Ingredients

- 1 tbsp. olive oil
- 1 onion, chopped
- 2 cloves crushed garlic
- 1 tbsp. capers
- 1 (14.5 ounce) can crushed tomatoes
- 1 tbsp. lemon juice
- 1 tbsp. chopped fresh parsley
- 1/4 tsp. red pepper flakes
- 2 (5 ounce) cans tuna, drained
- 1 (16 ounce) package dry pasta

Directions

- Over low heat, heat oil in a large sauté pan, and add garlic and onion. Cook while stirring until the onion becomes tender. Mix in parsley, lemon juice, capers and tomatoes. Add red pepper flakes to taste. Let to simmer slowly for about three minutes to make the sauce thick. Roll in tuna and then heat through.
- As the sauce cooks, pour in pasta into a pot with rapidly boiling water and let to cook until tender. Drain pasta thoroughly.
- Combine the pasta together with the sauce before serving.

Nutrition Information

- Nutritionist's Calories: 384 kcal 19%
- Total Fat: 6.2 g 10%
- Carbohydrates: 59.6g 19%
- Protein: 23 g 46%
- Cholesterol: 102 mg 34%
- Sodium: 174 mg 7%

227. Pat's Baked Beans

"I got this delicious recipe from my step mother when I didn't know what to carry to a barbecue. I have brought this dish to a few parties and never enough!"

Ingredients

- 6 slices bacon
- 1 c chopped onion
- 1 clove garlic, minced
- 1 (16 ounce) can pinto beans
- 1 (16 ounce) can great Northern beans, drained
- 1 (16 ounce) can baked beans
- 1 (16 ounce) can red kidney beans, drained
- 1 (15 ounce) can garbanzo beans, drained
- 3/4 c ketchup
- 1/2 c molasses
- 1/4 c packed brown sugar
- 2 tbsps. Worcestershire sauce
- 1 tbsp. yellow mustard
- 1/2 tsp. pepper

Directions

- Preheat an oven to 190 degrees C (375 degrees F).
- Into a large and deep skillet, put bacon. Over medium high heat, cook until browned evenly. Drain and reserve two tbsps. of the drippings. Crumble bacon and reserve in a bowl. Cook garlic and onion in the drippings reserved until the onion becomes tender. Drain any excess grease and then pour into bowl containing bacon.
- Add pinto beans, kidney beans, northern beans, garbanzo beans and baked beans to the bacon and onions. Mix in Worcestershire sauce, ketchup, molasses, black pepper, brown sugar and mustard. Combine well and place into a casserole dish of 9x12 inch.
- Cover the dish and then bake for one hour in oven.

Nutrition Information

- Nutritionist's Calories: 399 kcal 20%
- Total Fat: 9.1 g 14%
- Carbohydrates: 68g 22%
- Protein: 14.1 g 28%
- Cholesterol: 12 mg 4%
- Sodium: 950 mg 38%

228. Peachy Pork Chops

"I love recipes that are great and simple just like this one. Lovely when served together with wild rice."

Servings: 4

Ingredients

- 4 (1 1/4 inch) thick pork chops
- salt and pepper to taste
- 1 tbsp. vegetable oil
- 1 (29 ounce) can sliced peaches, drained and syrup reserved
- 3 tbsps. brown sugar
- 1 tsp. ground ginger

Directions

- Over medium heat, heat oil in a skillet. Trim any fat that is visible from the chops and then season with pepper and salt. Cook the chops in vegetable oil until brown.
- Mix ginger, brown sugar and the peach syrup reserved. Spread on top of chops and heat to boil. Pour in peaches and then let to cook without covering for about 15 to 20 minutes or until the liquid becomes thick and reduced to half. Flip the chops frequently to cook even.

Nutrition Information

- Nutritionist's Calories: 388 kcal 19%
- Total Fat: 9.4 g 14%
- Carbohydrates: 48.4g 16%
- Protein: 26.4 g 53%

- Cholesterol: 69 mg 23%
- Sodium: 93 mg 4%

229. Penne Pasta with Cannellini Beans and Escarole

"A nice pasta recipe. Chopping the escarole is the hardest part of this recipe. It's quick, easy and tasty! Goes well together with a loaf of Italian bread."

Servings: 8 | Prep: 15 m | Ready In: 30 m

Ingredients

- 1 (16 ounce) package dry penne pasta
- 1 head escarole, chopped
- 1 (15.5 ounce) can cannellini beans, with liquid
- 1 (14.5 ounce) can diced tomatoes with garlic and onion, drained
- salt and ground black pepper to taste

Directions

- Bring to boil lightly salted water in a pot and penne pasta. Cook until al dente or for about 8 to 10 minutes and then drain.
- Over medium heat, cook while stirring diced tomatoes along with garlic and onion, escarole and cannellini beans and liquid in a skillet until the ingredients are heated through. Add pepper and salt to taste. Combine with cooked pasta and then serve.

Nutrition Information

- Nutritionist's Calories: 310 kcal 16%
- Total Fat: 2 g 3%
- Carbohydrates: 60.1g 19%
- Protein: 13.7 g 27%
- Cholesterol: 0 mg 0%
- Sodium: 268 mg 11%

230. Penne Pasta with Spinach and Bacon

"This meal is fast and light. Penne pasta is combined with tomatoes, wilted spinach and bacon. It's great for all seasons and complements everything."

Servings: 4 | Prep: 10 m | Ready In: 25 m

Ingredients

- 1 (12 ounce) package penne pasta
- 2 tbsps. olive oil, divided
- 6 slices bacon, chopped
- 2 tbsps. minced garlic
- 1 (14.5 ounce) can diced tomatoes
- 1 bunch fresh spinach, rinsed and torn into bite-size pieces

Directions

- Bring to boil lightly salted water in a pot and add penne pasta. Cook until tender or for about 8 to 10 minutes.
- In the meantime, over medium heat, heat one tbsp. olive oil in a skillet and add bacon. Cook until crispy and browned. Pour in garlic and then let to cook for about one minute. Add tomatoes, stir and let to cook until heated through.
- Into a colander, put spinach and then drain the hot pasta on top of it to make it wilt. Place in a serving bowl and combine with the mixture of bacon and tomato and the olive oil remaining.

Nutrition Information

- Nutritionist's Calories: 517 kcal 26%
- Total Fat: 14.8 g 23%
- Carbohydrates: 73.8g 24%

- Protein: 21 g 42%
- Cholesterol: 15 mg 5%
- Sodium: 547 mg 22%

- Protein: 24.5 g 49%
- Cholesterol: 95 mg 32%
- Sodium: 399 mg 16%

231. Penne with Shrimp

"This Italian dish is light and delicious!"

Servings: 8 | Prep: 10 m | Ready In: 35 m

Ingredients

- 1 (16 ounce) package penne pasta
- 2 tbsps. olive oil
- 1/4 c chopped red onion
- 1 tbsp. chopped garlic
- 1/4 c white wine
- 2 (14.5 ounce) cans diced tomatoes
- 1 pound shrimp, peeled and deveined
- 1 c grated Parmesan cheese

Directions

- Bring to boil lightly salted water in a pot and add pasta. Cook until al dente or for about 8 to 10 minutes and then drain.
- Over medium heat, heat oil in a skillet and mix in garlic and onion. Let to cook until the onion becomes tender. Add in tomatoes and wine and stir. Continue to cook while stirring frequently for about 10 minutes.
- Stir shrimp into skillet and let to cook for about five minutes or until opaque. Combine with the pasta, add Parmesan cheese on top and serve.

Nutrition Information

- Nutritionist's Calories: 385 kcal 19%
- Total Fat: 8.5 g 13%
- Carbohydrates: 48.5g 16%

232. Peppered Bacon and Tomato Linguine

"This is a fast and tasty dish!"

Servings: 6 | Prep: 15 m | Ready In: 30 m

Ingredients

- 1/2 pound peppered bacon, diced
- 2 tbsps. chopped green onion
- 2 tsps. minced garlic
- 1 (14.5 ounce) can diced tomatoes
- 1 tsp. dried basil
- 1 tsp. salt
- ground black pepper to taste
- 1 (16 ounce) package linguine pasta
- 3 tbsps. grated Parmesan cheese

Directions

- Into a large and deep skillet, put bacon. Over medium high heat, cook until browned evenly. Drain bacon and reserve the drippings. Set bacon aside.
- Over medium heat, sauté garlic and green onion in the bacon drippings for about 1 minute. Mix in ground black pepper, tomatoes, salt and basil. Let to simmer for five minutes.
- In the meantime, bring to boil lightly salted water in a pot and add pasta. Cook until al dente or for about 8 to 10 minutes and then drain.
- Mix the hot pasta together with the sauce and top with Parmesan cheese.

Nutrition Information

- Nutritionist's Calories: 362 kcal 18%
- Total Fat: 7.6 g 12%
- Carbohydrates: 57.5g 19%
- Protein: 16.2 g 32%
- Cholesterol: 16 mg 5%
- Sodium: 821 mg 33%

233. Pesto Chicken Florentine

"This dish contains a very rich combo of creamy pesto sauce, chicken and spinach. Best served together with romaine salad and crunchy bread!"

***Servings:** 4 | **Prep:** 20 m | **Ready In:** 55 m*

Ingredients

- 2 tbsps. olive oil
- 2 cloves garlic, finely chopped
- 4 skinless, boneless chicken breast halves - cut into strips
- 2 c fresh spinach leaves
- 1 (4.5 ounce) package dry Alfredo sauce mix
- 2 tbsps. pesto
- 1 (8 ounce) package dry penne pasta
- 1 tbsp. grated Romano cheese

Directions

- Over medium high heat, heat oil in a skillet, pour in garlic and then sauté for one minute. Place chicken in skillet and let to cook for about 7 to 8 minutes per side. Once the chicken is almost cooked through (no pink remains inside), pour in spinach and then sauté for about 3 to 4 minutes.
- In the meantime, make Alfredo sauce by following the package instructions. Once done, add in two tbsps. pesto, stir and reserve.
- Cook pasta in a pot containing salted boiling water until al dente or for about 8 to 10 minutes. Use cold water to rinse and then drain.
- Into the pasta, add the chicken/spinach mixture and then mix in the pesto/Alfredo sauce. Combine well, add cheese on top and then serve.

Nutrition Information

- Nutritionist's Calories: 572 kcal 29%
- Total Fat: 19.3 g 30%
- Carbohydrates: 57.3g 18%
- Protein: 41.9 g 84%
- Cholesterol: 84 mg 28%
- Sodium: 1707 mg 68%

234. Pesto Pasta with Chicken

"Pasta that is simple and tasty together with chicken. For a quick dinner, serve together with salad and crusty bread. Adjust the amount of pesto sauce to suit your taste. Even better to use homemade pesto but requires more time."

***Servings:** 8 | **Prep:** 10 m | **Ready In:** 30 m*

Ingredients

- 1 (16 ounce) package bow tie pasta
- 1 tsp. olive oil
- 2 cloves garlic, minced
- 2 boneless skinless chicken breasts, cut into bite-size pieces
- crushed red pepper flakes to taste
- 1/3 c oil-packed sun-dried tomatoes, drained and cut into strips
- 1/2 c pesto sauce

Directions

- Bring to boil lightly salted water in a pot and add pasta. Cook until al dente or for about 8 to 10 minutes. Drain.
- Over medium heat, heat oil in a skillet, add garlic and then sauté until tender. Mix in chicken. Add red pepper flakes to taste. Let to cook until the chicken is cooked through and golden.
- Mix pesto, pasta, sun-dried tomatoes and chicken in a large bowl. Mix to evenly coat.

Nutrition Information

- Nutritionist's Calories: 328 kcal 16%
- Total Fat: 10.1 g 15%
- Carbohydrates: 43.3g 14%
- Protein: 17.4 g 35%
- Cholesterol: 22 mg 7%
- Sodium: 154 mg 6%

235. Pesto Pasta

"This recipe is simple to prepare and rich in flavor! Great either hot or cold."

Servings: 8

Ingredients

- 1/2 c chopped onion
- 2 1/2 tbsps. pesto
- 2 tbsps. olive oil
- 2 tbsps. grated Parmesan cheese
- 1 (16 ounce) package pasta
- salt to taste
- ground black pepper to taste

Directions

- In a large pot containing boiling water, cook pasta until done and then drain.
- In the meantime, over medium low heat, heat oil in a frying pan and add onion, pesto, pepper and salt. Let to cook for about 5 minutes or until the onions become soft.
- Combine the pesto mixture into the pasta in a bowl. Add grated cheese, stir and serve.

Nutrition Information

- Nutritionist's Calories: 225 kcal 11%
- Total Fat: 7.2 g 11%
- Carbohydrates: 32g 10%
- Protein: 7.8 g 16%
- Cholesterol: 44 mg 15%
- Sodium: 71 mg 3%

236. Pesto Polenta Lasagna

"This meal is simple and fast and rich in flavor. Ready in 10 minutes."

Servings: 8 | Prep: 10 m | Ready In: 40 m

Ingredients

- 1 (18 ounce) package polenta, cut into 1/4 inch thick slices
- 1/2 (24 ounce) jar bottled marinara sauce
- 1/4 c pesto
- 1/4 c pine nuts
- 1 c shredded mozzarella cheese

Directions

- Preheat an oven to 190 degrees C (375 degrees F). Coat a baking dish of 11x7x2 inch with oil.

- At the bottom of the baking dish prepared, spread a layer of polenta. Add a thin layer of pesto on top of polenta. Pour ½ of sauce on top of polenta. Spread on top, another layer of the polenta and the sauce.
- Bake without covering for about 25 minutes. Switch the broiler on. Add pine nuts and cheese on top of polenta and then broil until the nuts become toasted and the cheese turns browns.

Nutrition Information

- Nutritionist's Calories: 179 kcal 9%
- Total Fat: 9.1 g 14%
- Carbohydrates: 16.7g 5%
- Protein: 7.9 g 16%
- Cholesterol: 12 mg 4%
- Sodium: 515 mg 21%

237. Picante Chicken

"Super simple and fast. I got this from a checker at a grocery store. If desired, serve on top of rice."

Servings: 2

Ingredients

- 2 skinless, boneless chicken breasts
- 1 c picante sauce

Directions

- Open the jar containing picante sauce and pour in a saucepan. To the picante sauce, add chicken breasts and then heat to a steady boil. Let to boil slowly for about 20 to 25 minutes or until the juice runs clear and no pink color of chicken remains inside.

Nutrition Information

- Nutritionist's Calories: 175 kcal 9%
- Total Fat: 1.8 g 3%
- Carbohydrates: 8.7g 3%
- Protein: 28.8 g 58%
- Cholesterol: 68 mg 23%
- Sodium: 1082 mg 43%

238. Pico De Gallo

"At times when enjoying a classic Mexican food, you get this salsa made with jalapenos, tomatoes and onions. Feel free to add some lime juice but I like this simple basic recipe. The moment you serve this dish together with a Mexican dish like tacos, you'll probably want to have it with all Mexican dishes!"

Servings: 4 | Prep: 20 m | Ready In: 50 m

Ingredients

- 1 medium tomato, diced
- 1 onion, finely chopped
- 1/2 fresh jalapeno pepper, seeded and chopped
- 2 sprigs fresh cilantro, finely chopped
- 1 green onion, finely chopped
- 1/2 tsp. garlic powder
- 1/8 tsp. salt
- 1/8 tsp. pepper

Directions

- Mix tomato, cilantro, onion, green onion and jalapeno pepper (to taste) in a medium bowl. Add pepper, salt and garlic powder to taste. Mix until distributed evenly. Chill for half an hour.

Nutrition Information

- Nutritionist's Calories: 21 kcal 1%
- Total Fat: 0.1 g < 1%
- Carbohydrates: 4.7g 2%
- Protein: 0.8 g 2%
- Cholesterol: 0 mg 0%
- Sodium: 76 mg 3%

---

239. Pineapple Chicken Tenders

"These bites are tasty for a light meal with salad or for an appetizer!"

Servings: 10 | Prep: 30 m | Ready In: 1 h 10 m

Ingredients

- 1 c pineapple juice
- 1/2 c packed brown sugar
- 1/3 c light soy sauce
- 2 pounds chicken breast tenderloins or strips
- skewers

Directions

- Over medium heat, combine soy sauce, pineapple juice and brown sugar in a small saucepan. Take out from the heat source before mixture starts to boil.
- In a medium bowl, put chicken tenders. Add the pineapple marinade to cover and chill for a minimum of 30 minutes.
- Preheat the grill over medium heat. Onto wooden skewers, thread the chicken lengthwise.
- Polish grill grate lightly with oil. Let the chicken grill for about 5 minutes on each side or until the juice runs clear. Take care because the tenders cook fast.

Nutrition Information

- Nutritionist's Calories: 160 kcal 8%
- Total Fat: 2.2 g 3%
- Carbohydrates: 14.7g 5%
- Protein: 19.4 g 39%
- Cholesterol: 52 mg 17%
- Sodium: 332 mg 13%

---

240. Pineapple Chicken

"This chicken recipe is super simple to prepare and very delicious!"

Servings: 5 | Prep: 10 m | Ready In: 40 m

Ingredients

- 5 skinless, boneless chicken breast halves
- 1 1/2 (1 ounce) packages dry onion soup mix
- 2 c water
- 1 (15 ounce) can pineapple, drained
- 1 large orange, sliced in rounds
- 1 tbsp. vegetable oil

Directions

- Use vegetable spray to coat an electric skillet or large frying pan. Then brown the chicken breasts in the pan with the meat side facing downwards.
- Flip over the chicken. Pour in onion soup, water and pineapple chunks.
- Cover and then decrease the heat to low. Let to simmer for half an hour. Decorate with fresh slices of orange and cooked pineapple chunks.

Nutrition Information

- Nutritionist's Calories: 245 kcal 12%
- Total Fat: 5.8 g 9%

- Carbohydrates: 22.8g 7%
- Protein: 25.8 g 52%
- Cholesterol: 67 mg 22%
- Sodium: 802 mg 32%

241. Pineapple Cranberry Chicken

"This poultry dish is tongue-tantalizing and makes chicken to something you have been searching for!"

Servings: 8 | Prep: 5 m | Ready In: 45 m

Ingredients

- 4 pounds skinless, boneless chicken breast halves
- 1 (16 ounce) can whole cranberry sauce
- 1 (20 ounce) can crushed pineapple, drained
- 1/2 tsp. ground cinnamon

Directions

- Preheat an oven to 190 degrees C (375 degrees F).
- Into a baking dish of 9x13 inch that is lightly greased, put chicken and then poke with a fork. Spread a layer pineapple and cranberry sauce on top of chicken and drizzle cinnamon on top.
- Cover the dish and then bake for 25 minutes in oven. Uncover and then bake for about 15 more minutes or until the chicken is done (the juice runs clear).

Nutrition Information

- Nutritionist's Calories: 374 kcal 19%
- Total Fat: 5.5 g 8%
- Carbohydrates: 31.9g 10%
- Protein: 47.5 g 95%
- Cholesterol: 129 mg 43%

- Sodium: 125 mg 5%

242. Pineapple Salsa

"This salsa is made with a vegetable and fruit! You can serve as a side dish or on top of pork, chicken or fish."

Servings: 8 | Prep: 20 m | Ready In: 20 m

Ingredients

- 1 c finely chopped fresh pineapple
- 1/2 c diced red bell pepper
- 1/2 c diced green bell pepper
- 1 c frozen corn kernels, thawed
- 1 (15 ounce) can black beans, drained and rinsed
- 1/4 c chopped onions
- 2 green chile peppers, chopped
- 1/4 c orange juice
- 1/4 c chopped fresh cilantro
- 1/2 tsp. ground cumin
- salt and pepper to taste

Directions

- Combine together pineapple, green chile peppers, red bell pepper, orange juice, green bell pepper, cilantro, corn, onions and black beans in a large bowl. Add pepper, cumin and salt. Cover the bowl and refrigerate until when ready to serve.

Nutrition Information

- Nutritionist's Calories: 92 kcal 5%
- Total Fat: 0.5 g < 1%
- Carbohydrates: 19.3g 6%
- Protein: 4.5 g 9%
- Cholesterol: 0 mg 0%

- Sodium: 207 mg 8%

243. P.J.'s Fresh Corn Salad

"During summer, my son in-law usually prepares this salad. It's satisfying on a hot day."

Servings: 8 | Prep: 15 m | Ready In: 1 h 15 m

Ingredients

- 8 ears fresh corn
- 1 tomato, chopped
- 1 zucchini, chopped
- 1 cucumber, peeled and chopped
- 1 red onion, chopped
- 1 red bell pepper, chopped
- 1/2 c Italian-style salad dressing

Directions

- Husk corn and then chop the kernels from cob. Combine together red bell pepper, corn, cucumber, onion, tomato and zucchini in a large bowl. Spread the dressing on top of the veggies and stir to coat. Chill for at least one hour.

Nutrition Information

- Nutritionist's Calories: 141 kcal 7%
- Total Fat: 5.4 g 8%
- Carbohydrates: 23g 7%
- Protein: 3.9 g 8%
- Cholesterol: 0 mg 0%
- Sodium: 261 mg 10%

244. Pork Chops for the Slow Cooker

"This is a delicious and tender recipe just like other recipes that are slow cooked."

Servings: 6 | Prep: 5 m | Ready In: 6 h 5 m

Ingredients

- 6 boneless pork chops
- 1/4 c brown sugar
- 1 tsp. ground ginger
- 1/2 c soy sauce
- 1/4 c ketchup
- 2 cloves garlic, crushed
- salt and pepper to taste

Directions

- Into a slow cooker, put pork chops. Mix the ingredients remaining and spread on top of the pork chops.
- Let to cook for 6 hours on Low setting until the temperature at the center of the pork is 63 degrees C (145 degrees F).

Nutrition Information

- Nutritionist's Calories: 146 kcal 7%
- Total Fat: 4.3 g 7%
- Carbohydrates: 10.6g 3%
- Protein: 16 g 32%
- Cholesterol: 36 mg 12%
- Sodium: 1337 mg 53%

245. Pork Chops in Beer

"A simple recipe for pork chops with brown sugar, beer and ketchup. Easy and tastes great."

Ingredients

- 2 c ketchup
- 1 (12 fluid ounce) can or bottle beer
- 3/4 c packed brown sugar
- 8 pork chops

Directions

- Preheat an oven to 175 degrees C (350 degrees F).
- Mix beer, ketchup and brown sugar in a medium bowl. Combine well and transfer to a baking dish of 9x13 inch. Onto this mixture in dish, add pork chops.
- Bake without covering for 1 hour at 175 degrees C (350 degrees F) or the temperature at the center of the pork is 63 degrees C (145 degrees F). (Note that you can put foil on top of the pork chops in case they begin to brown too fast).

Nutrition Information

- Nutritionist's Calories: 256 kcal 13%
- Total Fat: 6.4 g 10%
- Carbohydrates: 36.9g 12%
- Protein: 11.7 g 23%
- Cholesterol: 34 mg 11%
- Sodium: 697 mg 28%

---

246. Pork Chops with Apples, Sweet Potatoes, and Sauerkraut

"A sweet and savory mix of sauerkraut, apples, onions and sweet potatoes that cook well in a slow cooker! Do not have worries of sauerkraut because it becomes mild and sweet."

Ingredients

- 4 (1 inch thick) boneless pork chops
- 2 medium sweet potatoes, peeled and sliced 1/2 inch thick
- 1 medium onion, sliced
- 2 apples - peeled, cored and sliced
- 1 tbsp. brown sugar
- 1/2 tsp. ground nutmeg
- 1/4 tsp. salt
- freshly ground black pepper to taste
- 1 (16 ounce) can sauerkraut, drained

Directions

- Over medium-high heat, heat a skillet and use cooking spray to coat it. Brown pork chops quickly on each side. Reserve.
- At the bottom of a slow cooker of 3 to 4 quart, spread slices of sweet potato. Add slices of onion and then slices of apple to cover. Drizzle salt, brown sugar and nutmeg on top apples, and then grind some pepper. Onto the pile, put the pork chops and then add sauerkraut to cover. Cover and let to cook for about 5 hours on Low. Note that you can cook for 1 more hour without drying out.
- Serve the veggies and pork along with juice from cooker on top.

Nutrition Information

- Nutritionist's Calories: 276 kcal 14%
- Total Fat: 5.6 g 9%
- Carbohydrates: 43.4g 14%
- Protein: 14.6 g 29%
- Cholesterol: 30 mg 10%
- Sodium: 968 mg 39%

247. Pork Tenderloin

"A nice pork tenderloin recipe that is marinated overnight and then smothered in apple jelly."

Servings: 6 | Prep: 10 m | Ready In: 1 h 10 m

Ingredients

- 2 1/2 pounds pork tenderloin
- 1/8 tsp. mustard powder to taste
- 1/8 tsp. dried thyme
- 1/2 c dry sherry
- 1/2 c soy sauce
- 3 cloves garlic, minced
- 2 tbsps. fresh ginger root, minced
- 3/4 c apple jelly
- 2 tbsps. dry sherry
- 1 tbsp. soy sauce

Directions

- Season the meat with thyme and mustard powder to taste. Transfer to a non-reactive dish and pour in ginger, garlic, 1/2 c of soy sauce and 1/2 c of sherry. Coat loin thoroughly, cover the dish and chill overnight.
- Preheat an oven to 165 degrees C (325 degrees F).
- Bake for about 25 minutes per pound or until the temperature at the center is 63 degrees C (145 degrees F). Baste pork frequently as you cook.
- In the meantime, over medium heat, heat apple jelly in a saucepan. Pour in one tbsp. of soy sauce and two tbsps. of sherry and combine well. Decrease the heat to low and simmer. When done, spread on top of the tenderloin.

Nutrition Information

- Nutritionist's Calories: 367 kcal 18%
- Total Fat: 6.7 g 10%
- Carbohydrates: 30.7g 10%
- Protein: 40.7 g 81%
- Cholesterol: 123 mg 41%
- Sodium: 1454 mg 58%

248. Pork with Peach and Black Bean Salsa

"This dish is surprisingly easy and flavorful! Can serve together with a glass of red wine, rice and a green salad. Contains little amounts of fat!"

Servings: 4 | Prep: 10 m | Ready In: 40 m

Ingredients

- 1 pound pork tenderloin, cubed
- salt and pepper to taste
- 1/4 c cornmeal
- 1 tbsp. olive oil
- 1/4 c beer
- 1 c prepared salsa
- 1 (15 ounce) can sliced canned peaches, drained
- 1/2 (15 ounce) can black beans; drain and reserve liquid
- 1 tbsp. chopped fresh cilantro

Directions

- Use pepper and salt to season cubed pork to taste. In a large plastic bag containing cornmeal add the meat and then shake thoroughly to coat meat.
- Over medium high heat, heat oil in a skillet and add the coated meat. Sauté for about 5 to 10 minutes or until browned. Low the heat to medium.
- Add peaches, salsa, beer and beans along with two tbsps. of the liquid reserved. Combine well and allow to simmer for about 15 to 20 minutes. Add cilantro and stir.

Nutrition Information

- Nutritionist's Calories: 317 kcal 16%
- Total Fat: 7.8 g 12%
- Carbohydrates: 32.4g 10%
- Protein: 29 g 58%
- Cholesterol: 74 mg 25%
- Sodium: 657 mg 26%

249. Potato Soup

"This is my recipe and simple to prepare. All types of homemade soups are loved by my family."

Servings: 7 | Prep: 5 m | Ready In: 25 m

Ingredients

- 1 tbsp. butter
- 1 large onion, chopped
- 6 c mashed cooked potatoes
- 2 (14.5 ounce) cans chicken broth
- 1/2 c milk

Directions

- Over low heat, melt butter in a medium soup pot, add onions and then sauté until tender. Add mashed potatoes, stir and gently pour in chicken broth. Pour in milk while stirring until you achieve the creaminess desired. Let to cook until heated through. Add pepper and salt to taste.

Nutrition Information

- Nutritionist's Calories: 190 kcal 9%
- Total Fat: 3.3 g 5%
- Carbohydrates: 35.1g 11%

- Protein: 4.9 g 10%
- Cholesterol: 12 mg 4%
- Sodium: 1060 mg 42%

250. Quick and Easy 20-Minute Chicken Posole

"A fast and awesome dish to make posole for the guests or bring to a potluck party. A favorite for my hubby. I've adjusted this recipe a lot. Feel free to replace hominy with one (10 ounce) package of frozen corn or omit olives and chilies. I usually make mine and consider whether the kids will eat it or not."

Servings: 6 | Prep: 5 m | Ready In: 20 m

Ingredients

- 1 tbsp. olive oil
- 1 large onion, thinly sliced
- 2 cloves garlic, minced
- 2 tsps. dried oregano
- 1/2 tsp. ground cumin
- 2 (14.5 ounce) cans chicken broth
- 1 (15 ounce) can white hominy
- 1 (7 ounce) can chopped green chile peppers, drained
- 1 (2 ounce) can sliced black olives, drained
- 3/4 pound skinless, boneless chicken breast meat - cut into cubes

Directions

- Over medium heat, mix cumin, oregano, oil, garlic and onion in a large pot. Let to cook while covered for about 5 minutes until the onions become tender.
- Mix in olives, broth, chile peppers and hominy. Heat to boil and low the heat to medium. Mix chicken into the pot. Cover the pot and let to cook for about 5 to 10 minutes until no pink color of chicken remains.

Nutrition Information

- Nutritionist's Calories: 174 kcal 9%
- Total Fat: 5 g 8%
- Carbohydrates: 16.1g 5%
- Protein: 15.6 g 31%
- Cholesterol: 36 mg 12%
- Sodium: 1230 mg 49%

---

251. Quick and Easy Ham with Sweet Potatoes

"Sweet potatoes and ham are my favorite throughout the year. I developed this simple dish of ham and sweet potato and has very few dishes to clean. For a complete meal, serve together with rolls and a vegetable and/or side salad."

Servings: 2 | Prep: 5 m | Ready In: 45 m

Ingredients

- 2 ham steaks
- 1/4 c packed brown sugar
- 1 (8 ounce) can crushed pineapple, drained
- 1 (15 ounce) can sweet potatoes, drained
- 1 c miniature marshmallows

Directions

- Preheat an oven to 175 degrees C (350 degrees F).
- Cut off 2 big aluminum foil sheets. Onto each sheet of foil, put a ham slice and drizzle brown sugar on each side. Onto the ham, spread some crushed pineapple and add sweet potatoes on top. Drizzle some more pineapple and brown sugar on top of sweet potatoes. Seal aluminum foil all-round the ham tightly and transfer to a baking sheet.

- Bake for about 30 minutes. Take out from oven and open packets carefully. Drizzle miniature marshmallows on top and take back to oven with foil still open. Bake for 10 more minutes. You can brown the marshmallows under a broiler for a few minutes in case you want them toasty. The end result is a sweet and juicy ham dish and few dishes to clean.

Nutrition Information

- Nutritionist's Calories: 511 kcal 26%
- Total Fat: 2.5 g 4%
- Carbohydrates: 110.5g 36%
- Protein: 13.3 g 27%
- Cholesterol: 27 mg 9%
- Sodium: 859 mg 34%

---

252. Quick and Easy Vegetable Curry

"This curry is fast and simple that can be served with a salad and rice."

Servings: 5

Ingredients

- 1 tbsp. olive oil
- 1 onion, chopped
- 2 cloves crushed garlic
- 2 1/2 tbsps. curry powder
- 2 tbsps. tomato paste
- 1 (14.5 ounce) can diced tomatoes
- 1 cube vegetable bouillon
- 1 (10 ounce) package frozen mixed vegetables
- 1 1/2 c water
- salt and pepper to taste
- 2 tbsps. chopped fresh cilantro

Directions

- Over medium-high, heat oil in a saucepan, add garlic and onion and then sauté until golden. Add tomato paste and curry powder and stir. Let to cook for about 2 to 3 minutes.
- Mix in mixed vegetables, tomatoes, water, vegetable bouillon cube, pepper and salt. Let to cook for about 30 minutes until the veggies are cooked through (shouldn't be crunchy). Drizzle fresh cilantro on top before you serve.

Nutrition Information

- Nutritionist's Calories: 103 kcal 5%
- Total Fat: 3.5 g 5%
- Carbohydrates: 15.7g 5%
- Protein: 3.5 g 7%
- Cholesterol: 0 mg 0%
- Sodium: 267 mg 11%

253. Quick Black Beans and Rice

"It's believed rice and beans is a well-balanced meal and rich in nutrients. When serving, add salsa or chutney you love!"

Servings: 4 | Prep: 5 m | Ready In: 25 m

Ingredients

- 1 tbsp. vegetable oil
- 1 onion, chopped
- 1 (15 ounce) can black beans, undrained
- 1 (14.5 ounce) can stewed tomatoes
- 1 tsp. dried oregano
- 1/2 tsp. garlic powder
- 1 1/2 c uncooked instant brown rice

Directions

- Over medium-high, heat oil in a saucepan and add onion. Cook while stirring until tender. Pour in garlic powder, oregano, beans and tomatoes. Heat to boil and mix in rice. Cover the pan, low the heat and allow to simmer for five minutes. Take out from the heat and allow to sit for five minutes prior to serving.

Nutrition Information

- Nutritionist's Calories: 271 kcal 14%
- Total Fat: 5.3 g 8%
- Carbohydrates: 47.8g 15%
- Protein: 10 g 20%
- Cholesterol: 0 mg 0%
- Sodium: 552 mg 22%

254. Quick Chick!

"You can easily increase the recipe for carry-in dinners. This recipe always has rave reviews and requested for."

Servings: 4 | Prep: 15 m | Ready In: 6 h 15 m

Ingredients

- 3 boneless, skinless chicken breast halves
- 1 (12 ounce) jar turkey gravy
- 1/2 tsp. paprika
- 1/2 tsp. salt-free herb seasoning blend
- 1 tsp. soy sauce

Directions

- Into a slow cooker, put gravy and chicken. Add soy sauce, paprika and seasoning blend. Let to cook for about 6 to 8 hours on medium or for 4 hours on high. Cut the chicken into pieces and then serve on top of potatoes, rice or noodles.

Nutrition Information

- Nutritionist's Calories: 135 kcal 7%
- Total Fat: 2.6 g 4%
- Carbohydrates: 4.7g 2%
- Protein: 22 g 44%
- Cholesterol: 51 mg 17%
- Sodium: 530 mg 21%

- Carbohydrates: 11.1g 4%
- Protein: 28.2 g 56%
- Cholesterol: 76 mg 25%
- Sodium: 455 mg 18%

256. Quick Chinese-Style Vermicelli (Rice Noodles)

"These Chinese-style rice noodles are fast and delicious."

Servings: 4 | Prep: 15 m | Ready In: 18 m

Ingredients

- 1 (8 ounce) package dried rice noodles
- 2 tbsps. vegetable oil
- 1 clove garlic, minced
- 1 tbsp. soy sauce
- 1/2 tbsp. chili sauce
- salt and pepper to taste
- 1 green onion, chopped

Directions

- Bring to boil water in a pot, add rice noodles and then let to cook until al dente or for about for 2 to 3 minutes. Avoid overcooking because they can become mushy. Drain rice.
- Over medium heat, heat oil in a skillet, add garlic and then sauté until tender. Add noodles, stir and then season with pepper, salt, soy sauce and chili sauce. Add chopped green onion on top.

Nutrition Information

- Nutritionist's Calories: 271 kcal 14%
- Total Fat: 7.1 g 11%
- Carbohydrates: 48g 15%
- Protein: 2.3 g 5%

255. Quick Chicken Marsala

"This chicken Marsala is simple to make! Serve on top of egg noodles or linguini. (Keep in mind that at times sauté fresh chopped mushrooms and/or onions together with chicken. Can replace Marsala wine with sherry or white wine)."

Servings: 6 | Prep: 5 m | Ready In: 25 m

Ingredients

- 1 tbsp. butter
- 6 skinless, boneless chicken breasts
- 1 (10.75 ounce) can condensed golden mushroom soup
- 1 1/4 c Marsala wine

Directions

- Sauté chicken breasts in butter in a skillet. Add Marsala wine and soup (undiluted) when the chicken becomes browned lightly on all sides. Cover the skillet and let to simmer for about 20minutes until no pink color of chicken remains inside. Serve immediately.

Nutrition Information

- Nutritionist's Calories: 262 kcal 13%
- Total Fat: 4.8 g 7%

- Cholesterol: 0 mg 0%
- Sodium: 357 mg 14%

257. Quick Lemon Dijon Chicken

"This is a chicken dish is spicy, tangy and rich in flavor and ready in no time! Adjust the Ingredients to suit your taste."

Servings: 2 | Prep: 10 m | Ready In: 25 m

Ingredients

- 2 skinless, boneless chicken breast halves - cut into 2 inch pieces
- 1/4 lime, juiced
- 1/2 lemon, juiced
- 4 tbsps. Dijon mustard
- freshly ground black pepper
- Creole-style seasoning to taste

Directions

- Over medium heat, put chicken in a skillet and add lemon and lime juices. Mix in Creole-seasoning, Dijon and black pepper. Cook the chicken while turning frequently for about 15 minutes until the pieces of chicken are cooked through.

Nutrition Information

- Nutritionist's Calories: 301 kcal 15%
- Total Fat: 3.1 g 5%
- Carbohydrates: 10.5g 3%
- Protein: 55 g 110%
- Cholesterol: 137 mg 46%
- Sodium: 984 mg 39%

258. Quick Tuna Casserole

"The fastest tuna casserole available! For a classy treat, place in a baking dish, add fried onions on top and then broiling for several minutes."

Servings: 4 | Prep: 5 m | Ready In: 25 m

Ingredients

- 1 (7.25 ounce) package macaroni and cheese mix
- 1 (10.75 ounce) can condensed cream of mushroom soup
- 1 (9 ounce) can tuna, drained
- 1 (10 ounce) can peas, drained

Directions

- Follow the package instructions on how to cook macaroni and cheese mix. Mix in peas, tuna and cream of mushroom soup. Combine thoroughly and heat until bubbling.

Nutrition Information

- Nutritionist's Calories: 363 kcal 18%
- Total Fat: 7.1 g 11%
- Carbohydrates: 46.1g 15%
- Protein: 28.1 g 56%
- Cholesterol: 26 mg 9%
- Sodium: 1062 mg 42%

259. Quinoa and Black Beans

"A good replacement to rice and black beans. Quinoa, a nutty grain, comes from South America."

Servings: 10 | Prep: 15 m | Ready In: 50 m

Ingredients

- 1 tsp. vegetable oil
- 1 onion, chopped
- 3 cloves garlic, chopped
- 3/4 c quinoa
- 1 1/2 c vegetable broth
- 1 tsp. ground cumin
- 1/4 tsp. cayenne pepper
- salt and ground black pepper to taste
- 1 c frozen corn kernels
- 2 (15 ounce) cans black beans, rinsed and drained
- 1/2 c chopped fresh cilantro

Directions

- Over medium heat, heat oil in a saucepan and add garlic and onion. Cook while stirring for about 10 minutes until browned lightly.
- Combine quinoa into the mixture of onion and add vegetable broth to cover. Season with pepper, salt, cumin and cayenne pepper. Heat the mixture to boil. Cover the pan, low the heat and allow to simmer for about 20 minutes until broth has been absorbed and the quinoa becomes tender.
- Mix frozen corn into saucepan and continue simmering for about 5 minutes until heated through. Add cilantro and black beans and mix.

Nutrition Information

- Nutritionist's Calories: 153 kcal 8%
- Total Fat: 1.7 g 3%
- Carbohydrates: 27.8g 9%
- Protein: 7.7 g 15%
- Cholesterol: 0 mg 0%
- Sodium: 517 mg 21%

260. Quinoa Side Dish

"You can replace rice with quinoa because it is lighter and ready in about half the time."

Servings: *4* | **Prep:** *15 m* | **Ready In:** *35 m*

Ingredients

- 1 tbsp. butter
- 1 c uncooked quinoa
- 2 c vegetable broth
- 2 tsps. chopped garlic
- 2 tbsps. chopped fresh parsley
- 1/2 tbsp. chopped fresh thyme
- 1/4 tsp. salt
- 1 small onion, finely chopped
- 1 dash fresh lemon juice (optional)

Directions

- Over medium heat, heat butter in a saucepan, pour in toast and quinoa while stirring frequently for about 5 minutes until browned lightly. Mix in broth and heat to boil. Low to a simmer, cover the pan and let to cook for about 15 minutes or until the quinoa becomes tender.
- Mix quinoa with onion, salt, thyme, garlic and parsley in a bowl. Drizzle lemon juice on top and then serve.

Nutrition Information

- Nutritionist's Calories: 207 kcal 10%
- Total Fat: 5.8 g 9%
- Carbohydrates: 32g 10%
- Protein: 6.9 g 14%
- Cholesterol: 8 mg 3%
- Sodium: 400 mg 16%

261. RamJam Chicken

"I love this chicken marinade. I can make it every night! The flavor is more intense the longer it marinates. I normally reserve in the fridge overnight but a couple of hours will do."

Servings: 8 | Prep: 20 m | Ready In: 3 h 35 m

Ingredients

- 1/4 c soy sauce
- 3 tbsps. dry white wine
- 2 tbsps. lemon juice
- 2 tbsps. vegetable oil
- 3/4 tsp. dried Italian-style seasoning
- 1 tsp. grated fresh ginger root
- 1 clove garlic, crushed
- 1/4 tsp. onion powder
- 1 pinch ground black pepper
- 8 skinless, boneless chicken breast halves - cut into strips

Directions

- Mix soy sauce, Italian-style seasoning, wine, onion powder, lemon juice, oil, garlic, ginger and ground black pepper in a large plastic bag that is sealable. Add chicken into the bag. Seal the bag and refrigerate for a minimum of three hours or overnight to marinate.
- Preheat the outdoor grill over medium-high heat.
- Onto skewers, thread the chicken and reserve. Transfer the marinade a saucepan and heat to boil on high heat.
- Polish grill grate lightly with oil. Let the chicken cook on the grill prepared for about 8 minutes on each side as you baste with the sauce a few times. The chicken is cooked once the juice runs clear.

Nutrition Information

- Nutritionist's Calories: 303 kcal 15%
- Total Fat: 9.1 g 14%
- Carbohydrates: 1.5g < 1%
- Protein: 49.6 g 99%
- Cholesterol: 134 mg 45%
- Sodium: 568 mg 23%

262. Ranch Crispy Chicken

"A super simple and yummy recipe!"

Servings: 8 | Prep: 15 m | Ready In: 45 m

Ingredients

- 8 skinless, boneless chicken breast halves
- 2 (1 ounce) packages ranch dressing mix
- 1/4 c dry bread crumbs

Directions

- Preheat an oven to 190 degrees C (375 degrees F).
- In a plastic bag, mix bread crumbs and dressing mix. Pour in chicken and then shake to coat.
- Onto an ungreased cookie sheet, put the coated chicken pieces and then bake for about 25 to 30 minutes or until the chicken juice runs clear and cooked through. If desired, serve with potatoes and rice.

Nutrition Information

- Nutritionist's Calories: 162 kcal 8%
- Total Fat: 1.7 g 3%
- Carbohydrates: 6.1g 2%
- Protein: 27.8 g 56%
- Cholesterol: 68 mg 23%
- Sodium: 633 mg 25%

263. Roasted and Curried Butternut Squash Soup

"I developed this recipe and it can be meat based or vegan. Chills well. You can thaw, heat and top with yoghurt or cream prior to serving. Very tasty and worth the extra effort roasting and pureeing."

Servings: 8 | Prep: 30 m | Ready In: 1 h 40 m

Ingredients

- 1 butternut squash, halved and seeded
- 2 large onions, peeled and quartered
- 1 medium head garlic
- 6 c vegetable broth
- 1 bay leaf
- 1 tsp. brown sugar
- 1 tsp. mild curry powder
- 1/2 tsp. dried oregano
- 1/2 tsp. ground cinnamon
- 1/4 tsp. ground nutmeg
- salt and pepper to taste
- 1 c plain yogurt
- 1/4 c chopped fresh parsley (optional)

Directions

- Preheat an oven to 175 degrees C (350 degrees F). Use aluminum foil or parchment paper to line a baking sheet.
- Onto the baking sheet prepared, put onion and squash halves. Use foil to wrap garlic and position with the other veggies. .
- Roast for about 45 to 60 minutes at the middle of oven until squash becomes tender. Take out from oven and reserve until when cool enough to handle.
- Press out garlic cloves out of their skin into a food processor. Remove flesh from squash and transfer to the food processor together with roasted onion and then puree until the mix is smooth. If need be, add vegetable broth. Onto a stockpot, place the pureed mixture, add in vegetable broth and stir. Season with pepper, salt, bay leaf, nutmeg, brown sugar, oregano, curry powder and cinnamon. Heat to boil and allow to simmer gently for about ten minutes. Take out from the heat and mix in yogurt.
- Take out bay leaf and then serve while hot. If desired, decorate with fresh parsley.

Nutrition Information

- Nutritionist's Calories: 142 kcal 7%
- Total Fat: 1.2 g 2%
- Carbohydrates: 31.1g 10%
- Protein: 4.9 g 10%
- Cholesterol: 2 mg < 1%
- Sodium: 377 mg 15%

264. Roasted Brussels Sprouts

"My mom gave me this recipe. Sounds strange but they great and super simple to prepare. When done, the Brussels sprouts should be dark brown outside. You can reheat the leftovers or eat cold from fridge. Surprisingly tastes sweet and salt at the same time!"

Servings: 6 | Prep: 15 m | Ready In: 1 h

Ingredients

- 1 1/2 pounds Brussels sprouts, ends trimmed and yellow leaves removed
- 3 tbsps. olive oil
- 1 tsp. kosher salt
- 1/2 tsp. freshly ground black pepper

Directions

- Preheat an oven to 205 degrees C (400 degrees F).
- In a large plastic bag that is sealable, put olive oil, trimmed Brussels sprouts, pepper and kosher salt. Seal the bag tightly and then shake to coat. Transfer to a baking sheet and put at the middle of oven rack.
- Roast for about 30 to 45 minutes while shaking the pan after every 5 to 7 minutes to ensure even browning. Low the heat if need be to keep from burning. The Brussels sprouts will be dark brown and almost black when cooked through. If desired, adjust the seasoning with kosher salt. Serve right away.

Nutrition Information

- Nutritionist's Calories: 104 kcal 5%
- Total Fat: 7.3 g 11%
- Carbohydrates: 10g 3%
- Protein: 2.9 g 6%
- Cholesterol: 0 mg 0%
- Sodium: 344 mg 14%

265. Roasted Garlic

"It's great to serve roasted garlic with apples, bread or crackers. Guest can easily remove a clove of garlic and press garlic out of shell onto a cracker or bread."

Servings: 15 | Prep: 5 m | Ready In: 1 h 5 m

Ingredients

- 10 medium heads garlic
- 3 tbsps. olive oil

Directions

- Preheat an oven to 200 degrees C (400 degrees F).
- Onto a baking sheet, spread heads of garlic and then drizzle olive oil on top. Bake for about 40 minutes to 1 hour until garlic becomes soft and squeezable. Take out, cool and then serve.

Nutrition Information

- Nutritionist's Calories: 79 kcal 4%
- Total Fat: 2.9 g 4%
- Carbohydrates: 12.3g 4%
- Protein: 2.4 g 5%
- Cholesterol: 0 mg 0%
- Sodium: 6 mg < 1%

266. Roasted Pork Tenderloin

"Simple and very delicious pork tenderloin. Adjust the amount of sage to suit your taste."

Servings: 6 | Prep: 10 m | Ready In: 3 h 10 m

Ingredients

- 2 pounds pork tenderloin
- 1/2 tsp. ground sage
- garlic salt to taste
- 1 (32 ounce) jar sauerkraut, drained
- 1/2 apple
- 1/2 onion
- 1/3 c brown sugar

Directions

- Preheat an oven to 165 degrees C (325 degrees F).
- Use garlic salt and sage to rub tenderloin. Into a casserole or baking pan, put tenderloin. Add

half of the sauerkraut to cover the meat. Onto the sauerkraut, put onion and apple with the cut side facing downwards. Add the sauerkraut remaining to cover. Drizzle brown sugar on top.

- Cover the pan and then bake for about 2 to 3 hours until the temperature at the center is 63 degrees C (145 degrees F).

Nutrition Information

- Nutritionist's Calories: 199 kcal 10%
- Total Fat: 3.8 g 6%
- Carbohydrates: 16.5g 5%
- Protein: 24.8 g 50%
- Cholesterol: 65 mg 22%
- Sodium: 1063 mg 43%

---

267. Roasted Red Bell Pepper Soup

"This is a creamy textured soup that is delicious and has no cream. The key is beans! A family favorite. Can serve cold or hot along with goat cheese or a dollop of sour cream. Add chopped watercress on top."

Servings: 6

Ingredients

- 3 red bell peppers
- 1 onion, chopped
- 1 tbsp. minced garlic
- 1 tbsp. olive oil
- 2 (15 ounce) cans cannellini beans, drained and rinsed
- 2 (14.5 ounce) cans chicken broth
- salt and pepper to taste

Directions

- Preheat an oven so that it broils.
- Onto a baking sheet, put bell peppers and then broil on top oven's rack. Turn when each side blackens with tongs. Transfer the blackened peppers to a paper bag, seal tightly and let to cool for about 20 to 30 minutes. Remove skin of the peppers and get rid of the stem and seeds. Cut the peppers and reserve.
- Over medium heat, sauté garlic and onion for 5 minutes in a large pot or until the onion becomes translucent. Pour in the chopped and roasted red bell peppers and then sauté for about 2 to 3 minutes.
- Pour in beans and chicken broth while stirring well. Puree soup in small batches in a blender and then take back to pot. Heat for 5 minutes on low heat.

Nutrition Information

- Nutritionist's Calories: 207 kcal 10%
- Total Fat: 2.9 g 4%
- Carbohydrates: 35.4g 11%
- Protein: 11 g 22%
- Cholesterol: 0 mg 0%
- Sodium: 10 mg < 1%

---

268. Roasted Tomatillo and Garlic Salsa

"This is a rich and earthy flavor salsa made with charred spicy jalapenos, tomatillos and lots of garlic under a broiler. Replace jalapeno with roasted Jamaican scotch bonnets if you like a very hot salsa."

Servings: 20 | Prep: 10 m | Ready In: 40 m

Ingredients

- 1 pound fresh tomatillos, husks removed

- 1 head garlic cloves, separated and peeled
- 3 fresh jalapeno peppers
- 1 bunch fresh cilantro
- 1/2 c water, or as needed
- salt and pepper to taste

Directions

- Preheat the broiler of oven. Onto a baking sheet, spread jalapenos, tomatillos and whole cloves of garlic. Put under broiler and let to cook for several minutes. Take out garlic cloves first when they are toasted to prevent development of bitter flavor. Continue roasting tomatillos and jalapenos while turning frequently until charred evenly. Reserve to cool. Avoid removing the charred portions of peppers or tomatillos because they add a nice flavor.
- In a blender, put the tomatillos and peppers along with cilantro and garlic. If need be, add some water to the mixture to facilitate the blending process. Add pepper and salt to taste. Chill until serving.

Nutrition Information

- Nutritionist's Calories: 13 kcal < 1%
- Total Fat: 0.3 g < 1%
- Carbohydrates: 2.5g < 1%
- Protein: 0.5 g < 1%
- Cholesterol: 0 mg 0%
- Sodium: 2 mg < 1%

269. Rosemary Turkey Meatloaf

"A tasty meatloaf that is different from the usual one."

Servings: 8 | Prep: 15 m | Ready In: 1 h 15 m

Ingredients

- 1 1/2 pounds ground turkey
- 2 c dry bread crumbs
- 1 onion, chopped
- 1 egg, beaten
- 1 c milk
- 1/2 c balsamic vinegar
- 1 clove garlic, minced
- 1 tsp. salt
- 1 tsp. pepper
- 1 1/2 tbsps. chopped fresh rosemary
- 1 c canned tomato sauce
- 3/4 c brown sugar
- 1 tbsp. Dijon mustard

Directions

- Preheat an oven to 175 degrees C (350 degrees F). Coat a loaf pan of 9x5 inch lightly with grease.
- Combine together egg, milk, onion, ground turkey and bread crumbs in a large mixing bowl. Season with rosemary, pepper, salt and balsamic vinegar. Transfer to the pan prepared. Combine together mustard, tomato sauce and brown sugar. Spread evenly onto the loaf.
- Bake for about one hour or until the juice run clear when poked with a knife.

Nutrition Information

- Nutritionist's Calories: 362 kcal 18%
- Total Fat: 9.8 g 15%
- Carbohydrates: 47.1g 15%
- Protein: 20.9 g 42%
- Cholesterol: 93 mg 31%
- Sodium: 807 mg 32%

270. Salsa Chicken Burrito Filling

"This burrito/taco filling is fast, simple tasty and chills well. Serve with some sour cream, tortillas and shredded Cheddar cheese. Stuff the tortillas, place in a baking dish, cover with cheese and salsa and then bake for around 10 minutes."

Servings: 4 | Prep: 5 m | Ready In: 35 m

Ingredients

- 2 skinless, boneless chicken breast halves
- 1 (4 ounce) can tomato sauce
- 1/4 c salsa
- 1 (1.25 ounce) package taco seasoning mix
- 1 tsp. ground cumin
- 2 cloves garlic, minced
- 1 tsp. chili powder
- hot sauce to taste

Directions

- Over medium high heat, put tomato sauce and chicken breasts in a medium saucepan. Heat to boil, and pour in salsa, chili powder, garlic, seasoning and cumin. Allow to simmer for about 15 minutes.
- Start to pull chicken meat apart with a fork into thin strings. Continue to cook the pulled chicken and sauce while covered for about 5 to 10 more minutes. Pour in hot sauce and combine together (Keep in remind you may add some water in case the mixture becomes cooked too high and becomes very thick.)

Nutrition Information

- Nutritionist's Calories: 107 kcal 5%
- Total Fat: 1.5 g 2%
- Carbohydrates: 9.6g 3%
- Protein: 12.3 g 25%
- Cholesterol: 30 mg 10%
- Sodium: 923 mg 37%

271. Salsa De Tomatillo

"I grew up with this 'salsa de tomatillo'. You can use it as a dipping sauce for chips, as a sauce for grilled fish, shrimp or chicken and as basis for green chilaquiles (spread on top of shredded Monterey Jack, shredded cooked chicken and tortilla chips and heat under the broiler),"

Servings: 16 | Prep: 20 m | Ready In: 30 m

Ingredients

- 10 tomatillos, husked
- 1 small onion, chopped
- 3 cloves garlic, chopped
- 2 jalapeno peppers, chopped
- 1/4 c chopped fresh cilantro
- salt and pepper to taste

Directions

- In a nonreactive saucepan, put tomatillos along with plenty of water to cover. Heat to boil. Let to simmer for about 10 minutes until the tomatillos start to burst and soften.
- Drain the tomatillos and transfer to a blender or food processor along with cilantro, pepper, salt, onion, garlic and jalapeno peppers. Puree to the consistency desired.

Nutrition Information

- Nutritionist's Calories: 10 kcal < 1%
- Total Fat: 0.2 g < 1%
- Carbohydrates: 2g < 1%
- Protein: 0.3 g < 1%
- Cholesterol: 0 mg 0%
- Sodium: < 1 mg < 1%

272. Salsa II

"A great salsa recipe. It's made of ingredients that are boiled and combined to create flavorful and spicy mix that goes well on Mexican-style foods or with tortilla chips. You can adjust the amounts of jalapenos and onions. Can replace canned crushed tomatoes with fresh ones."

Servings: 96 | Prep: 30 m | Ready In: 50 m

Ingredients

- 6 pounds roma (plum) tomatoes
- 1/4 pound roma (plum) tomatoes, chopped
- 2 tbsps. garlic powder
- 1/4 c lemon juice
- 1 1/2 tbsps. salt
- 1 tbsp. ground cayenne pepper
- 1 1/2 tsps. ground cumin
- 1 red onion, chopped
- 1 white onion, chopped
- 1 yellow onion, chopped
- 1 pound jalapeno peppers, chopped
- 1/3 bunch fresh cilantro, chopped

Directions

- Bring to boil water in a saucepan and briefly add six pounds tomatoes to make the skins loose and setting the color. Drain tomatoes, remove skin and then crush.
- Into the saucepan containing crushed tomatoes, combine cayenne pepper, chopped tomatoes, lemon juice, cumin, salt and cumin garlic powder. Then whip to the thickness desired. Heat to boil. Stir in cilantro, red onion, yellow onion, white onion and jalapeno peppers. Continue to boil until and the mixture reaches the consistency desired and the veggies become soft. Take out from the heat source. Chill until when ready to serve.

Nutrition Information

- Nutritionist's Calories: 9 kcal < 1%
- Total Fat: 0.1 g < 1%
- Carbohydrates: 2g < 1%
- Protein: 0.4 g < 1%
- Cholesterol: 0 mg 0%
- Sodium: 111 mg 4%

273. Salsa

"I simple recipe I often make and it's popular. You can serve together with tortilla chips."

Servings: 4 | Prep: 10 m | Ready In: 10 m

Ingredients

- 4 large tomatoes, chopped
- 1 onion, chopped
- 1/2 c chopped fresh cilantro
- 3 cloves garlic, minced
- 1 tbsp. lime juice
- 1 tomatillo, diced (optional)
- salt to taste
- 1 jalapeno pepper, minced

Directions

- Mix tomatillo, tomatoes, lime juice, onion, salt, cilantro and garlic in a medium-size mixing bowl. Combine well. Pour in half jalapeno pepper and check the taste. You can add the half jalapeno remaining if you want a salsa with more of a kick. Don't add the other half of jalapeno if ok with the salsa's heat. Cover salsa and refrigerate until serving.

Nutrition Information

- Nutritionist's Calories: 53 kcal 3%
- Total Fat: 0.5 g < 1%
- Carbohydrates: 11.7g 4%
- Protein: 2.3 g 5%
- Cholesterol: 0 mg 0%
- Sodium: 13 mg < 1%

- Carbohydrates: 1.7g < 1%
- Protein: 0.4 g < 1%
- Cholesterol: 0 mg 0%
- Sodium: 95 mg 4%

274. Sarah's Salsa

"A simple salsa recipe prepare in a blender. A family favorite including families that I know of. Adjust to suit your taste and great on anything."

Servings: 32 | Prep: 15 m | Ready In: 15 m

Ingredients

- 2 (14.5 ounce) cans diced tomatoes
- 1 1/2 (10 ounce) cans diced tomatoes with green chile peppers
- 2 tbsps. lemon juice
- 1 fresh jalapeno pepper, chopped
- 1/3 c chopped fresh cilantro
- 1/2 large yellow onion, chopped
- 3 drops hot pepper sauce
- 1 clove garlic, minced

Directions

- Put diced tomatoes, jalapeno pepper, diced tomatoes along with green chile peppers, yellow onion, garlic, lemon juice, cilantro and hot pepper sauce in a blender. Puree until smooth. Refrigerate until when ready to serve.

Nutrition Information

- Nutritionist's Calories: 9 kcal < 1%
- Total Fat: 0 g < 1%

275. Scallop Scampi

"A hearty and tasty scallop Scampi recipe with a great taste. If desired, serve together with a green salad and crusty bread. Add one tsp. of corn starch if you want a thicker sauce at the end."

Servings: 8 | Prep: 15 m | Ready In: 45 m

Ingredients

- 4 tbsps. margarine
- 3 cloves garlic, minced
- 1 large onion, minced
- 1/2 c dry white wine
- 1 tsp. salt
- 1/4 tsp. ground black pepper
- 1/2 c grated Romano cheese
- 1 (10.75 ounce) can chicken broth
- 1 pound bay scallops
- 1 pound linguine pasta
- 1/4 c chopped fresh parsley

Directions

- Over medium heat, heat margarine, add onion and garlic and then sauté in a skillet until translucent. Pour in 1/4 c cheese, wine, ground black pepper and salt.
- Pour in scallops and chicken broth. Raise the heat and let to boil rapidly for about 7 to 8 minutes.
- In the meantime, bring to boil lightly salted water in a pot and add pasta. Cook until al dente or for about 8 to 10 minutes. Drain.
- Decrease the heat for the scallop mixture and then pour in parsley. Pour the sauce over

linguine. Drizzle remaining cheese on top and then serve.

Nutrition Information

- Nutritionist's Calories: 360 kcal 18%
- Total Fat: 9.3 g 14%
- Carbohydrates: 43.5g 14%
- Protein: 21.3 g 43%
- Cholesterol: 31 mg 10%
- Sodium: 799 mg 32%

276. Seafood Cioppino

"A great dish that resembles that of a restaurant! You can serve together with a salad and rice."

Servings: 8 | Prep: 30 m | Ready In: 2 h 45 m

Ingredients

- 1/4 c olive oil
- 1 onion, chopped
- 4 cloves garlic, minced
- 1 green bell pepper, chopped
- 1 fresh red chile pepper, seeded and chopped
- 1/2 c chopped fresh parsley
- salt and pepper to taste
- 2 tsps. dried basil
- 1 tsp. dried oregano
- 1 tsp. dried thyme
- 1 (28 ounce) can crushed tomatoes
- 1 (8 ounce) can tomato sauce
- 1/2 c water
- 1 pinch paprika
- 1 pinch cayenne pepper
- 1 c white wine
- 1 (10 ounce) can minced clams, drained with juice reserved
- 25 mussels, cleaned and debearded
- 25 shrimp
- 10 ounces scallops

- 1 pound cod fillets, cubed

Directions

- Over medium heat, heat olive oil in a pot and then sauté chile pepper, onion, bell pepper and garlic until tender. Pour in parsley, oregano, pepper, juice from the clams, salt, basil, thyme, cayenne pepper, tomatoes paprika, tomato sauce and water. Combine well, decrease the heat and allow to simmer for about 1 to 2 hours while adding wine little by little.
- In the last 10 minutes prior to serving, pour in cod, scallops, clams, prawns and mussels. Raise the heat a little and mix. Serve cioppino once the seafood is done (mussels should open up, cod should be flaky and prawns should turn pink).

Nutrition Information

- Nutritionist's Calories: 303 kcal 15%
- Total Fat: 9.1 g 14%
- Carbohydrates: 16.5g 5%
- Protein: 34.3 g 69%
- Cholesterol: 98 mg 33%
- Sodium: 564 mg 23%

277. Sesame Green Beans

"Green beans are not my thing until I experimented this dish I got from a friend. It's a simple dish but very flavorful! You can even prepare broccoli this way."

Servings: 4 | Prep: 5 m | Ready In: 30 m

Ingredients

- 1 tbsp. olive oil
- 1 tbsp. sesame seeds

- 1 pound fresh green beans, cut into 2 inch pieces
- 1/4 c chicken broth
- 1/4 tsp. salt
- freshly ground black pepper to taste

Directions

- Over medium heat, heat oil in a wok or skillet and then add sesame seeds. Mix in green beans once the seeds begin to darken. Cook while stirring until beans become bright green.
- Add chicken broth, pepper and salt. Cover the skillet and let to cook for about 10 minutes until the beans become tender-crisp. Remove cover and let to cook until the liquid has evaporated.

Nutrition Information

- Nutritionist's Calories: 78 kcal 4%
- Total Fat: 4.6 g 7%
- Carbohydrates: 8.6g 3%
- Protein: 2.5 g 5%
- Cholesterol: 0 mg 0%
- Sodium: 152 mg 6%

278. Shrimp and Okra Gumbo

"I usually add crabmeat to this delicious soup. You can serve on top of rice along with crusty French bread. Top with fresh parsley."

Servings: 6 | Prep: 15 m | Ready In: 2 h 15 m

Ingredients

- 2 pounds medium shrimp - peeled and deveined
- salt and pepper to taste
- cayenne pepper to taste
- 1/2 c olive oil

- 2 pounds chopped okra
- 1 tbsp. tomato paste
- 1 tomato, chopped
- 1 c chopped onion
- 4 cloves garlic, minced
- 1/2 c chopped celery
- 1/2 c chopped green bell pepper
- 12 c water
- 1/2 c chopped green onions

Directions

- Season shrimp with cayenne, pepper and salt. Reserve. Over medium heat, heat oil in a pot. Pour in okra and then sauté while stirring frequently for 30 minutes. Pour in green bell pepper, tomato paste, celery, garlic, tomato and onion. Sauté for about 15 minutes.
- Pour in water and then season to taste. Heat to boil, decrease the heat to low and allow to simmer for about 45 minutes. Pour in the shrimp and let to simmer for about 20 minutes. Lastly, to the soup, pour in green onion and combine well.

Nutrition Information

- Nutritionist's Calories: 394 kcal 20%
- Total Fat: 20.9 g 32%
- Carbohydrates: 18.1g 6%
- Protein: 34.8 g 70%
- Cholesterol: 230 mg 77%
- Sodium: 270 mg 11%

279. Shrimp Durango

"This shrimp is sautéed with lime juice and white wine and then seasoned with cayenne pepper and cilantro. Easy, fast and tasty. You can serve together with a salsa salad and grilled corn."

Servings: 6 | Prep: 5 m | Ready In: 25 m

Ingredients

- 1 pound dry fettuccine pasta
- 3 tbsps. butter
- 1 pound shrimp, peeled and deveined
- 1/2 c white wine
- 2 tbsps. lime juice
- 1/2 bunch cilantro, finely chopped
- 1/8 tsp. cayenne pepper
- salt and pepper to taste

Directions

- Bring water to boil in a pot and then add fettuccine noodles. Return the water to boil and let the noodles cook until al dente. Drain noodles thoroughly.
- In the meantime, over medium heat, heat butter in a skillet and add shrimp. Let to cook about three minutes until the shrimp turns pink. Take out the shrimp from the heat and reserve.
- Add lime juice and wine to skillet that was used to cook shrimp. Heat the mixture to boil. Let to boil for about 2 minutes until mixture decreases by half. Take back shrimp to the skillet. Pour in pepper, salt, cilantro and cayenne pepper. Mix to heat mixture through for approximately 2 minutes and then combine with pasta. Serve.

Nutrition Information

- Nutritionist's Calories: 422 kcal 21%
- Total Fat: 8.8 g 14%
- Carbohydrates: 56.9g 18%
- Protein: 25.6 g 51%
- Cholesterol: 130 mg 43%
- Sodium: 160 mg 6%

280. Sicilian Spaghetti

"This recipe is for those that love pasta and anchovies. It's fast, simple and delicious. If desired, you can serve together with crusty Italian bread."

Servings: 8 | Prep: 10 m | Ready In: 15 m

Ingredients

- 1 pound spaghetti
- 4 tbsps. olive oil
- 3 cloves garlic, crushed
- 1 (2 ounce) can anchovy fillets, chopped
- 1 c fine bread crumbs
- 1 c chopped fresh parsley
- ground black pepper to taste
- 4 tbsps. freshly grated Parmesan cheese

Directions

- Bring to boil lightly salted water in a pot and add pasta. Cook until al dente or for about 8 to 10 minutes and then drain.
- In the meantime, over medium heat, heat olive oil in a skillet and then pour in anchovies and garlic. Let to cook while stirring frequently for approximately two minutes.
- Add in breadcrumbs, stir and switch off the heat. Pour in black ground pepper and parsley and combine together.
- Mix the anchovy sauce together with hot pasta and drizzle cheese on top. Serve.

Nutrition Information

- Nutritionist's Calories: 355 kcal 18%
- Total Fat: 9.8 g 15%
- Carbohydrates: 53.6g 17%
- Protein: 12.4 g 25%
- Cholesterol: 7 mg 2%
- Sodium: 516 mg 21%

281. Simple Baked Beans

"In this recipe for baked bean, canned beans are used instead of the dry type. It's fast and simple to make."

Servings: 10 | Prep: 15 m | Ready In: 3 h 15 m

Ingredients

- 2 (16 ounce) cans baked beans with pork
- 1/4 c molasses
- 1/4 c chopped onions
- 4 tbsps. brown sugar
- 1 tbsp. prepared mustard
- 2 tbsps. ketchup
- 2 slices bacon, chopped

Directions

- Preheat an oven to 175 degrees C (350 degrees F).
- Combine baked beans together with pork, ketchup, brown sugar, molasses and onions and transfer to a greased casserole dish. Add bacon on top, cover and then bake for about three hours or until thick.

Nutrition Information

- Nutritionist's Calories: 176 kcal 9%
- Total Fat: 3.9 g 6%
- Carbohydrates: 31.7g 10%
- Protein: 5.6 g 11%
- Cholesterol: 10 mg 3%
- Sodium: 402 mg 16%

282. Six Can Chicken Tortilla Soup

"This tasty and simple soup recipe has just six canned ingredients! Feel free to serve on top of tortilla chips and then add shredded Cheddar cheese on top. Get rid of the cans and nobody will know how you made it!"

Servings: 6 | Prep: 5 m | Ready In: 20 m

Ingredients

- 1 (15 ounce) can whole kernel corn, drained
- 2 (14.5 ounce) cans chicken broth
- 1 (10 ounce) can chunk chicken
- 1 (15 ounce) can black beans
- 1 (10 ounce) can diced tomatoes with green chile peppers, drained

Directions

- Open the cans of chunk chicken, corn, diced tomatoes with green chilies chicken broth and black beans. Transfer all the contents to a large stock pot or saucepan. Over medium heat, let to simmer until the chicken is heated through.

Nutrition Information

- Nutritionist's Calories: 214 kcal 11%
- Total Fat: 4.9 g 8%
- Carbohydrates: 27.2g 9%
- Protein: 17.2 g 34%
- Cholesterol: 32 mg 11%
- Sodium: 1482 mg 59%

283. Skillet Herbed Chicken with Mustard

"I have created this classy French recipe so that I can have a fast and simple meal. Adjust the amounts of tarragon to suit your taste."

Servings: 4 | Prep: 10 m | Ready In: 35 m

Ingredients

- 3 tbsps. Dijon mustard
- 2 tbsps. honey
- 2 tbsps. dried tarragon
- 2 tsps. dried basil
- 2 tsps. dried thyme
- 1/8 tsp. salt
- 1/8 tsp. freshly ground black pepper
- 2 tbsps. vegetable oil
- 4 boneless, skinless chicken breast halves
- 1 c white wine

Directions

- Blend honey and Dijon mustard in a small bowl. Stir in thyme, tarragon, basil, pepper and salt.
- Over medium heat, heat oil in a skillet and add chicken. Use the Dijon mustard mixture to polish on each side. Spread 1/4 c of wine all-round the chicken. Low the heat, cover the skillet and allow to simmer for approximately 10 minutes until the liquid reduces.
- Spread another 1/4 c of wine all-round chicken and continue cooking for approximately 5 minutes until the juice runs clear and no pink color of chicken remains. Take out from the heat source and set the remaining liquid aside.
- Stir the wine remaining into skillet. Raise the heat to medium and then scrape up the browned parts. Cook while stirring until the liquid decreases by about 1/3. You can serve as a sauce on top of chicken.

Nutrition Information

- Nutritionist's Calories: 298 kcal 15%
- Total Fat: 8.5 g 13%
- Carbohydrates: 14.8g 5%
- Protein: 28.1 g 56%
- Cholesterol: 68 mg 23%
- Sodium: 437 mg 17%

284. Slow Cooker Chicken and Noodles

"A simple and nice soup to make when busy or at work! It can be 'soupy' with extra broth or thicken it with cornstarch mixture and water and cook until thick. Great when served on top of mashed potatoes!"

Servings: 6 | Prep: 30 m | Ready In: 8 h 30 m

Ingredients

- 4 skinless, boneless chicken breast halves
- 6 c water
- 1 onion, chopped
- 2 stalks celery, chopped (optional)
- salt and pepper to taste
- 1 (12 ounce) package frozen egg noodles

Directions

- Into a slow cooker, put chicken, onion, water, pepper and salt to taste. If desired, add celery. Adjust the temperature to low and let to cook for about 6 to 8 hours.
- Once chicken becomes tender, take out from slow cooker and then cut or tear into small pieces. Reserve in a casserole dish and keep them warm. Switch slow cooker to high heat and add frozen egg noodles and stir. Let to cook until the noodles become tender and then take back the pieces of chicken to the broth. Seasoning to taste.

Nutrition Information

- Nutritionist's Calories: 311 kcal 16%
- Total Fat: 3.5 g 5%
- Carbohydrates: 42g 14%
- Protein: 26.4 g 53%
- Cholesterol: 93 mg 31%
- Sodium: 81 mg 3%

285. Slow Cooker Chicken Cacciatore

"Chicken cacciatore that is simple and slow cooker. Can serve on top of angel hair pasta. 'Cacciatore' is an Italian word meaning 'hunter' and this American-Italian term means that food is made 'hunter style,' together with onions and mushrooms. "

Servings: 6 | Prep: 15 m | Ready In: 9 h 15 m

Ingredients

- 6 skinless, boneless chicken breast halves
- 1 (28 ounce) jar spaghetti sauce
- 2 green bell pepper, seeded and cubed
- 8 ounces fresh mushrooms, sliced
- 1 onion, finely diced
- 2 tbsps. minced garlic

Directions

- In the slow cooker, place chicken and then add garlic, onion, mushrooms, spaghetti sauce and green bell peppers on top.
- Cover and let to cook for about 7 to 9 hours on Low.

Nutrition Information

- Nutritionist's Calories: 261 kcal 13%
- Total Fat: 6.1 g 9%
- Carbohydrates: 23.7g 8%
- Protein: 27.1 g 54%
- Cholesterol: 63 mg 21%
- Sodium: 590 mg 24%

286. Slow Cooker Chicken Creole

"A slow cooked recipe with a Creole zing due to addition of jalapeno pepper and stewed tomatoes together with seasoning and vegetables. A simple and delicious recipe for Creole chicken. Throw the ingredients into a slow cooker and leave to simmer the whole day. Great on top of egg noodles. To the leftovers, add more veggies and water have a delicious afternoon soup."

Servings: 4 | Prep: 10 m | Ready In: 12 h 10 m

Ingredients

- 4 skinless, boneless chicken breast halves
- salt and pepper to taste
- Creole-style seasoning to taste
- 1 (14.5 ounce) can stewed tomatoes, with liquid
- 1 stalk celery, diced
- 1 green bell pepper, diced
- 3 cloves garlic, minced
- 1 onion, diced
- 1 (4 ounce) can mushrooms, drained
- 1 fresh jalapeno pepper, seeded and chopped

Directions

- In the slow cooker, put chicken breasts and then season with Creole-style seasoning, pepper and salt. Mix in mushrooms, tomatoes with liquid, onion, celery, jalapeno pepper and bell pepper.
- Cook for 5 to 6 hours on High or for 10 to 12 hours on Low.

Nutrition Information

- Nutritionist's Calories: 189 kcal 9%
- Total Fat: 1.9 g 3%
- Carbohydrates: 13.8g 4%
- Protein: 29.6 g 59%
- Cholesterol: 68 mg 23%
- Sodium: 431 mg 17%

287. Slow Cooker Chili II

"For the best chili, use a slow cooker. This beefy chili is made with spice, beans and veggies."

Servings: 8 | Prep: 15 m | Ready In: 8 h 15 m

Ingredients

- 1 pound ground beef
- 3/4 c diced onion
- 3/4 c diced celery
- 3/4 c diced green bell pepper
- 2 cloves garlic, minced
- 2 (10.75 ounce) cans tomato puree
- 1 (15 ounce) can kidney beans with liquid
- 1 (15 ounce) can kidney beans, drained
- 1 (15 ounce) can cannellini beans with liquid
- 1/2 tbsp. chili powder
- 1/2 tsp. dried parsley
- 1 tsp. salt
- 3/4 tsp. dried basil
- 3/4 tsp. dried oregano
- 1/4 tsp. ground black pepper
- 1/8 tsp. hot pepper sauce

Directions

- Over medium heat, cook beef in a skillet until browned evenly and then drain off grease.
- In a slow cooker, add beef and stir in cannellini beans, onion, kidney beans, celery, tomato puree, green bell pepper and garlic. Season with oregano, hot pepper sauce, chili powder, black pepper, parsley, basil and salt.
- Cover and let to cook on Low for 8 hours.

Nutrition Information

- Nutritionist's Calories: 273 kcal 14%
- Total Fat: 7.6 g 12%
- Carbohydrates: 33.4g 11%
- Protein: 18.9 g 38%
- Cholesterol: 34 mg 11%
- Sodium: 975 mg 39%

288. Slow Cooker Ham and Beans

"A great recipe for those busy days, have no time to cook and want a nutritious meal for the family. It's super simple and healthy meal!"

Servings: 8 | Prep: 10 m | Ready In: 20 h 10 m

Ingredients

- 1 pound dried great Northern beans, soaked overnight
- 1/2 pound cooked ham, chopped
- 1/2 c brown sugar
- 1 tbsp. onion powder
- 1 tbsp. dried parsley
- 1/2 tsp. garlic salt
- 1/2 tsp. black pepper
- 1/4 tsp. cayenne pepper
- water to cover

Directions

- In a slow cooker, mix beans, cayenne pepper, ham, black pepper, brown sugar, garlic salt, onion powder and parsley. Add to the slow cooker plenty of water to cover mixture by approximately two inches. Switch the slow cooker to Low and let to simmer while stirring frequently for 12 hours.

Nutrition Information

- Nutritionist's Calories: 318 kcal 16%
- Total Fat: 5.9 g 9%

- Carbohydrates: 49.8g 16%
- Protein: 17.8 g 36%
- Cholesterol: 16 mg 5%
- Sodium: 492 mg 20%

289. Slow Cooker Homemade Beans

"Homemade beans that are delicious and can be served as a side dish or by itself. Perfect for football Sundays or chill for a later use."

Servings: 12 | Prep: 20 m | Ready In: 10 h 20 m

Ingredients

- 3 c dry navy beans, soaked overnight or boiled for one hour
- 1 1/2 c ketchup
- 1 1/2 c water
- 1/4 c molasses
- 1 large onion, chopped
- 1 tbsp. dry mustard
- 1 tbsp. salt
- 6 slices thick cut bacon, cut into 1 inch pieces
- 1 c brown sugar

Directions

- Drain off the soaking liquid from beans and then transfer the beans to a Slow Cooker.
- Mix ketchup, bacon, water, brown sugar, onion, mustard molasses and salt into the beans until combine well.
- Cover and let to cook for about 8 to 10 hours on LOW while stirring frequently if possible but it's not necessary.

Nutrition Information

- Nutritionist's Calories: 296 kcal 15%
- Total Fat: 3 g 5%
- Carbohydrates: 57g 18%
- Protein: 12.4 g 25%
- Cholesterol: 5 mg 2%
- Sodium: 1312 mg 52%

290. Slow Cooker Honey Garlic Chicken

"This dish is simple to make and delicious. You can even bake and have the same results just like in a slow cooker. Can serve on top of rice."

Servings: 10 | Prep: 20 m | Ready In: 4 h 20 m

Ingredients

- 1 tbsp. vegetable oil
- 10 boneless, skinless chicken thighs
- 3/4 c honey
- 3/4 c lite soy sauce
- 3 tbsps. ketchup
- 2 cloves garlic, crushed
- 1 tbsp. minced fresh ginger root
- 1 (20 ounce) can pineapple tidbits, drained with juice reserved
- 2 tbsps. cornstarch
- 1/4 c water

Directions

- Over medium heat, heat oil in a skillet, add chicken thighs and cook until browned evenly on all sides. Transfer the thighs to the slow cooker.
- Combine the pineapple juice reserved, honey, garlic, soy sauce, ginger and ketchup in a bowl. Transfer to the slow cooker.

- Cover and let to cook on High for four hours. Mix in pineapple tidbits prior to serving.
- In a small bowl, combine water and cornstarch. Take out the thighs from the slow cooker. Combine the mixture of cornstarch into the sauce remaining in the slow cooker to make it thick. Can serve the sauce on top of chicken.

Nutrition Information

- Nutritionist's Calories: 235 kcal 12%
- Total Fat: 6 g 9%
- Carbohydrates: 34.4g 11%
- Protein: 13 g 26%
- Cholesterol: 42 mg 14%
- Sodium: 724 mg 29%

291. Slow Cooker Italian Beef

"A fast and tasty recipe! Use broth as an au jus together with sandwiches."

Servings: 6 | Prep: 5 m | Ready In: 1 h 5 m

Ingredients

- 1 pound thinly sliced roast beef
- 1 (.7 ounce) package dry Italian-style salad dressing mix
- 1 (16 ounce) jar pepperoncini, sliced
- 1 (10.5 ounce) can beef broth

Directions

- In a slow cooker, mix beef broth, roast beef, pepperoncini and dry dressing mix. Over medium-high heat, heat while covered for about one hour until hot.

Nutrition Information

- Nutritionist's Calories: 113 kcal 6%
- Total Fat: 2.8 g 4%
- Carbohydrates: 5.2g 2%
- Protein: 16.5 g 33%
- Cholesterol: 36 mg 12%
- Sodium: 3033 mg 121%

292. Slow Cooker Rosemary and Red Pepper Chicken

"Peasant-style chicken or 'pollo alla contadina' refers to Italian spirited chicken dishes. Can serve together with pasta like linguine or fettuccine."

Servings: 8 | Prep: 20 m | Ready In: 7 h 20 m

Ingredients

- 1 small onion, thinly sliced
- 1 medium red bell pepper, seeded and thinly sliced
- 4 cloves garlic, minced
- 2 tsps. dried rosemary
- 1/2 tsp. dried oregano
- 8 ounces turkey Italian sausages, casings removed
- 8 (4 ounce) skinless, boneless chicken breast halves
- 1/4 tsp. coarsely ground pepper
- 1/4 c dry vermouth
- 1 1/2 tbsps. cornstarch
- 2 tbsps. cold water
- salt to taste
- 1/4 c chopped fresh parsley

Directions

- Mix oregano, onion, garlic, rosemary and bell pepper in a 5 to 6 quart slow cooker. Then crumble the sausages on top of the onion mixture. Rinse the chicken, pat dry and then spread a single layer onto the sausage. Drizzle pepper on top and add vermouth. Cover and let to cook for about 5 to 7 hours on Low setting or until the chicken is cooked through and tender when poked.

- Into a warm and deep platter, put the chicken and then cover to keep it warm.
- Mix cold water and cornstarch together in a small bowl. Mix with the cooking liquid in the slow cooker. Raise the heat to High and then cover. Cook while stirring for about 2 to 3 times for ten minutes until the sauce becomes thick. Add salt to taste. Ladle the sauce on top of chicken and then drizzle with parsley.

Nutrition Information

- Nutritionist's Calories: 201 kcal 10%
- Total Fat: 4.4 g 7%
- Carbohydrates: 5g 2%
- Protein: 32 g 64%
- Cholesterol: 87 mg 29%
- Sodium: 457 mg 18%

293. Slow Cooker Venison Roast

"This is a slow coked venison roast together with spices, creamy mushroom soup and onion. It's a delicious and easy way to eat game meat."

Servings: 6 | Prep: 10 m | Ready In: 6 h 10 m

Ingredients

- 3 pounds boneless venison roast
- 1 large onion, sliced
- 1 tbsp. soy sauce
- 1 tbsp. Worcestershire sauce
- 1 tbsp. garlic salt
- 1/4 tsp. ground black pepper
- 1 (1 ounce) package dry onion soup mix

- 1 (10.75 ounce) can condensed cream of mushroom soup

Directions

- In a slow cooker, place cleaned meat and then add onion to cover. Drizzle with Worcestershire sauce, soy sauce, pepper and garlic salt.
- Mix the soup together with the soup mix in a small bowl. Spread the mixture on top of venison. Let to cook for 6 hours on Low setting.

Nutrition Information

- Nutritionist's Calories: 314 kcal 16%
- Total Fat: 8 g 12%
- Carbohydrates: 10g 3%
- Protein: 48 g 96%
- Cholesterol: 171 mg 57%
- Sodium: 1882 mg 75%

294. Snow on the Mountain Green Beans

"These green beans are cooked in lemon juice and olive oil, topped with feta cheese and served as a side dish."

Servings: 8 | Prep: 15 m | Ready In: 25 m

Ingredients

- 2 pounds fresh green beans
- 2 tbsps. butter
- 1 tbsp. extra virgin olive oil
- sea salt and ground black pepper to taste
- 1 1/2 tbsps. lemon juice
- 1/2 c crumbled feta cheese

Directions

- Bring to boil lightly salted water in a pot and add green beans. Let to cook without covering for 3 to 4 minutes until tender. In the meantime, over medium-high heat, heat butter together with olive oil in a skillet. Once beans are almost tender, drain and then transfer to skillet. Continue to cook green beans in butter for around two minutes until tender.
- Season beans with lemon juice, pepper and salt. Transfer to a warmed serving dish and drizzle crumbled feta cheese on top.

Nutrition Information

- Nutritionist's Calories: 101 kcal 5%
- Total Fat: 6.7 g 10%
- Carbohydrates: 8.7g 3%
- Protein: 3.4 g 7%
- Cholesterol: 16 mg 5%
- Sodium: 172 mg 7%

295. Southwest Chicken

"These are chicken breasts together with tomatoes, corn, black beans and chile peppers. The dish is fast, simple and contains Low amounts of fat. If desired, serve on top of hot cooked rice."

Servings: 4

Ingredients

- 1 tbsp. vegetable oil
- 4 skinless, boneless chicken breast halves
- 1 (10 ounce) can diced tomatoes with green chile peppers
- 1 (15 ounce) can black beans, rinsed and drained
- 1 (8.75 ounce) can whole kernel corn, drained
- 1 pinch ground cumin

Directions

- Over medium high heat, heat oil in a skillet and then brown chicken breasts on each side. Pour in beans, corn and tomatoes with green chile peppers. Decrease the heat and allow to simmer for about 25 to 30 minutes or until the juice runs clear and the chicken is cooked through. Add a pinch of cumin before serving.

Nutrition Information

- Nutritionist's Calories: 310 kcal 15%
- Total Fat: 6.4 g 10%
- Carbohydrates: 27.9g 9%
- Protein: 35 g 70%
- Cholesterol: 68 mg 23%
- Sodium: 863 mg 35%

296. Southwestern Vegetarian Pasta

"A vegan pasta meal with protein-rich chickpeas and a southwestern flavor!"

Servings: 6 | Prep: 10 m | Ready In: 30 m

Ingredients

- 1 tbsp. vegetable oil
- 1 onion, chopped
- 1/2 green bell pepper, diced
- 2 cloves garlic, chopped
- 2 tbsps. chili powder
- 1 tsp. ground cumin
- 1 (28 ounce) can diced tomatoes with juice
- 1 (15 ounce) can chickpeas
- 1 (10 ounce) package frozen corn kernels, thawed
- 1 (12 ounce) package uncooked elbow macaroni
- 1/2 c shredded Monterey Jack cheese

Directions

- In a deep skillet, heat oil, add cumin, chili powder, garlic, onion and green pepper and sauté. Mix in corn, tomatoes and chickpeas. Decrease the heat to low and allow to simmer for about 15 to 20 minutes or until heated through and thickened.
- In the meantime, bring to boil lightly salted water in a pot and add macaroni. Cook until al dente or for about 8 to 10 minutes. Drain pasta.
- Mix sauce and pasta. Drizzle Monterey Jack cheese onto each serving.

Nutrition Information

- Nutritionist's Calories: 421 kcal 21%
- Total Fat: 7.9 g 12%
- Carbohydrates: 72.1g 23%
- Protein: 16 g 32%
- Cholesterol: 8 mg 3%
- Sodium: 426 mg 17%

---

297. Soy and Garlic Marinated Chicken

"A super simple marinade and often used in my family. Goes well any slice of chicken whether legs, thighs, etc."

Servings: 4

Ingredients

- 4 cloves garlic, minced
- 1/2 c soy sauce
- 4 skinless, boneless chicken breasts

Directions

- Mix soy sauce and garlic in a nonporous bowl. Pour in chicken and then turn to coat thoroughly. Cover the bowl and refrigerate for at least 1 hour to marinate.
- Preheat the outdoor grill over medium high heat and polish grate lightly with oil.
- Over medium high heat, grill the chicken for about 10 to 15 minutes on each side or until the temperature at the center is 80 degrees C (180 degrees F). Get rid of the marinade remaining.

Nutrition Information

- Nutritionist's Calories: 152 kcal 8%
- Total Fat: 2.8 g 4%
- Carbohydrates: 3.4g 1%
- Protein: 26.7 g 53%
- Cholesterol: 67 mg 22%
- Sodium: 1863 mg 75%

---

298. Spaghetti Italian

"Not very sweet but tasty dish. It's a great meal!!"

Servings: 6 | Prep: 20 m | Ready In: 1 h 20 m

Ingredients

- 1/2 pound Italian sausage
- 4 (6.5 ounce) cans tomato sauce
- 1 (14.5 ounce) can diced tomatoes
- 2 bay leaves
- 1 tsp. Italian seasoning
- 1/2 tsp. garlic powder
- 1 tsp. dried basil
- 1 tsp. dried oregano
- salt and pepper to taste
- 1 (8 ounce) package spaghetti

Directions

- Over medium heat, brown sausage in a skillet. Drain and then reserve.
- Over medium heat, mix tomato sauce, oregano, diced tomatoes, garlic powder, bay leaves, Italian sausage, Italian seasoning, basil, pepper and salt in a large saucepan. Combine well.
- Over medium-low heat, let to simmer for at least 1 hour. Best when simmered the whole day.
- Bring to boil lightly salted water in a pot and add pasta. Cook until al dente or for about 8 to 10 minutes and then drain.
- Combine the sauce together with the hot pasta before serving.

Nutrition Information

- Nutritionist's Calories: 275 kcal 14%
- Total Fat: 8 g 12%
- Carbohydrates: 38.5g 12%
- Protein: 12.2 g 24%
- Cholesterol: 15 mg 5%
- Sodium: 1069 mg 43%

299. Spiced Chicken Loaf

"This is a combo of ground chicken, seasonings, onion, egg, stuffing mix and cheese that is baked into a tangy delicious loaf."

Servings: 6

Ingredients

- 1 pound ground chicken
- 2/3 c herb stuffing mix, crushed into fine crumbs
- 1/4 c grated Parmesan cheese
- 1 egg
- 1 c diced onion

- 1/2 tsp. salt
- 1/2 tsp. ground black pepper
- 1 pinch garlic pepper seasoning
- 2 tsps. ketchup
- 2 tsps. barbeque sauce

Directions

- Preheat an oven to 175 degrees C (350 degrees F).
- Mix chicken, onion, egg, stuffing mix crumbs, garlic pepper, seasoning cheese, pepper and salt in a large bowl. Combine together and mix in barbeque sauce and ketchup. Combine well and spread the mixture onto a bread loaf pan.
- Bake for 50 minutes in oven. Switch off the oven and allow to rest in the hot oven for about 15 minutes.

Nutrition Information

- Nutritionist's Calories: 194 kcal 10%
- Total Fat: 4.7 g 7%
- Carbohydrates: 15.5g 5%
- Protein: 21.5 g 43%
- Cholesterol: 80 mg 27%
- Sodium: 665 mg 27%

300. Spiced Sweet Roasted Red Pepper Hummus

"Can serve along with pita bread. Chop the pita bread into wedges and then toast for taste variation. Tahini, a sesame paste, is available in Mediterranean section at a grocery store."

Servings: 8 | Prep: 15 m | Ready In: 1 h 15 m

Ingredients

- 1 (15 ounce) can garbanzo beans, drained

- 1 (4 ounce) jar roasted red peppers
- 3 tbsps. lemon juice
- 1 1/2 tbsps. tahini
- 1 clove garlic, minced
- 1/2 tsp. ground cumin
- 1/2 tsp. cayenne pepper
- 1/4 tsp. salt
- 1 tbsp. chopped fresh parsley

Directions

- Puree chickpeas, cayenne, red peppers, tahini, lemon juice, salt, garlic and cumin in a food processor or electric blender. Process with long pulses until mixture becomes fluffy a little and is fairly smooth. In between pulses, scrape mixture off the sides of blender or food processor. Place in a serving bowl and then chill for a minimum of one hour. (You can prepare hummus up to three days ahead and then chill. Heat to room temperature prior to serving).
- Drizzle chopped parsley on top of hummus prior to serving.

Nutrition Information

- Nutritionist's Calories: 64 kcal 3%
- Total Fat: 2.2 g 3%
- Carbohydrates: 9.6g 3%
- Protein: 2.5 g 5%
- Cholesterol: 0 mg 0%
- Sodium: 370 mg 15%

Servings: 6 | Prep: 10 m | Ready In: 1 h 10 m

Ingredients

- 6 sweet potatoes, cut into French fries
- 2 tbsps. canola oil
- 3 tbsps. taco seasoning mix
- 1/4 tsp. cayenne pepper

Directions

- Preheat an oven to 220 degrees C (425 degrees F).
- Mix sweet potatoes, cayenne pepper, taco seasoning and canola oil in a plastic bag. Seal and then shake the bag until fries are coated evenly. Onto 2 large baking sheets, arrange a single layer of fries.
- Bake in oven for about 30 minutes or until browned on one side and crispy. Use a spatula to flip over the fries and then let to cook for about 30 minutes or until they are tender inside and crispy outside. Thin fries cook fast.

Nutrition Information

- Nutritionist's Calories: 169 kcal 8%
- Total Fat: 4.7 g 7%
- Carbohydrates: 29.2g 9%
- Protein: 2.1 g 4%
- Cholesterol: 0 mg 0%
- Sodium: 399 mg 16%

---

301. Spicy Baked Sweet Potato Fries

"Very delicious dish for the family and won't believe it's healthy! It tastes great and surprisingly very simple to cook. Tasty when eaten plain but you can dip in guacamole, honey mustard sauce or ketchup."

---

302. Spicy Black Bean Cakes

"Simple to prepare black bean cakes with less fat content than other fried cakes."

Servings: 8 | Prep: 20 m | Ready In: 35 m

Ingredients

- Lime Sour Cream:
- 1/2 c reduced fat sour cream
- 2 tsps. fresh lime juice
- 1 small fresh jalapeno pepper, minced
- salt to taste
- Bean Cakes:
- 2 tbsps. olive oil, divided
- 4 green onions, thinly sliced
- 6 cloves garlic, pressed
- 2 fresh jalapeno peppers, finely diced
- 1 tbsp. ground cumin
- 2 (14.5 ounce) cans black beans, drained and rinsed
- salt and black pepper to taste
- 2 c grated raw sweet potato
- 1 egg, lightly beaten
- 1/2 c plain dried bread crumbs

Directions

- To make lime sour cream, in a bowl, combine together salt, sour cream, one small minced jalapeno and lime juice. Cover the bowl and chill.
- Over medium heat, heat one tbsp. of olive oil in a skillet, add green onions and cook for about one minute until softened. Mix in cumin, garlic and two diced jalapenos. Let to cook for about 30 seconds until fragrant.
- Into a large bowl, put the contents from skillet. Add black beans, stir and use a fork to mash. Add pepper and salt to taste. Stir in bread crumbs, sweet potatoes and egg. Subdivide into eight balls and then flatten them into patties.
- Position the cooking rack in oven about four inches away from the heat. Bring the oven to broil. Use one tbsp. oil to polish a baking dish lightly with grease.
- Transfer the bean patties to the baking sheet and let to broil for about 8 to 10 minutes. Flip over the cakes and let to broil for 3 minutes until crispy. Can serve along with lime sour cream.

Nutrition Information

- Nutritionist's Calories: 219 kcal 11%
- Total Fat: 6.7 g 10%
- Carbohydrates: 31.3g 10%
- Protein: 9.4 g 19%
- Cholesterol: 29 mg 10%
- Sodium: 481 mg 19%

---

303. Spicy Chicken Breasts

"A recipe for chicken breast with no skin that is great when served as an appetizer or on top of salad greens! In case you're serving on top of salad greens, chop chicken into strips and add dressing or salsa you like on top."

Servings: 4 | Prep: 15 m | Ready In: 30 m

Ingredients

- 2 1/2 tbsps. paprika
- 2 tbsps. garlic powder
- 1 tbsp. salt
- 1 tbsp. onion powder
- 1 tbsp. dried thyme
- 1 tbsp. ground cayenne pepper
- 1 tbsp. ground black pepper
- 4 skinless, boneless chicken breast halves

Directions

- Combine together cayenne pepper, paprika, thyme, garlic powder, salt, ground black pepper and onion powder in a medium bowl. For the chicken, reserve about three tbsps. of this seasoning mixture. Transfer the rest to an airtight container for use later (for seasoning veggies, fish or meats).
- Preheat the grill over medium-high heat. Use the 3 tbsps. of seasoning reserved to coat each side of the chicken breasts.

- Polish grill grate lightly with oil. Transfer the chicken to the grill and let to cook for about 6 to 8 minutes per side until the juice is clear.

Nutrition Information

- Nutritionist's Calories: 173 kcal 9%
- Total Fat: 2.4 g 4%
- Carbohydrates: 9.2g 3%
- Protein: 29.2 g 58%
- Cholesterol: 68 mg 23%
- Sodium: 1826 mg 73%

304. Spicy Fish Soup

"A low fat tasty fish soup! I love spicy foods since when grown up on the Texas/Mexico border. Adjust seasonings to suit your taste. I usually add hot pepper sauce when serving."

Servings: 4 | Prep: 10 m | Ready In: 40 m

Ingredients

- 1/2 onion, chopped
- 1 clove garlic, minced
- 1 tbsp. chili powder
- 1 1/2 c chicken broth
- 1 (4 ounce) can canned green chile peppers, chopped
- 1 tsp. ground cumin
- 1 1/2 c canned peeled and diced tomatoes
- 1/2 c chopped green bell pepper
- 1/2 c shrimp
- 1/2 pound cod fillets
- 3/4 c plain nonfat yogurt

Directions

- Over medium high heat, use vegetable cooking spray to coat a large saucepan. Pour in onions and then sauté while stirring frequently for around five minutes. Pour in chili powder and garlic and then sauté for about two 2 minutes.
- Then stir in cumin, chicken broth and chile peppers. Combine well. Heat to boil, decrease the heat to low, cover the pan and let to simmer for 20 minutes.
- Pour in cod, tomatoes, shrimp and green bell pepper. Heat to boil, decrease the heat to low, cover the pan and let to simmer for about five minutes. Slowly mix in yogurt until heated through.

Nutrition Information

- Nutritionist's Calories: 146 kcal 7%
- Total Fat: 1.7 g 3%
- Carbohydrates: 12.2g 4%
- Protein: 19.3 g 39%
- Cholesterol: 46 mg 15%
- Sodium: 874 mg 35%

305. Spicy Indian Dahl

"This Indian lentil soup is spicy and can be served with Naan (Indian bread) or rice. This dish is nutritious."

Servings: 6

Ingredients

- 1 c red lentils
- 2 tbsps. ginger root, minced
- 1 tsp. mustard seed
- 2 tbsps. chopped fresh cilantro
- 4 tomatoes, chopped
- 3 onions, chopped
- 3 jalapeno peppers, seeded and minced

- 1 tbsp. ground cumin
- 1 tbsp. ground coriander seed
- 6 cloves garlic, minced
- 2 tbsps. olive oil
- 1 c water
- salt to taste

Directions

- Cook lentils by pressure cooking or boiling until the lentils become soft. (For fast results, use pressure cooking).
- Heat oil in a skillet and pour in mustard seeds. Once the mustard seeds start to flutter, add garlic, ginger, onions and jalapeno peppers. Sauté until garlic and onions become golden brown. Pour in cumin and coriander. Pour in chopped tomatoes. Sauté mixture thoroughly until the tomatoes are cooked well.
- Pour in water. Let to boil for six minutes. Pour in the cooked lentils and stir thoroughly. Season with salt while stirring well. Pour in finely chopped cilantro and then take out from the heat. Serve immediately.

Nutrition Information

- Nutritionist's Calories: 209 kcal 10%
- Total Fat: 5.7 g 9%
- Carbohydrates: 30.6g 10%
- Protein: 10.4 g 21%
- Cholesterol: 0 mg 0%
- Sodium: 12 mg < 1%

Ingredients

- 1 pound dry black beans, soaked overnight
- 4 tsps. diced jalapeno peppers
- 6 c chicken broth
- 1/2 tsp. garlic powder
- 1 tbsp. chili powder
- 1 tsp. ground cumin
- 1 tsp. cayenne pepper
- 3/4 tsp. ground black pepper
- 1/2 tsp. hot pepper sauce

Directions

- Drain the black beans and then rinse them.
- In a slow cooker, mix chicken broth, beans and jalapenos. Season with hot pepper sauce, garlic powder, cayenne, chili powder, pepper and cumin.
- Cook for four hours on High. Decrease the heat to Low and continue to cook for about two hours or until serving.

Nutrition Information

- Nutritionist's Calories: 281 kcal 14%
- Total Fat: 2 g 3%
- Carbohydrates: 49.7g 16%
- Protein: 17.7 g 35%
- Cholesterol: 5 mg 2%
- Sodium: 1012 mg 40%

---

306. Spicy Slow Cooker Black Bean Soup

"You can serve this soup the way it is or blend in a blender to have a creamy version. Adjust the spice to suit your taste."

Servings: 6 | Prep: 5 m | Ready In: 6 h 5 m

---

307. Spicy Three Pepper Hummus

"This 3 pepper hummus is loved by my family. They like it so much such that they can finish a container! The dish yields three times the amount in store bought containers of around same price just like that of one 8 ounce tub."

Servings: 24 | Prep: 15 m | Ready In: 8 h 15 m

Ingredients

- 2 (16 ounce) cans garbanzo beans, drained
- 2 tbsps. olive oil
- 1/8 c lemon juice
- 2 tbsps. tahini
- 8 cloves garlic, minced
- 2 slices jarred jalapeno pepper, chopped
- 1 tsp. liquid from the jar of jalapeno peppers
- 1/2 tsp. ground black pepper
- 1 1/2 tsps. cayenne pepper
- 1/2 tsp. ground cumin
- 3/4 tsp. dried oregano

Directions

- Mix garbanzo beans, lemon juice, olive oil, garlic, tahini, juice from jalapeno jar and jalapeno in the bowl of a stand mixer. Then season with oregano, cumin, black pepper and cayenne.
- Use the whisk attachment to combine on low speed until ingredients begin to blend and then adjust the speed to medium. Blend to the consistency desired. Cover and then chill overnight to enable flavors to blend. Ensure the container is properly sealed to prevent the refrigerator from smelling garlic!

Nutrition Information

- Nutritionist's Calories: 65 kcal 3%
- Total Fat: 2.3 g 3%
- Carbohydrates: 9.4g 3%
- Protein: 2.2 g 4%
- Cholesterol: 0 mg 0%
- Sodium: 122 mg 5%

308. Spinach and Pasta Shells

"This is for those that like spice and garlic in their pasta. It's a super simple recipe. Adjust the amount of red pepper flakes to the spiciness you like. If desired, it works well some garlic bread and a salad."

Servings: 8

Ingredients

- 1 pound seashell pasta
- 1 (10 ounce) package frozen chopped spinach
- 2 tbsps. olive oil
- 7 cloves garlic, minced
- 1 tsp. dried red pepper flakes (optional)
- salt to taste

Directions

- Bring to boil lightly salted water in a pot and add spinach and pasta. Cook until pasta is al dente or for about 8 to 10 minutes. Drain and set aside.
- Over medium heat, heat oil in a skillet, add red pepper flakes and garlic and then sauté for about five minutes or until garlic is light gold. Pour in spinach and cooked pasta to skillet and combine well. Add salt to taste and mix before serving.

Nutrition Information

- Nutritionist's Calories: 248 kcal 12%
- Total Fat: 4.9 g 8%
- Carbohydrates: 43.8g 14%
- Protein: 9 g 18%
- Cholesterol: 0 mg 0%
- Sodium: 30 mg 1%

309. Spinach and Sun-Dried Tomato Pasta

"I made this easy Sicilian-style pasta dish on a day I wanted to make use of sun-dried tomatoes."

Servings: 4 | Prep: 15 m | Ready In: 40 m

Ingredients

- 1 c vegetable broth
- 12 dehydrated sun-dried tomatoes
- 1 (8 ounce) package uncooked penne pasta
- 2 tbsps. pine nuts
- 1 tbsp. olive oil
- 1/4 tsp. crushed red pepper flakes
- 1 clove garlic, minced
- 1 bunch fresh spinach, rinsed and torn into bite-size pieces
- 1/4 c grated Parmesan cheese

Directions

- Bring broth to boil in a small saucepan and then take out from the heat. Into the broth, add sun-dried tomatoes and let to stand for about 15 minutes or until softened. Then drain, set the broth aside and chop coarsely.
- Bring to boil lightly salted water in a pot and add penne pasta. Let to cook until al dente or for about 9 to 12 minutes. Drain.
- Over medium heat, put pine nuts in a skillet and then cook while stirring until toasted lightly.
- Over medium heat, heat red pepper flakes and olive oil in a skillet and then sauté garlic for one minute until tender. Add spinach, stir and let to cook until almost wilted. Add the broth reserved and mix in sliced sun-dried tomatoes. Continue to cook for two minutes or until heated through.
- Mix cooked pasta together with pine nuts and the mixture of tomato and spinach in a large bowl. Add Parmesan cheese on top and serve.

Nutrition Information

- Nutritionist's Calories: 340 kcal 17%
- Total Fat: 8.9 g 14%
- Carbohydrates: 52g 17%
- Protein: 14.7 g 29%
- Cholesterol: 4 mg 1%
- Sodium: 386 mg 15%

310. Spinach Chickpea Curry

"This is a fast and tasty Indian-style curry containing onions, chickpeas, spinach and/or other vegetables you like. You can add sweet potatoes, cauliflower and potatoes to this dish. They are great. If desired, you can serve with rice, nan or pita."

Servings: 4 | Prep: 5 m | Ready In: 20 m

Ingredients

- 1 tbsp. vegetable oil
- 1 onion, chopped
- 1 (14.75 ounce) can creamed corn
- 1 tbsp. curry paste
- salt to taste
- ground black pepper to taste
- 1/2 tsp. garlic powder, or to taste
- 1 (15 ounce) can garbanzo beans (chickpeas), drained and rinsed
- 1 (12 ounce) package firm tofu, cubed
- 1 bunch fresh spinach, stems removed
- 1 tsp. dried basil or to taste

Directions

- Over medium heat, heat oil in a skillet or wok, add onions and sauté until translucent. Mix in curry paste and creamed corn. Cook while stirring often for five minutes. Add garlic, salt and pepper while stirring.

- Mix in garbanzo beans and slowly roll in tofu. Pour in spinach and cover the skillet. Once the spinach becomes tender, take out from the heat source and mix in basil.

Nutrition Information

- Nutritionist's Calories: 346 kcal 17%
- Total Fat: 12.3 g 19%
- Carbohydrates: 44.7g 14%
- Protein: 21.7 g 43%
- Cholesterol: 0 mg 0%
- Sodium: 849 mg 34%

311.Spinach, Red Lentil, and Bean Curry

"This is a delicious vegan curry that make taste buds water! Can serve on naan or with rice."

Servings: 4 | Prep: 25 m | Ready In: 35 m

Ingredients

- 1 c red lentils
- 1/4 c tomato puree
- 1/2 (8 ounce) container plain yogurt
- 1 tsp. garam masala
- 1/2 tsp. ground dried turmeric
- 1/2 tsp. ground cumin
- 1/2 tsp. ancho chile powder
- 2 tbsps. vegetable oil
- 1 onion, chopped
- 2 cloves garlic, chopped
- 1 (1 inch) piece fresh ginger root, grated
- 4 c loosely packed fresh spinach, coarsely chopped
- 2 tomatoes, chopped
- 4 sprigs fresh cilantro, chopped
- 1 (15.5 ounce) can mixed beans, rinsed and drained

Directions

- Rinse the lentils and transfer to saucepan containing plenty of water to cover. Heat to boil. Decrease the heat to low, cover and allow to simmer for 20 minutes on low heat. Drain lentils.
- Mix together yoghurt and tomato puree in a bowl. Season with chile powder, garam masala, cumin and turmeric. Mix until creamy.
- Over medium heat, heat oil in a skillet. Mix in ginger, onion and garlic and let to cook until the onion starts to brown. Add spinach, stir and let to cook until wilted and dark green. Slowly mix in the yogurt mixture. Stir in cilantro and tomatoes.
- Mix mixed beans and lentils into the mixture until combined well. Heat for about five minutes.

Nutrition Information

- Nutritionist's Calories: 328 kcal 16%
- Total Fat: 8.3 g 13%
- Carbohydrates: 51.9g 17%
- Protein: 18 g 36%
- Cholesterol: 2 mg < 1%
- Sodium: 633 mg 25%

---

312. Spinach-Stuffed Flounder with Mushrooms and Feta

"This dish is fantastic and low in fat."

Servings: 4 | Prep: 15 m | Ready In: 30 m

Ingredients

- 8 large fresh mushrooms, sliced
- 8 ounces spinach, rinsed and chopped

- 1 tbsp. crumbled feta cheese
- 4 (4 ounce) fillets flounder

Directions

- Preheat an oven to 175 degrees C (350 degrees F).
- Use non-stick spray to coat an unheated skillet. Over medium heat, heat the skillet and then add mushrooms. Cook for about five minutes while stirring often or until liquid released from mushrooms evaporates.
- To the skillet, add spinach. Cook while stirring for about two minutes or until the spinach wilts. Take out from the heat source and then drain the excess moisture. Drizzle feta cheese on top of the veggies and mix.
- To prepare fish rolls, onto the wide end of every filet, put one-quarter spinach mixture. Fold fillet around spinach mixture carefully. Hold the end of each roll with wooden toothpicks.
- Use non-stick spray to coat a baking dish of 8x8 inch. Transfer the fish rolls to the baking dish with the seam side facing down. Pour in two tbsps. water. Cover loosely with foil.
- Bake for about 15 to 20 minutes or until the fish is opaque all the way through and easily flakes with a fork.

Nutrition Information

- Nutritionist's Calories: 131 kcal 7%
- Total Fat: 2.2 g 3%
- Carbohydrates: 3.6g 1%
- Protein: 24.5 g 49%
- Cholesterol: 56 mg 19%
- Sodium: 164 mg 7%

---

you like. Remember to serve together with buttered bread toasted."

*Servings: 4 | Prep: 5 m | **Ready In:** 2 h 30 m*

Ingredients

- 1 c chopped onion
- 1 tsp. vegetable oil
- 1 pound dried split peas
- 1 pound ham bone
- 1 pinch salt and pepper to taste

Directions

- Sauté onions in oil in a pot. Pour in ham bone, split peas and plenty of water to cover the ingredients. Add pepper and salt.
- Cover the pot and let to cook for two hours until no peas are left but just a green liquid. As you cook, check the amount of water present. If necessary add more water while the soup cooks.
- Take out from the heat when the soup becomes a green liquid and leave it to stand to make it thick. When thickened, you can heat through and serve.

Nutrition Information

- Nutritionist's Calories: 413 kcal 21%
- Total Fat: 2.5 g 4%
- Carbohydrates: 72.2g 23%
- Protein: 28.3 g 57%
- Cholesterol: 0 mg 0%
- Sodium: 116 mg 5%

---

313. Split Pea and Ham Soup I

"A cheap and delicious way to make use leftover ham. You definitely like it. Feel free to add carrots or other veggies

314. Stir Fried Snow Peas and Mushrooms

"Easy to make side dish served along with Asian dishes.

Grilled tuna is our favorite."

Servings: 4 | Prep: 15 m | Ready In: 25 m

Ingredients

- 1 tbsp. sesame seeds
- 1 tbsp. olive oil
- 1/2 pound snow peas
- 4 ounces fresh mushrooms, thinly sliced
- 2 tbsps. teriyaki sauce

Directions

- Over medium heat, cook sesame seeds in a skillet for about five minutes while stirring often until browned lightly. Take out from the heat and reserve.
- Over medium high heat, heat oil in skillet and mix in mushrooms and snow peas. Let to cook for about 3 to 4 minutes until tender.
- Into a bowl, place the mushrooms and snow peas. Mix with teriyaki sauce and sesame seeds and then serve while warm.

Nutrition Information

- Nutritionist's Calories: 83 kcal 4%
- Total Fat: 5 g 8%
- Carbohydrates: 7.6g 2%
- Protein: 2.9 g 6%
- Cholesterol: 0 mg 0%
- Sodium: 84 mg 3%

315. Sugar Snap Peas

"This is a tasty and simple sugar snap peas recipe!"

Servings: 4 | Prep: 10 m | Ready In: 20 m

Ingredients

- 1/2 pound sugar snap peas
- 1 tbsp. olive oil
- 1 tbsp. chopped shallots
- 1 tsp. chopped fresh thyme
- kosher salt to taste

Directions

- Preheat an oven to 230 degrees C (450 degrees F).
- Onto a medium baking sheet, arrange a single layer of sugar snap peas and polish with olive oil. Drizzle with kosher salt, shallots and thyme.
- Bake for about 6 to 8 minutes until tender but still firm.

Nutrition Information

- Nutritionist's Calories: 59 kcal 3%
- Total Fat: 3.4 g 5%
- Carbohydrates: 5.3g 2%
- Protein: 1.4 g 3%
- Cholesterol: 0 mg 0%
- Sodium: 100 mg 4%

316. Summerly Squash

"A recipe that will be loved by even those who dislike squash. Great with fresh veggies from the market. This is side dish is great during summer!"

Servings: 6 | Prep: 15 m | Ready In: 45 m

Ingredients

- 2 tbsps. vegetable oil
- 1 small onion, sliced
- 2 medium tomatoes, coarsely chopped

- 1 tsp. salt
- 1/4 tsp. pepper
- 2 small zucchini, cut into 1/2 inch slices
- 2 small yellow summer squash, cut into 1/2-inch slices
- 1 bay leaf
- 1/2 tsp. dried basil

Directions

- Over medium heat, heat oil in a skillet and add onion. Cook while stirring for about five minutes until tender. Stir in tomatoes and then season with pepper and salt. Continue cooking while stirring for about five minutes. Stir in basil, zucchini, bay leaf and yellow squash. Cover the skillet, decrease the heat to low and allow to simmer while stirring often for about 20 minutes. Take out leaf prior to serving.

Nutrition Information

- Nutritionist's Calories: 65 kcal 3%
- Total Fat: 4.8 g 7%
- Carbohydrates: 5.4g 2%
- Protein: 1.5 g 3%
- Cholesterol: 0 mg 0%
- Sodium: 395 mg 16%

317. Sun-dried Tomatoes I

"This recipe takes some time to prepare but worth the effort. When these delicious gems dry, keep them in the fridge."

Servings: 32

Ingredients

- 4 pounds tomatoes
- salt to taste

Directions

- Preheat an oven to 95 degrees C (200 degrees F).
- Clean and cut tomatoes in half. Slowly press out the seeds. Onto a non-stick cookie sheet, put the tomatoes and season with salt.
- Bake in oven until the tomatoes have a leathery texture. May take the whole day but smaller pieces take less time in oven.

Nutrition Information

- Nutritionist's Calories: 10 kcal < 1%
- Total Fat: 0.1 g < 1%
- Carbohydrates: 2.2g < 1%
- Protein: 0.5 g < 1%
- Cholesterol: 0 mg 0%
- Sodium: 3 mg < 1%

318. Super Easy Slow Cooker Chicken

"A simple and delicious dish. I normally prepare it for my family of four. It's easy to increase or decrease this recipe. It's a favorite for my hubby who can eat this dish every night without complaining."

Servings: 4 | Prep: 15 m | Ready In: 3 h 15 m

Ingredients

- 1 (10.75 ounce) can condensed low fat cream of chicken and herbs soup
- 1 (4 ounce) can mushroom pieces, drained
- 1/2 red onion, chopped
- 1 1/2 pounds skinless, boneless chicken breast halves - cut into strips
- 1 dash Marsala wine

Directions

- In slow cooker, mix chicken, onion, wine, soup and mushroom pieces.
- Cook for about 2 1/2 to 3 hours on Low setting.

Nutrition Information

- Nutritionist's Calories: 234 kcal 12%
- Total Fat: 5.7 g 9%
- Carbohydrates: 8.2g 3%
- Protein: 34.9 g 70%
- Cholesterol: 91 mg 30%
- Sodium: 684 mg 27%

---

319. Sweet 'n' Hot Glazed Salmon

"This is the best salmon recipe. This dish is both delicious and very healthy. This is perfect for dinner parties alongside salad, rice pilaf and green beans."

Servings: 4 | Prep: 30 m | Ready In: 42 m

Ingredients

- 1 1/2 c apricot nectar
- 1/3 c chopped dried apricots
- 2 tbsps. honey
- 2 tbsps. reduced sodium soy sauce
- 1 tbsp. grated fresh ginger
- 2 cloves garlic, minced
- 1/8 tsp. cayenne pepper
- 1/4 tsp. ground cinnamon
- 1 (3/4 pound) salmon filet without skin

Directions

- Preheat the broiler of oven and then polish a broiling pan with grease.
- Over medium heat, Combine together cinnamon, apricot nectar, ginger dried apricots, cayenne, honey, garlic and soy sauce in a saucepan. Heat to boil, decrease the heat to medium-low and allow to simmer for approximately 20 minutes or until decreased by about ½. Mix often to keep from burning. Take out 1/4 c glaze for basting and reserve the remaining.
- Onto the greased broiling pan, put salmon filet and polish with glaze. Let to broil for three inches away from heat source for about 8 to 12 minutes or until the salmon easily flakes with a fork. Slowly flip over once while cooking and then baste occasionally during the final four minutes. Serve together with the glaze remaining.

Nutrition Information

- Nutritionist's Calories: 275 kcal 14%
- Total Fat: 9.4 g 14%
- Carbohydrates: 30.6g 10%
- Protein: 18.2 g 36%
- Cholesterol: 50 mg 17%
- Sodium: 321 mg 13%

---

320. Swiss Chard with Garbanzo Beans and Fresh Tomatoes

"Green and beans are a great combination and filling. A Swiss chard recipe with fresh tomatoes, garbanzo beans, onion and lemon juice. It makes a tantalizing side dish for meat/fish or a great vegan main dish."

Servings: 4 | Prep: 10 m | Ready In: 25 m

Ingredients

- 2 tbsps. olive oil
- 1 shallot, chopped
- 2 green onions, chopped
- 1/2 c garbanzo beans, drained
- salt and pepper to taste

- 1 bunch red Swiss chard, rinsed and chopped
- 1 tomato, sliced
- 1/2 lemon, juiced

Directions

- In a skillet, heat olive oil. Mix in green onions and shallot. Cook while stirring for about 3 to 5 minutes or until fragrant and soft. Add garbanzo beans, stir, then add pepper and salt to taste and heat through. Transfer chard to pan and then cook until wilted. Pour in slices of tomato, squeeze lemon juice on top of greens and then heat through. Transfer to a plate and add pepper and salt to taste.

Nutrition Information

- Nutritionist's Calories: 122 kcal 6%
- Total Fat: 7.3 g 11%
- Carbohydrates: 13.3g 4%
- Protein: 3.2 g 6%
- Cholesterol: 0 mg 0%
- Sodium: 253 mg 10%

321. Szechwan Shrimp

"Do not be fooled by some of the ingredients. This shrimp is spicy and yields a simple and nice dish for company. Adjust the amount of red pepper to suit your taste. You can serve on top of hot steamed rice."

Servings: 4 | Prep: 10 m | Ready In: 20 m

Ingredients

- 4 tbsps. water
- 2 tbsps. ketchup
- 1 tbsp. soy sauce
- 2 tsps. cornstarch
- 1 tsp. honey

- 1/2 tsp. crushed red pepper
- 1/4 tsp. ground ginger
- 1 tbsp. vegetable oil
- 1/4 c sliced green onions
- 4 cloves garlic, minced
- 12 ounces cooked shrimp, tails removed

Directions

- Combine together honey, water, ground ginger, ketchup, soy sauce, crushed red pepper and cornstarch in a bowl. Reserve.
- Over medium-high heat, heat oil in a skillet and mix in garlic and green onions. Let to cook for 30 seconds. Add shrimp, stir and mix to coat with oil. Add sauce and stir. Cook while stirring until the sauce is thickened and bubbly.

Nutrition Information

- Nutritionist's Calories: 142 kcal 7%
- Total Fat: 4.4 g 7%
- Carbohydrates: 6.7g 2%
- Protein: 18.3 g 37%
- Cholesterol: 164 mg 55%
- Sodium: 500 mg 20%

322. Tandoori Chicken II

"The key for this spicy grilled chicken is the blend of dried peppers and spices. The marinating time is short. While the coals get hot, prepare the chicken."

Servings: 4 | Prep: 15 m | Ready In: 50 m

Ingredients

- 1/2 tsp. curry powder
- 1/2 tsp. red pepper flakes
- 1/2 tsp. kosher salt

- 1/4 tsp. ground ginger
- 1/4 tsp. paprika
- 1/4 tsp. ground cinnamon
- 1/4 tsp. ground turmeric
- 2 tbsps. water
- 4 skinless, boneless chicken breast halves

Directions

- Preheat the grill over high heat.
- Combine ginger, curry powder, cinnamon, red pepper flakes, salt, turmeric, paprika and water in a medium bowl to form a smooth paste. Use the paste to polish chicken breasts and then transfer to a plate. Cover the plate and let to marinate for about 20 minutes.
- Use oil to polish grate. Onto the grill, put chicken and let to cook for about 6 to 8 minutes per side until the juice runs clear when poked with a fork.

Nutrition Information

- Nutritionist's Calories: 264 kcal 13%
- Total Fat: 5.8 g 9%
- Carbohydrates: 0.7g < 1%
- Protein: 49.1 g 98%
- Cholesterol: 134 mg 45%
- Sodium: 358 mg 14%

323. Tangy Grilled Pork Tenderloin

"A recipe that is fast, simple and very flavorful. Have prepared it a lot. Since pork needs to marinate, prepare in advance."

Servings: 6 | Prep: 15 m | Ready In: 4 h 40 m

Ingredients

- 2 pounds pork tenderloin

- 2/3 c honey
- 1/2 c Dijon mustard
- 1/4 tsp. chili powder
- 1/4 tsp. salt

Directions

- Into a large plastic bag that is sealable, put meat. Combine together chili powder, honey, salt and Dijon mustard in a medium bowl. Spread the marinade on top of the tenderloins, seal the bag and chill for a minimum of 4 hours.
- Prepare a grill over indirect heat.
- Polish grill grate lightly with oil. Take out the meat from the marinade and get rid of liquid. Let to grill for about 15 to 25 minutes or until the temperature at the center is 63 degrees C (145 degrees F).

Nutrition Information

- Nutritionist's Calories: 267 kcal 13%
- Total Fat: 3.6 g 5%
- Carbohydrates: 35.3g 11%
- Protein: 23.4 g 47%
- Cholesterol: 65 mg 22%
- Sodium: 651 mg 26%

324. Tasty Collard Greens

"This is an authentic collard greens recipe with smoked turkey for some flavor. The greens are allowed to simmer in chicken stock and drizzled with some red chile flakes."

Servings: 10 | Prep: 30 m | Ready In: 2 h 30 m

Ingredients

- 1/4 c olive oil
- 2 tbsps. minced garlic
- 5 c chicken stock

- 1 smoked turkey drumstick
- 5 bunches collard greens - rinsed, trimmed and chopped
- salt and black pepper to taste
- 1 tbsp. crushed red pepper flakes (optional)

Directions

- Over medium heat, heat olive oil in a pot and add garlic. Sauté gently until garlic is light brown. Add chicken stock and then place in turkey leg. Cover and allow to simmer for about 30 minutes.
- To the cooking pot, add collard greens and raise the heat to medium-high. Cook the greens cook while stirring often for about 45 minutes.
- Low the heat to medium and add pepper and salt. Continue cooking for about 45 to 60 minutes until greens become dark green and tender. Drain the greens and set aside the liquid. If desired, add red pepper flakes and stir. Reheat the leftovers with liquid.

Nutrition Information

- Nutritionist's Calories: 142 kcal 7%
- Total Fat: 7.9 g 12%
- Carbohydrates: 10.6g 3%
- Protein: 9.6 g 19%
- Cholesterol: 23 mg 8%
- Sodium: 689 mg 28%

325. Tasty Orange Chops

"You should experiment this recipe. It's great. My family loves eating pork this way."

Servings: 4 | Prep: 15 m | Ready In: 6 h 23 m

Ingredients

- 1/4 c cider vinegar
- 1 tbsp. soy sauce
- 1/2 c frozen orange juice concentrate, thawed
- 1/2 onion, shredded
- 1 tsp. dried rosemary
- 1 tsp. ground sage
- 2 tsps. salt, or to taste
- 1 large clove garlic, crushed
- 1/2 c barbeque sauce
- 4 thick cut pork chops

Directions

- Combine together sage, vinegar, barbecue sauce, soy sauce, orange juice, garlic, onion, salt and rosemary in a mixing bowl. In a large plastic bag that is sealable, put chops. Add marinade and then seal. Chill for about 6 to 8 hours or overnight.
- Preheat the grill over high heat. Into a small saucepan, place the marinade, heat to boil and allow cooking for a few minutes.
- Polish the grill preheated lightly with oil. Let the chops grill for about 6 to 8 minutes, flip once, or to the doneness desired. Polish the chops with the cooked marinade on the last minutes of cooking.

Nutrition Information

- Nutritionist's Calories: 258 kcal 13%
- Total Fat: 6.9 g 11%
- Carbohydrates: 27.3g 9%
- Protein: 20.2 g 40%
- Cholesterol: 56 mg 19%
- Sodium: 1788 mg 72%

326. Terry's Texas Pinto Beans

"A traditional recipe for 'pot of beans'. Begin with

chicken broth, onion and dry pinto beans. For a spicy kick, add cumin, jalapeno and green chili salsa."

Servings: 8 | Prep: 15 m | Ready In: 2 h 15 m

Ingredients

- 1 pound dry pinto beans
- 1 (29 ounce) can reduced sodium chicken broth
- 1 large onion, chopped
- 1 fresh jalapeno pepper, chopped
- 2 cloves garlic, minced
- 1/2 c green salsa
- 1 tsp. cumin
- 1/2 tsp. ground black pepper
- water, if needed

Directions

- Into a large pot, put pinto beans and add chicken broth. Mix in pepper, salsa, onion, jalapeno, cumin and garlic. Heat to boil, decrease the heat to medium-low and then continue to cook for two hours while stirring occasionally until the beans become tender. Keep the beans moist by adding water as required.

Nutrition Information

- Nutritionist's Calories: 210 kcal 10%
- Total Fat: 1.1 g 2%
- Carbohydrates: 37.9g 12%
- Protein: 13.2 g 26%
- Cholesterol: 1 mg < 1%
- Sodium: 95 mg 4%

327. Texas Enchilada Sauce

"Since am from South Texas, I've learned lots of ways to make Mexican and Tex-Mex foods. I love this recipe!"

Servings: 7 | Prep: 15 m | Ready In: 45 m

Ingredients

- 2 (6.5 ounce) cans tomato sauce
- 1 (28 ounce) can crushed tomatoes
- 1/3 c chili powder
- 1 tbsp. dried oregano
- 1 tsp. paprika
- 2 tsps. ground cumin
- 2 tsps. ground black pepper
- 1/4 tsp. salt
- 1 clove garlic, minced
- 1 tbsp. butter
- 1 onion, minced
- 1 green bell pepper, chopped

Directions

- Mix chili powder, tomato sauce, cumin, crushed tomatoes, garlic, oregano, paprika, salt and pepper in a medium saucepan. Cover the pan and let to cook on medium heat.
- In the meantime, over medium heat, heat butter in a skillet, add onion and then sauté for about four minutes. Mix into the sauce.   Let the sauce cook for 20 minutes while stirring often. Add in bell pepper, stir and let to cook for about 10 minutes.

Nutrition Information

- Nutritionist's Calories: 100 kcal 5%
- Total Fat: 3.4 g 5%
- Carbohydrates: 18.2g 6%
- Protein: 4 g 8%
- Cholesterol: 4 mg 1%
- Sodium: 582 mg 23%

328. Thai Chicken Balls

"Delicious chicken balls! Experiment them!"

Servings: 8 | Prep: 20 m | Ready In: 1 h

Ingredients

- 2 pounds ground chicken
- 1 c dry bread crumbs
- 4 green onions, sliced
- 1 tbsp. ground coriander seed
- 1 c chopped fresh cilantro
- 1/4 c sweet chili sauce
- 2 tbsps. fresh lemon juice
- oil for frying

Directions

- Combine together bread crumbs and chicken in a large bowl. Season with chili sauce, green onion, lemon juice, ground coriander and cilantro. Combine well.
- Form the mixture, with damp hands, into balls that are evenly shaped. The balls should be either small and bite size or big enough to use as burgers.
- Over medium heat, heat oil in a skillet and then fry chicken balls in batches until browned well around.

Nutrition Information

- Nutritionist's Calories: 313 kcal 16%
- Total Fat: 15.5 g 24%
- Carbohydrates: 14.8g 5%
- Protein: 27.6 g 55%
- Cholesterol: 69 mg 23%
- Sodium: 247 mg 10%

329. Thai Spiced Barbecue Shrimp

"This barbecue shrimp recipe is the best and it's very delicious! You'll be glued to this shrimp recipe."

Servings: 8 | Prep: 1 m | Ready In: 1 h 6 m

Ingredients

- 3 tbsps. fresh lemon juice
- 1 tbsp. soy sauce
- 1 tbsp. Dijon mustard
- 2 cloves garlic, minced
- 1 tbsp. brown sugar
- 2 tsps. curry paste
- 1 pound medium shrimp - peeled and deveined

Directions

- Combine together mustard, lemon juice, curry paste, soy sauce, brown sugar and garlic in a resealable bag or shallow dish. Place in shrimp and then cover or seal. Chill for 1 hour to marinate.
- Preheat the grill over high heat. Once grill becomes hot, polish the grate lightly with oil. Onto skewers, thread shrimp or transfer to a grill basket for ease of handling. Into a saucepan, place the marinade and let to boil for several minutes.
- Let shrimp grill for about three minutes on each side or until opaque. Use the marinade to baste often.

Nutrition Information

- Nutritionist's Calories: 73 kcal 4%
- Total Fat: 1 g 2%
- Carbohydrates: 3.6g 1%
- Protein: 11.7 g 23%
- Cholesterol: 86 mg 29%
- Sodium: 268 mg 11%

330. The Best Vegetarian Chili in the World

"Prepare this tasty and spicy vegan chili in your soup pot! Prep time is short and contains beans, veggies and flavor!"

Servings: 8 | Prep: 15 m | Ready In: 1 h 15 m

Ingredients

- 1 tbsp. olive oil
- 1/2 medium onion, chopped
- 2 bay leaves
- 1 tsp. ground cumin
- 2 tbsps. dried oregano
- 1 tbsp. salt
- 2 stalks celery, chopped
- 2 green bell peppers, chopped
- 2 jalapeno peppers, chopped
- 3 cloves garlic, chopped
- 2 (4 ounce) cans chopped green chile peppers, drained
- 2 (12 ounce) packages vegetarian burger crumbles
- 3 (28 ounce) cans whole peeled tomatoes, crushed
- 1/4 c chili powder
- 1 tbsp. ground black pepper
- 1 (15 ounce) can kidney beans, drained
- 1 (15 ounce) can garbanzo beans, drained
- 1 (15 ounce) can black beans
- 1 (15 ounce) can whole kernel corn

Directions

- Over medium heat, heat olive oil in a pot and mix in onion. Season with salt, cumin, bay leaves and oregano. Cook while stirring until the onion becomes tender. Stir in green chile peppers, celery, jalapeno peppers, green bell peppers and garlic. Once the veggies are heated through, add vegetarian burger crumbles and stir. Decrease the heat to low, cover the pot and allow to simmer for five minutes.
- Into the pot, add tomatoes and mix. Season the chili with pepper and chili powder. Mix in black beans, kidney beans and garbanzo beans. Heat to boil, decrease the heat to low and allow to simmer for 45 minutes. Add corn, stir and continue to cook for five minutes prior to serving.

Nutrition Information

- Nutritionist's Calories: 391 kcal 20%
- Total Fat: 7.9 g 12%
- Carbohydrates: 58.7g 19%
- Protein: 28.2 g 56%
- Cholesterol: 0 mg 0%
- Sodium: 2571 mg 103%

331. The Easiest Blackened Chicken

"This recipe is for those that like spicy chicken! It's easy and fast and great when served together with rice and a cool drink!"

Servings: 4

Ingredients

- 4 skinless, boneless chicken breast halves
- 1 c Worcestershire sauce
- 2 tsps. ground black pepper

Directions

- Mix ground black pepper and Worcestershire sauce in a large skillet. Over medium heat, add chicken and then let to simmer until sauce starts to boil. Decrease the heat to low and simmer for about 15 to 20 minutes. Flip the chicken often while spooning the sauce on top of it. Sauce should thicken. Cool before serving.

Nutrition Information

- Nutritionist's Calories: 186 kcal 9%
- Total Fat: 1.5 g 2%
- Carbohydrates: 13.9g 4%
- Protein: 27.4 g 55%
- Cholesterol: 68 mg 23%
- Sodium: 744 mg 30%

332. The Ultimate Chili

"This is a simple recipe and ready in no time. Feel free to make with ground turkey and tastes great the following day!"

Servings: 6 | Prep: 10 m | Ready In: 6 h 20 m

Ingredients

- 1 pound lean ground beef
- salt and pepper to taste
- 3 (15 ounce) cans dark red kidney beans
- 3 (14.5 ounce) cans Mexican-style stewed tomatoes
- 2 stalks celery, chopped
- 1 red bell pepper, chopped
- 1/4 c red wine vinegar
- 2 tbsps. chili powder
- 1 tsp. ground cumin
- 1 tsp. dried parsley
- 1 tsp. dried basil
- 1 dash Worcestershire sauce
- 1/2 c red wine

Directions

- Over medium-high heat, cook ground beef in a large skillet until browned evenly. Then drain off the grease and add pepper and salt to taste.
- Mix celery, cooked beef, red bell pepper, kidney beans, red wine vinegar and tomatoes in a slow cooker. Season with Worcestershire sauce, chili powder, basil, cumin and parsley. Mix to disperse the ingredients evenly.
- Cook for 8 hours on Low or for 6 hours on High. During the last two hours, add wine.

Nutrition Information

- Nutritionist's Calories: 414 kcal 21%
- Total Fat: 11 g 17%
- Carbohydrates: 49.5g 16%
- Protein: 28.4 g 57%
- Cholesterol: 50 mg 17%
- Sodium: 1015 mg 41%

333. Three Bean Salad

"I got this recipe from a vegan friend in college. It's a great bean salad and like it because you can try out with ingredients to have delicious side dish. You will love it!"

Servings: 8 | Prep: 15 m | Ready In: 2 h 15 m

Ingredients

- 1 (15 ounce) can garbanzo beans (chickpeas), drained and rinsed
- 1 (15 ounce) can kidney beans, drained and rinsed
- 1 (15 ounce) can green beans, drained and rinsed
- 4 green onions, chopped
- 1 stalk celery, sliced
- 1/2 c cider vinegar
- 1/4 c vegetable oil
- 1 tbsp. honey

- 1/2 tsp. ground dry mustard
- 1/4 tsp. garlic powder
- 1/4 tsp. ground black pepper
- 1/4 tsp. onion powder (optional)
- 1/4 tsp. ground cayenne pepper (optional)

Directions

- Gently combine green onions, garbanzo beans, celery, kidney beans and green beans in a bowl. Whisk together garlic powder, vinegar, onion powder, oil, cayenne pepper, mustard, black pepper and honey in a separate bowl. Spread the dressing on top of salad and mix slowly to coat. Cover the bowl, chill for a minimum of two hours and slowly mix prior to serving.

Nutrition Information

- Nutritionist's Calories: 170 kcal 9%
- Total Fat: 7.6 g 12%
- Carbohydrates: 20.7g 7%
- Protein: 5.2 g 10%
- Cholesterol: 0 mg 0%
- Sodium: 310 mg 12%

334. Tilapia with Tomatoes, Black Olives and Corn

"Tilapia cooked together with sauce. I ate something just like this in a restaurant and then created this based with what I ate (made some changes). Plate the tilapia, add sauce on top along with salad and a steamed vegetable and serve."

Servings: 4 | Prep: 10 m | Ready In: 40 m

Ingredients

- 1 1/2 tbsps. olive oil

- 4 cloves garlic, thinly sliced
- 2 (16 ounce) cans diced tomatoes
- 1 c dry white wine
- 1 (2.25 ounce) can sliced black olives
- 3 ears fresh corn, kernels cut from cob
- 4 (4 ounce) fillets tilapia

Directions

- Over medium heat, heat oil in a skillet, add garlic and cook for one minute. Mix in corn, black olives, 3/4 c of wine and diced tomatoes along with juice. Put fillets on top once the sauce becomes hot and then pour some tomato mixture on top of fish. Cover and let to cook for about 20 to 25 minutes or until the fish easily flakes with a fork. You can add another 1/4 c of white wine in case the sauce starts to dry out.

Nutrition Information

- Nutritionist's Calories: 336 kcal 17%
- Total Fat: 9.1 g 14%
- Carbohydrates: 24g 8%
- Protein: 27.4 g 55%
- Cholesterol: 41 mg 14%
- Sodium: 558 mg 22%

335. Tofu Stroganoff

"My family loves this tofu stroganoff. It's ready in s short while and good for weeknight dinners."

Servings: 8 | Prep: 15 m | Ready In: 45 m

Ingredients

- 1 (16 ounce) package uncooked egg noodles

- 2 (12 ounce) packages extra-firm tofu, drained and diced
- 1 tbsp. vegetable oil
- 2 onions, sliced
- 1 (12 ounce) container cottage cheese
- 2 tbsps. sour cream
- 1 sprig fresh dill weed, chopped
- 8 ounces mushrooms, sliced
- 1 tsp. garlic, minced
- 2 tbsps. soy sauce

Directions

- Bring to boil water in a large pot and add egg noodles. Cook until al dente, for about 8 to 10 minutes and then drain.
- Over medium heat, heat oil in a skillet, add tofu and then sauté for 5 minutes per side until browned lightly. Reserve. Add onions to skillet and let to cook until tender. Stir in soy sauce, mushrooms and garlic and then cook until heated through.
- Combine dill, cottage cheese and sour cream in a bowl. Mix into skillet. Place back tofu into skillet and continue to cook until heated through. You can serve on top of cooked noodles.

Nutrition Information

- Nutritionist's Calories: 356 kcal 18%
- Total Fat: 12.3 g 19%
- Carbohydrates: 42.1g 14%
- Protein: 21.5 g 43%
- Cholesterol: 49 mg 16%
- Sodium: 416 mg 17%

336. Tomato and Garlic Pasta

"Fresh tomatoes have a nice flavor. Can also use canned and it's worth the effort making this dish. Make the sauce as pasta cooks to reduce prep time. Fantastic for those that like meatless pasta."

Servings: 4

Ingredients

- 1 (8 ounce) package angel hair pasta
- 2 pounds tomatoes
- 4 cloves crushed garlic
- 1 tbsp. olive oil
- 1 tbsp. chopped fresh basil
- 1 tbsp. tomato paste
- salt to taste
- ground black pepper to taste
- 1/4 c grated Parmesan cheese

Directions

- In a kettle, put tomatoes and then add cold water to cover. Heat just to the boil. Drain water and add cold water again to cover. Remove skin. Chop into small pieces.
- In a large pot containing boiling salted water, cook pasta until al dente.
- Sauté garlic in a sauté pan or skillet along with plenty of olive oil that covers the pan's bottom. Garlic should be opaque and not brown. Add tomato paste and stir. Add pepper, salt and tomatoes immediately and stir. Decrease the heat and allow to simmer until pasta is done. Pour in basil.
- Drain pasta and don't rinse with cold water. Combine with a few tbsps. olive oil and stir into sauce. Decrease the heat to very low. Keep it warm without covering for around ten minutes until serving. Generously top with fresh Parmesan cheese.
- For variations: Sauté garlic with fresh quartered mushrooms or pour in shoestring zucchini together with tomato.

Nutrition Information

- Nutritionist's Calories: 260 kcal 13%

- Total Fat: 6.8 g 10%
- Carbohydrates: 41.9g 14%
- Protein: 10.3 g 21%
- Cholesterol: 4 mg 1%
- Sodium: 236 mg 9%

337. Tomato Cucumber Salad

"This easy and hearty salad can be served along with all types of food."

Servings: 4 | Prep: 10 m | Ready In: 10 m

Ingredients

- 2 tomatoes, chopped
- 1 cucumber, peeled and diced
- 1 onion, chopped
- 1 tbsp. lemon juice
- salt to taste
- ground black pepper to taste

Directions

- In a salad bowl, mix onions, tomatoes and cucumbers. Add black pepper and salt to taste. Drizzle with lemon juice and refrigerate.

Nutrition Information

- Nutritionist's Calories: 31 kcal 2%
- Total Fat: 0.3 g < 1%
- Carbohydrates: 7.1g 2%
- Protein: 1.3 g 3%
- Cholesterol: 0 mg 0%
- Sodium: 6 mg < 1%

338. Tomato-Curry Lentil Stew

"I developed this dish while experimenting with leftover celery and canned tomatoes. Easily to increase the recipe. If desired, add fresh tomatoes."

Servings: 2 | Prep: 10 m | Ready In: 1 h

Ingredients

- 1/2 c dry lentils
- 1 c water
- 5 ounces stewed tomatoes
- 1/8 c chopped onion
- 2 stalks celery, chopped, with leaves
- 1/4 tsp. curry powder
- 3 cloves garlic, minced
- salt to taste
- ground black pepper to taste

Directions

- Mix water and lentils and heat to boil.
- Reduce the heat to simmer, and then add celery, tomatoes and onion. Cover and allow to simmer for 45 minutes. Keep checking after every 15 minutes, stir and if need be, add water. During the last 15 minutes add spices to taste. Check the taste and adjust the spice if need be prior to serving.

Nutrition Information

- Nutritionist's Calories: 206 kcal 10%
- Total Fat: 0.8 g 1%
- Carbohydrates: 36.9g 12%
- Protein: 13.7 g 27%
- Cholesterol: 0 mg 0%
- Sodium: 194 mg 8%

339. Tortilla and Bean Soup

"A Mexican-style soup recipe with fresh chicken and lots of beans. The spiciness is from green chiles and taco seasoning. Adjust them to suit your taste. Can serve together with tortillas."

Servings: 12 | Prep: 10 m | Ready In: 1 h 20 m

Ingredients

- 6 c water
- 4 skinless, boneless chicken breasts
- 1 onion, chopped
- 1 (15 ounce) can kidney beans
- 1 (15 ounce) can ranch-style beans
- 1 (15 ounce) can pinto beans
- 1 (15 ounce) can black beans, rinsed and drained
- 1 (15 ounce) can white hominy
- 2 (10 ounce) cans diced tomatoes with green chile peppers
- 1 (1.25 ounce) package taco seasoning mix
- 1 (1 ounce) package ranch dressing mix

Directions

- Over high heat, mix water and chicken in a large pot. Let to cook for about 30 minutes to 1 hour or until the chicken is cooked through. Take out the chicken from pot and chop into small pieces.
- Take back the meat to pot. Pour in pinto beans, onion, kidney beans, tomatoes, hominy, ranch style beans, ranch dressing mix, black beans and taco seasoning. Combine well, decrease heat to low and allow to simmer for about 30 minutes or until heated through.

Nutrition Information

- Nutritionist's Calories: 205 kcal 10%
- Total Fat: 1.4 g 2%
- Carbohydrates: 29.6g 10%
- Protein: 16.9 g 34%
- Cholesterol: 23 mg 8%
- Sodium: 1091 mg 44%

340. Tuna Salad With Fresh Dill

"Tuna salad that is simple to prepare. Serve inside of hollowed out papayas or tomatoes."

Servings: 5 | Prep: 10 m | Ready In: 10 m

Ingredients

- 1 (5 ounce) can tuna
- 1/4 c diced celery
- 1/4 c chopped fresh dill weed
- 2 tbsps. chopped fresh parsley
- 2 tbsps. thinly sliced green onion
- 2 tbsps. fat-free mayonnaise
- 2 tbsps. plain low-fat yogurt
- 1/2 tsp. prepared Dijon-style mustard

Directions

- Mash tuna along with juices from can in a small bowl. Pour in chives, celery, mustard, dill, parsley, yogurt and mayonnaise and combine thoroughly.

Nutrition Information

- Nutritionist's Calories: 41 kcal 2%
- Total Fat: 0.3 g < 1%
- Carbohydrates: 2.3g < 1%
- Protein: 6.9 g 14%
- Cholesterol: 8 mg 3%
- Sodium: 78 mg 3%

341. Twelve Minute Pasta Toss

"A pasta dish that is simple, good and flavorful and will receive rave reviews! Friends often request for the recipe. Works great along with garlic bread and green salad."

Servings: 8 | Prep: 20 m | Ready In: 32 m

Ingredients

- 16 ounces rotini pasta
- 4 tbsps. olive oil
- 4 skinless, boneless chicken breast halves, cut into bite size pieces
- 3 cloves garlic, minced
- 1 1/4 tsps. salt
- 1 1/4 tsps. garlic powder
- 1 1/4 tsps. dried basil
- 1 1/4 tsps. dried oregano
- 1 c chopped sun-dried tomatoes
- 1/4 c grated Parmesan cheese

Directions

- Bring to boil lightly salted water in a pot and add rotini. Cook at a boil for about 8 minutes until tender but still firm when bitten. Drain.
- over medium-high heat, heat oil in a pot and then sauté chicken, oregano, garlic, salt, basil, and garlic powder for about 5 to 10 minutes until no pink color of chicken remains at the center. Pour in sun-dried tomatoes and then let to cook for about two minutes until heated through. Take out from the heat source.
- Add pasta into the pot and mix together with chicken until combined. Add Parmesan cheese on top.

Nutrition Information

- Nutritionist's Calories: 360 kcal 18%
- Total Fat: 10.2 g 16%
- Carbohydrates: 46.3g 15%
- Protein: 21.4 g 43%

- Cholesterol: 33 mg 11%
- Sodium: 437 mg 17%

342. Unbelievable Chicken

"Unique blend of popular ingredients that is awesome! Often requested for the recipe. You'll like it and also receive rave reviews!"

Servings: 6 | Prep: 15 m | Ready In: 9 h

Ingredients

- 1/4 c cider vinegar
- 3 tbsps. prepared coarse-ground mustard
- 3 cloves garlic, peeled and minced
- 1 lime, juiced
- 1/2 lemon, juiced
- 1/2 c brown sugar
- 1 1/2 tsps. salt
- ground black pepper to taste
- 6 tbsps. olive oil
- 6 skinless, boneless chicken breast halves

Directions

- Combine cider vinegar, lemon juice, mustard, garlic, brown sugar, lime juice, pepper and salt in a large glass bowl. Add olive oil and whisk. Add chicken into the mixture. Cover the bowl and chill for 8 hours or overnight to marinate.
- Preheat the outdoor grill over high heat.
- Polish grill grate lightly with oil. Transfer chicken to the grill prepared and let to cook for about 6 to 8 minutes on each side until the juice runs clear. Get rid of marinade.

Nutrition Information

- Nutritionist's Calories: 337 kcal 17%
- Total Fat: 16.4 g 25%

- Carbohydrates: 22.4g 7%
- Protein: 24.8 g 50%
- Cholesterol: 67 mg 22%
- Sodium: 736 mg 29%

- Protein: 7.5 g 15%
- Cholesterol: 0 mg 0%
- Sodium: 596 mg 24%

343. Vegan Bean Taco Filling

"Taco stuffed with fried bean. Fantastic with chips, tortillas, or taco shells."

Servings: 8 | Prep: 15 m | Ready In: 30 m

Ingredients

- 1 tbsp. olive oil
- 1 onion, diced
- 2 cloves garlic, minced
- 1 bell pepper, chopped
- 2 (14.5 ounce) cans black beans, rinsed, drained, and mashed
- 2 tbsps. yellow cornmeal
- 1 1/2 tbsps. cumin
- 1 tsp. paprika
- 1 tsp. cayenne pepper
- 1 tsp. chili powder
- 1 c salsa

Directions

- Over medium heat, heat olive oil in a skillet and mix in bell pepper, onion and garlic. Let to cook until tender. Add mashed beans and stir. Pour in cornmeal. Stir in salsa, cumin, cayenne, paprika and chili powder. Cover the skillet and let to cook for 5 minutes.

Nutrition Information

- Nutritionist's Calories: 142 kcal 7%
- Total Fat: 2.5 g 4%
- Carbohydrates: 24g 8%

344. Vegan Lasagna I

"A great lasagna and it's also vegan."

Servings: 8 | Prep: 30 m | Ready In: 2 h 30 m

Ingredients

- 2 tbsps. olive oil
- 1 1/2 c chopped onion
- 3 tbsps. minced garlic
- 4 (14.5 ounce) cans stewed tomatoes
- 1/3 c tomato paste
- 1/2 c chopped fresh basil
- 1/2 c chopped parsley
- 1 tsp. salt
- 1 tsp. ground black pepper
- 1 (16 ounce) package lasagna noodles
- 2 pounds firm tofu
- 2 tbsps. minced garlic
- 1/4 c chopped fresh basil
- 1/4 c chopped parsley
- 1/2 tsp. salt
- ground black pepper to taste
- 3 (10 ounce) packages frozen chopped spinach, thawed and drained

Directions

- For the sauce: over medium heat, heat olive oil in a heavy saucepan. Add onions and then sauté for about 5 minutes until soft. Pour in garlic and let to cook for 5 minutes.
- Into the saucepan, put basil, tomatoes, parsley and tomato paste. Combine well, decrease the heat to low and simmer the sauce while covered for one hour. Season with pepper and salt.

- As the sauce cooks, bring to boil salted water in a large kettle. Let the lasagna noodles to boil for 9 minutes, drain and then rinse thoroughly.
- Preheat an oven to 200 degrees C (400 degrees F).
- Into a large bowl, put tofu blocks. Pour in parsley, garlic and basil. Season with pepper and salt. Mash together the ingredients by squeezing tofu pieces through the fingers. Combine well.
- To prepare lasagna: At the bottom of a casserole pan of 9x13 inch, pour one c of tomato sauce. Spread a layer of lasagna noodles and then drizzle one-third tofu mixture on top of noodles. Disperse spinach evenly on top of tofu. On top of tofu, spoon 1 1/2 c of tomato sauce and spread another layer of noodles on top. Drizzle 1/3 tofu mixture on top of noodles, pour 1 1/2 c of the tomato sauce and then spread on top of tomato sauce, the last layer of noodles. Lastly, add 1/3 tofu on top of noodles and pour the tomato sauce remaining on top of all.
- Use foil to cover the pan and then bake lasagna for about 30 minutes. Serve while hot.

Nutrition Information

- Nutritionist's Calories: 511 kcal 26%
- Total Fat: 15.8 g 24%
- Carbohydrates: 69.9g 23%
- Protein: 32.5 g 65%
- Cholesterol: 0 mg 0%
- Sodium: 1074 mg 43%

---

345. Vegetable Lo Mein Delight

"This is a lovely meal that has onion, celery, red bell peppers, mushrooms, etc."

Servings: 4 | Prep: 15 m | Ready In: 30 m

Ingredients

- 8 ounces angel hair pasta
- 3/4 c chicken broth
- 1/4 c soy sauce
- 1 tbsp. cornstarch
- 2 tbsps. canola oil
- 1 3/4 c chopped celery
- 1 3/4 c sliced fresh mushrooms
- 1 3/4 c sliced red bell peppers
- 1/2 c sliced onion
- 2 c bean sprouts
- 2 c snow peas
- 1 c chow mein noodles

Directions

- Bring to boil lightly salted water in a pot and add angel hair pasta. Cook until al dente or for about 3 to 5 minutes and then drain.
- Whisk together cornstarch, chicken broth and soy sauce in a small bowl.
- Over medium-high heat, heat oil in a wok. Mix in onion, celery, peppers and mushrooms. Let to cook for about 3 minutes. Pour in snow peas, broth mixture and bean sprouts. Continue cooking while stirring for about five minutes until the veggies become tender but crispy.
- Combine together vegetable mixture and cooked pasta in a large bowl. Add chow mein noodles on top and serve.

Nutrition Information

- Nutritionist's Calories: 397 kcal 20%
- Total Fat: 12.6 g 19%
- Carbohydrates: 61.6g 20%
- Protein: 14.6 g 29%
- Cholesterol: 0 mg 0%
- Sodium: 1115 mg 45%

346. Vegetarian Chickpea Sandwich Filling

"You can serve this delicious sandwich filing over pita bread or crusty whole grain rolls along with tomato and lettuce. Can use celery instead of other raw sliced veggies. You can add mayo instead of the salad dressing you like."

Servings: 3 | Prep: 20 m | Ready In: 20 m

Ingredients

- 1 (19 ounce) can garbanzo beans, drained and rinsed
- 1 stalk celery, chopped
- 1/2 onion, chopped
- 1 tbsp. mayonnaise
- 1 tbsp. lemon juice
- 1 tsp. dried dill weed
- salt and pepper to taste

Directions

- Drain chickpeas and then rinse them. Into a medium size mixing bowl, put the chickpeas and use a fork to mash. Stir in dill, lemon juice, celery, onion, pepper, salt and mayonnaise (to taste).

Nutrition Information

- Nutritionist's Calories: 259 kcal 13%
- Total Fat: 5.8 g 9%
- Carbohydrates: 43.5g 14%
- Protein: 9.3 g 19%
- Cholesterol: 2 mg < 1%
- Sodium: 576 mg 23%

347. Vegetarian Chili

"No one will know this dish is vegan!"

Servings: 6 | Prep: 10 m | Ready In: 1 h 10 m

Ingredients

- 1 (12 ounce) package frozen burger-style crumbles
- 2 (15 ounce) cans black beans, rinsed and drained
- 2 (15 ounce) cans dark red kidney beans
- 1 (15 ounce) can light red kidney beans
- 1 (29 ounce) can diced tomatoes
- 1 (12 fluid ounce) can tomato juice
- 5 onions, chopped
- 3 tbsps. chili powder
- 1 1/2 tbsps. ground cumin
- 1 tbsp. garlic powder
- 2 bay leaves
- salt and pepper to taste

Directions

- Mix meat substitute, bay leaves, black beans, chili powder, kidney beans, garlic powder, diced tomatoes, onions, tomato juice, cumin, pepper and salt in a large pot. Heat to a simmer and then cover the pot. Simmer the chili for a minimum of one hour prior to serving.

Nutrition Information

- Nutritionist's Calories: 582 kcal 29%
- Total Fat: 4.9 g 8%
- Carbohydrates: 74.2g 24%
- Protein: 67.5 g 135%
- Cholesterol: 0 mg 0%
- Sodium: 2000 mg 80%

348. Vegetarian Meatloaf

"This is for vegans who love the taste of meatloaf. This delicious vegan dish matches the flavor."

***Servings:** 8 | **Prep:** 20 m | **Ready In:** 1 h 20 m*

Ingredients

- 1 (12 ounce) bottle barbeque sauce
- 1 (12 ounce) package vegetarian burger crumbles
- 1 green bell pepper, chopped
- 1/3 c minced onion
- 1 clove garlic, minced
- 1/2 c soft bread crumbs
- 3 tbsps. Parmesan cheese
- 1 egg, beaten
- 1/4 tsp. dried thyme
- 1/4 tsp. dried basil
- 1/4 tsp. parsley flakes
- salt and pepper to taste

Directions

- Preheat an oven to 165 degrees C (325 degrees F). Polish a loaf pan of 5x9 inch lightly with grease.
- Combine half barbeque sauce together with bread crumbs, vegetarian burger crumbles, parsley, green bell pepper, egg, onion, garlic and Parmesan cheese in a bowl. Season with pepper, salt, thyme and basil. Place into loaf pan.
- Bake for about 45 minutes. Add the barbeque sauce remaining on top of loaf and continue to bake for about 15 minutes or until the loaf sets.

Nutrition Information

- Nutritionist's Calories: 155 kcal 8%
- Total Fat: 3.3 g 5%
- Carbohydrates: 21.3g 7%
- Protein: 9.6 g 19%
- Cholesterol: 25 mg 8%
- Sodium: 688 mg 28%

349. Vegetarian Stuffed Peppers

"My first vegan recipe made with green peppers filled with a combo of cheese, tofu, nuts, brown rice and dried cranberries. For a vegan delight, replace soy cheese with Parmesan."

***Servings:** 6 | **Prep:** 10 m | **Ready In:** 1 h 20 m*

Ingredients

- 1 1/2 c brown rice
- 6 large green bell peppers
- 3 tbsps. soy sauce
- 3 tbsps. cooking sherry
- 1 tsp. vegetarian Worcestershire sauce
- 1 1/2 c extra firm tofu
- 1/2 c sweetened dried cranberries
- 1/4 c chopped pecans
- 1/2 c grated Parmesan cheese
- salt and pepper to taste
- 2 c tomato sauce
- 2 tbsps. brown sugar

Directions

- Preheat an oven to 175 degrees C (350 degrees F). Bring to boil three c of water in a saucepan. Add rice and stir. Low the heat, cover the pan and allow to simmer for 40 minutes.
- In the meantime, core and then remove seeds of green peppers leaving the bottoms intact. Transfer the peppers to a microwavable dish containing water approximately half inch from the bottom. Heat for 6 minutes in microwave on high.

- Bring Worcestershire sauce, soy sauce and wine to a simmer in a frying pan. Pour in tofu and let to simmer until liquid has been absorbed. Mix rice (after cooling), cheese, tofu, cranberries, pepper, nuts and salt. Combine and then firmly pack into peppers. Take back the peppers to dish that you had microwaved in and then bake for about 25 to 30 minutes or until browned lightly at the top.
- In the meantime, over low heat, mix brown sugar and tomato sauce in a saucepan and then heat until hot throughout. Pour the sauce on top of each serving.

Nutrition Information

- Nutritionist's Calories: 375 kcal 19%
- Total Fat: 10.2 g 16%
- Carbohydrates: 59.6g 19%
- Protein: 14.9 g 30%
- Cholesterol: 6 mg 2%
- Sodium: 1055 mg 42%

350. Very Simple Spelt Bread

"A very easy Spelt Bread with no yeast and ready in about one hour."

Servings: 30 | Prep: 5 m | Ready In: 1 h 15 m

Ingredients

- 8 c spelt flour
- 1/2 c sesame seeds
- 1/2 tsp. salt, or to taste
- 1 tbsp. blackstrap molasses
- 2 tsps. baking soda
- 4 1/4 c milk

Directions

- Preheat an oven to 175 degrees C (350 degrees F). Polish 2 loaf pans of 9x5 inch with grease.
- Combine together spelt flour, baking soda, sesame seeds, salt, milk and molasses in a bowl until blended well. Subdivide batter evenly in between the pans prepared.
- Bake in oven for about one hour and ten minutes or until golden. Put on top of loaf, a tin of the same size during baking process to have a nice crust.

Nutrition Information

- Nutritionist's Calories: 139 kcal 7%
- Total Fat: 2.4 g 4%
- Carbohydrates: 25g 8%
- Protein: 5.8 g 12%
- Cholesterol: 3 mg < 1%
- Sodium: 139 mg 6%

351. Wendy's Quick Pasta and Lentils

"This is a delicious lentil and pasta dish. Keeps you warm! You can serve with crusty bread and Parmesan."

Servings: 6 | Prep: 15 m | Ready In: 45 m

Ingredients

- 1 onion, chopped
- 3 cloves garlic, minced
- 2 tbsps. olive oil
- 1 (19 ounce) can lentil soup
- 1 c crushed tomatoes
- 1 (10 ounce) package frozen chopped spinach
- 1 (16 ounce) package ditalini pasta
- salt to taste
- ground black pepper to taste
- 1 pinch crushed red pepper

- 2 tbsps. grated Parmesan cheese

Directions

- Over medium heat, brown garlic and onion in oil. Mix in tomatoes and lentil soup. Heat to boil. Mix in spices and spinach and then let to simmer.
- In the meantime, in a pot containing boiling salted water, cook pasta until almost done and then drain. Stir pasta into the lentil sauce. Cover and then maintain warm for about 20 minutes. Add Parmesan cheese on top and serve.

Nutrition Information

- Nutritionist's Calories: 407 kcal 20%
- Total Fat: 7.1 g 11%
- Carbohydrates: 70.5g 23%
- Protein: 15.9 g 32%
- Cholesterol: 1 mg < 1%
- Sodium: 282 mg 11%

352. Whiskey Chicken

"My family loves this recipe. It is sweet, spicy and simple to prepare."

Servings: 2 | Prep: 10 m | Ready In: 30 m

Ingredients

- 2 skinless, boneless chicken breast halves - cut into 1/2 inch pieces
- 2 tbsps. soy sauce
- 1/4 tsp. garlic powder
- 1 c pineapple juice
- 3 tbsps. bourbon whiskey
- 1/8 tsp. ground black pepper
- 1 tbsp. brown sugar

Directions

- Over medium high heat, sauté chicken in a skillet until it's cooked through (no pink color remains).
- Mix pineapple juice, soy sauce, sugar, garlic powder, pepper and whiskey in a small bowl. Mix until the sugar dissolves and spread on top of chicken. Allow to simmer for about 10 to 15 minutes or until the sauce become thick.

Nutrition Information

- Nutritionist's Calories: 288 kcal 14%
- Total Fat: 1.6 g 3%
- Carbohydrates: 24.3g 8%
- Protein: 28.8 g 58%
- Cholesterol: 68 mg 23%
- Sodium: 983 mg 39%

353. White Bean Chicken Chili

"My friend gave me this recipe and it's my favorite! Great when you make use of leftover turkey or chicken! We love making this soup in California when cold! Can replace extra diced tomatoes with tomatillos. Pour in some salsa or red chili flakes if you want a spicier soup. You can serve together with these toppings for the guest to choose from: tortilla chips, limes, sour cream, cilantro, avocado and cheese."

Servings: 9 | Prep: 10 m | Ready In: 35 m

Ingredients

- 2 tbsps. vegetable oil
- 1 onion, chopped
- 2 cloves garlic, minced
- 1 (14.5 ounce) can chicken broth
- 1 (18.75 ounce) can tomatillos, drained and chopped

- 1 (16 ounce) can diced tomatoes
- 1 (7 ounce) can diced green chiles
- 1/2 tsp. dried oregano
- 1/2 tsp. ground coriander seed
- 1/4 tsp. ground cumin
- 2 ears fresh corn
- 1 pound diced, cooked chicken meat
- 1 (15 ounce) can white beans
- 1 pinch salt and black pepper to taste

Directions

- Heat oil and then cook garlic and onion until soft.
- Mix in broth, spices, chilies, tomatillos and tomatoes. Heat to boil and allow to simmer for ten minutes.
- Pour in beans, corn and chicken and allow to simmer for five minutes. Add pepper and salt to taste.

Nutrition Information

- Nutritionist's Calories: 220 kcal 11%
- Total Fat: 6.1 g 9%
- Carbohydrates: 21.2g 7%
- Protein: 20.1 g 40%
- Cholesterol: 40 mg 13%
- Sodium: 786 mg 31%

354. White Chili I

"You can serve together with salad and corn bread. In case you have chopped chicken in advance, prepare corn bread muffins as to make the chili. It's a quick meal to make. Add a bagged salad mix brought from a produce department."

Servings: 4 | Prep: 10 m | Ready In: 35 m

Ingredients

- 1 tbsp. olive oil
- 4 skinless, boneless chicken breast halves - cubed
- 1 onion, chopped
- 1 1/4 c chicken broth
- 1 (4 ounce) can diced green chiles
- 1 tsp. garlic powder
- 1 tsp. ground cumin
- 1/2 tsp. dried oregano
- 1/2 tsp. dried cilantro
- 1/8 tsp. cayenne pepper
- 1 (15 ounce) can cannellini beans, drained and rinsed
- 2 green onions, chopped
- 2 ounces shredded Monterey Jack cheese

Directions

- Over medium-high heat, heat oil in a saucepan, add onion and chicken and then cook for about 4 to 5 minutes or until the onion becomes tender.
- Mix in cayenne pepper chicken broth, oregano, green chiles, cumin, cilantro and garlic powder. Low the heat and allow to simmer for 15 minutes.
- Mix in beans and allow to simmer for about 5 minutes or until the juice runs clear and no pink color of chicken remains. Add shredded cheese and green onion on top.

Nutrition Information

- Nutritionist's Calories: 357 kcal 18%
- Total Fat: 9.7 g 15%
- Carbohydrates: 27.8g 9%
- Protein: 39.3 g 79%
- Cholesterol: 81 mg 27%
- Sodium: 490 mg 20%

355. Whole Wheat and Honey Pizza Dough

"This homemade pizza dough is fast, simple and delicious and can top with your favorite thing. Yields a thin crust but you can double to have a thick crust."

Servings: 12 | Prep: 10 m | Ready In: 20 m

Ingredients

- 1 (.25 ounce) package active dry yeast
- 1 c warm water
- 2 c whole wheat flour
- 1/4 c wheat germ
- 1 tsp. salt
- 1 tbsp. honey

Directions

- Preheat an oven to 175 degrees C (350 degrees F).
- Dissolve yeast in warm water in a bowl and leave it to stand for about 10 minutes until creamy.
- Mix flour, salt and wheat germ in a large bowl. Form a well at the center and then add yeast mixture and honey. Mix thoroughly to combine. Cover the bowl and let it to rise for several minutes in a warm place.
- On a floured pizza pan, roll the dough and then use a fork to make some holes.
- Bake for about 5 to 10 minutes or until the crispiness desired is achieved.

Nutrition Information

- Nutritionist's Calories: 83 kcal 4%
- Total Fat: 0.6 g < 1%
- Carbohydrates: 17.4g 6%
- Protein: 3.5 g 7%
- Cholesterol: 0 mg 0%
- Sodium: 196 mg 8%

356. Whole Wheat Apple Muffins

"This is a tasty muffin with low fat content. A favorite for kids. Add some raisins and/or sliced nuts if desired."

Servings: 12 | Prep: 15 m | Ready In: 35 m

Ingredients

- 2 c whole wheat flour
- 1 tbsp. baking powder
- 1/2 tsp. salt
- 1 tsp. ground cinnamon
- 3/4 c nonfat milk
- 2 egg whites
- 1/4 c vegetable oil
- 1/4 c honey
- 1 c chopped apples

Directions

- Preheat an oven to 190 degrees C (375 degrees F). Polish one 12-c muffin tin lightly with grease.
- Beat egg whites lightly.
- Combine dry ingredients well in a separate bowl.
- Combine the ingredients remaining in another bowl. Carefully roll in egg white. Pour into the dry ingredients. Mix until just moistened. The batter should be lumpy.
- Transfer batter to the greased muffin tins and fill to two-thirds full. Bake for about 20 minutes until browned lightly.

Nutrition Information

- Nutritionist's Calories: 144 kcal 7%
- Total Fat: 5 g 8%
- Carbohydrates: 23g 7%

- Protein: 3.9 g 8%
- Cholesterol: < 1 mg < 1%
- Sodium: 236 mg 9%

357. Whole Wheat Blueberry Pancakes

"Whole wheat pancakes with sweet and moist blueberries and don't need butter when served hot! My family usually eats this for breakfast every Saturday."

Servings: 5 | Prep: 5 m | Ready In: 13 m

Ingredients

- 1 1/4 c whole wheat flour
- 2 tsps. baking powder
- 1 egg
- 1 c milk, plus more if necessary
- 1/2 tsp. salt
- 1 tbsp. artificial sweetener
- 1/2 c blueberries

Directions

- Sift baking powder and flour together and reserve. In a bowl, beat artificial sweetener, salt, milk and egg. Mix in flour until barely moistened. Pour in blueberries and mix to incorporate.
- Over medium heat, preheat a heavy-bottomed skillet and then use cooking spray to coat it. Into the pan, spread about 1/4 c batter for every pancake. Let to cook for about 1 ½ minute until bubbly. Flip and continue to cook until golden brown.

Nutrition Information

- Nutritionist's Calories: 160 kcal 8%
- Total Fat: 2.6 g 4%

- Carbohydrates: 26.7g 9%
- Protein: 9.8 g 20%
- Cholesterol: 41 mg 14%
- Sodium: 464 mg 19%

358. Whole Wheat Pita Bread

"I developed this dish after looking for whole wheat pita bread. I replaced white flour with soy flour. The end product was a delicious pita with a wonderful nutty flavor. Fantastic dipped in hummus or with peanut butter or sandwich fillings. Hope you like this recipe."

Servings: 12 | Prep: 30 m | Ready In: 2 h 30 m

Ingredients

- 1 c warm water
- 1 (.25 ounce) package active dry yeast
- 1 tbsp. molasses
- 1 tsp. salt
- 1 1/2 c whole wheat flour
- 1 1/2 c soy flour
- cooking spray
- cornmeal for dusting

Directions

- Combine molasses, water, salt and yeast in a bowl. Allow to stand for about 5 to 10 minutes. Slowly stir in soy flour and whole wheat flour. Onto a floured surface, spread out and then knead until smooth. Transfer to a bowl that is coated lightly with cooking spray. Use towel to cover and leave it to rise for one hour in a warm place.
- Push the dough downwards and then knead for about 5 to 10 minutes. Subdivide dough into six pieces. Onto a surface that is lightly floured, use a rolling pin to flatten every piece to approximately 1/8 inch thick. Use towel to cover and leave to rise for about 30 minutes.

- Preheat an oven to 230 degrees C (450 degrees F). In the preheating oven, warm a baking sheet for approximately two minutes, take out from the heat and drizzle with cornmeal.
- Onto the baking sheet prepared, spread dough rounds and the bake for 6 minutes. Take out from the heat source and use a moist towel to cover the bread so that it can soften. Once cool, chop in half and then cut pockets in the bread with a knife.

Nutrition Information

- Nutritionist's Calories: 101 kcal 5%
- Total Fat: 1.1 g 2%
- Carbohydrates: 17.1g 6%
- Protein: 7.4 g 15%
- Cholesterol: 0 mg 0%
- Sodium: 197 mg 8%

359. Wonton Soup

"This is an easy, light and classy 'Chinese dumpling' in soup or fried. The wontons often bring the surprising great taste of Far East! Decorate with fresh scallions."

Servings: 8 | Prep: 30 m | Ready In: 1 h 15 m

Ingredients

- 1/2 pound boneless pork loin, coarsely chopped
- 2 ounces peeled shrimp, finely chopped
- 1 tsp. brown sugar
- 1 tbsp. Chinese rice wine
- 1 tbsp. light soy sauce
- 1 tsp. finely chopped green onion
- 1 tsp. chopped fresh ginger root
- 24 (3.5 inch square) wonton wrappers
- 3 c chicken stock
- 1/8 c finely chopped green onion

Directions

- Mix pork, one tsp. of chopped green onion, shrimp, ginger, sugar, soy sauce and wine in a bowl. Combine well and allow to rest for about 25 to 30 minutes.
- At the middle of every wonton skin, put about 1 tsp. of filling. Use water to moisten the four edges of wonton wrapper. Pull top corner down towards the bottom to wrap over the filling and form a triangle. Seal the edges firmly by pressing. Move the right and left corners together over the filling and overlap the tips of the corners. Use water to moisten and then squeeze together. Repeat this till the wrappers are used.
- To make soup: Heat to a rolling boil, chicken stock and then place in wontons. Let to cook for five minutes. Add sliced green onion on top and then serve.

Nutrition Information

- Nutritionist's Calories: 145 kcal 7%
- Total Fat: 4.2 g 7%
- Carbohydrates: 15.3g 5%
- Protein: 9.9 g 20%
- Cholesterol: 33 mg 11%
- Sodium: 589 mg 24%

360. Yummy Honey Chicken Kabobs

"These are honey chicken kabobs together with vegetables. Marinate throughout the night. You can substitute the usual barbecue fare with these chicken kabobs! Feel free to add cherry tomatoes and fresh mushrooms. (Also cooked in a broiler.)"

Servings: 12 | Prep: 15 m | Ready In: 2 h 30 m

Ingredients

- 1/4 c vegetable oil
- 1/3 c honey
- 1/3 c soy sauce
- 1/4 tsp. ground black pepper
- 8 skinless, boneless chicken breast halves - cut into 1 inch cubes
- 2 cloves garlic
- 5 small onions, cut into 2 inch pieces
- 2 red bell peppers, cut into 2 inch pieces
- skewers

Directions

- Whisk together oil, pepper, honey and soy sauce in a large bowl. Before you put in chicken, set aside a little amount of marinade that will be used to polish kabobs while cooking. In a bowl, add chicken, peppers, onions and garlic. Chill for at least two hours to marinate (better when marinated for longer).
- Preheat a grill over high heat.
- Drain the marinade from the veggies and chicken and get rid of marinade. Onto skewers, thread the veggies and chicken alternately.
- Polish grill grate lightly with oil. Transfer skewers to the grill. Let to cook for about 12 to 15 minutes until the chicken juice is clear. Flip and polish with the marinade reserved often.

Nutrition Information

- Nutritionist's Calories: 178 kcal 9%
- Total Fat: 6.6 g 10%
- Carbohydrates: 12.4g 4%
- Protein: 17.4 g 35%
- Cholesterol: 45 mg 15%
- Sodium: 442 mg 18%

361. Zesty Chicken Meatloaf

"A different way to enjoy meatloaf instead of the usual one."

Servings: 8 | Prep: 10 m | Ready In: 1 h 10 m

Ingredients

- 1 pound ground chicken
- 2 eggs
- 1 1/2 c bread crumbs
- 3 tbsps. salsa
- 2 tbsps. Ranch-style salad dressing
- 1 (1.25 ounce) package taco seasoning mix
- 1/2 c shredded Cheddar cheese
- sour cream (optional)

Directions

- Preheat an oven to 175 degrees C (350 degrees F). Polish a loaf pan of 8x4 inch with grease.
- Combine together salad dressing, ground chicken, salsa, eggs, taco seasoning mix and bread crumbs in a large bowl. Transfer to the loaf pan prepared.
- Bake for one hour. Add cheese on top and then serve together with sour cream.

Nutrition Information

- Nutritionist's Calories: 254 kcal 13%
- Total Fat: 10.4 g 16%
- Carbohydrates: 18.8g 6%
- Protein: 19.5 g 39%
- Cholesterol: 94 mg 31%
- Sodium: 649 mg 26%

362. Zesty Tuna Salad

"A dish that kicks up the boring canned tuna. Goes well

with dill pickle relish."

Servings: 2 | Prep: 5 m | Ready In: 5 m

Ingredients

- 1 (5 ounce) can tuna, drained
- 1 tsp. mayonnaise
- 1 tsp. sweet pickle relish
- 1 tsp. Dijon-style prepared mustard
- 1 stalk celery, chopped
- 1/4 c chopped onion
- 1/4 tsp. ground black pepper

Directions

- Use a fork to mash tuna in a bowl. Pour in celery, mayonnaise, black pepper, pickle relish, onion and mustard. Mix to blend. Refrigerate before serving.

Nutrition Information

- Nutritionist's Calories: 107 kcal 5%
- Total Fat: 2.4 g 4%
- Carbohydrates: 4.1g 1%
- Protein: 16.5 g 33%
- Cholesterol: 20 mg 7%
- Sodium: 145 mg 6%

363. Zesty Zucchini and Squash

"This side dish is super simple and quick. Great when served on top of pasta."

Servings: 6 | Prep: 15 m | Ready In: 40 m

Ingredients

- 3 medium small yellow squash, cubed
- 3 small zucchini, cubed
- 1 (10 ounce) can diced tomatoes with green chile peppers
- 1/2 onion, chopped
- salt to taste
- garlic powder to taste

Directions

- Mix garlic powder, squash, onion, zucchini, tomatoes along with chiles, salt and onion in a large saucepan. Over medium-high heat, heat to boil.
- Decrease the heat to low and then let to cook until tender-crisp.

Nutrition Information

- Nutritionist's Calories: 43 kcal 2%
- Total Fat: 0.4 g < 1%
- Carbohydrates: 9.7g 3%
- Protein: 1.8 g 4%
- Cholesterol: 0 mg 0%
- Sodium: 328 mg 13%

364. Zucchini Pasta II

"On one night, I made this dish to make use of zucchini available in the garden. For a complete meal, add leftover chicken! Fast and simple!"

Servings: 4 | Prep: 15 m | Ready In: 35 m

Ingredients

- 1 (8 ounce) package uncooked pasta shells
- 1 tsp. olive oil
- 1/2 onion, chopped
- 3 cloves garlic, sliced
- 1 zucchini, chopped
- 1/2 tsp. dried oregano
- salt and freshly ground black pepper to taste

- 1/4 tsp. crushed red pepper flakes
- 3/4 c chicken broth
- 1/2 c chopped cooked chicken
- 1 ounce diced roasted red peppers
- 2 tbsps. light cream cheese
- 1/4 c chopped fresh basil leaves
- 1/4 c grated Parmesan cheese

Directions

- Bring to boil lightly salted water in a pot and add pasta shells. Cook until al dente or for about 8 to 10 minutes. Drain.
- Over medium heat, heat olive oil in a skillet, add garlic and onion and cook until tender. Stir in zucchini and then season with red pepper, salt, pepper and oregano. Let to cook for 10 minutes until tender.
- Mix chicken broth into skillet and let to cook for about 5 minutes until heated through. Stir in cream cheese, chicken and roasted red peppers. Continue to cook for 5 minutes. You can serve on top of cooked pasta and add Parmesan cheese and fresh basil on top.

Nutrition Information

- Nutritionist's Calories: 321 kcal 16%
- Total Fat: 6.6 g 10%
- Carbohydrates: 48.2g 16%
- Protein: 16.7 g 33%
- Cholesterol: 21 mg 7%
- Sodium: 739 mg 30%

365. Zucchini with Chickpea and Mushroom Stuffing

"Use vegetable dish as a side dish or as a main meal Great served together with a green vegetable and tomato based sauce. Can also enjoy this dish at Christmas with old-fashioned roasted veggies."

Servings: 8 | Prep: 30 m | Ready In: 1 h

Ingredients

- 4 zucchini, halved
- 1 tbsp. olive oil
- 1 onion, chopped
- 2 cloves garlic, crushed
- 1/2 (8 ounce) package button mushrooms, sliced
- 1 tsp. ground coriander
- 1 1/2 tsps. ground cumin, or to taste
- 1 (15.5 ounce) can chickpeas, rinsed and drained
- 1/2 lemon, juiced
- 2 tbsps. chopped fresh parsley
- sea salt to taste
- ground black pepper to taste

Directions

- Preheat an oven to 175 degrees C (350 degrees F). Polish a shallow baking dish with grease.
- Scoop zucchini's fresh out, cut the flesh and reserve. Transfer the shells to the dish prepared.
- Over medium heat, heat oil in a skillet, add onions and sauté for 5 minutes. Pour in garlic and then sauté for two minutes. Mix in mushrooms and chopped zucchini and sauté for 5 minutes. Mix in lemon juice, coriander, parsley, cumin, chickpeas, pepper and salt. Ladle the mixture into the zucchini shells.
- Bake for about 30 to 40 minutes or until the zucchini becomes tender.

Nutrition Information

- Nutritionist's Calories: 107 kcal 5%
- Total Fat: 2.7 g 4%
- Carbohydrates: 18.4g 6%
- Protein: 4.5 g 9%
- Cholesterol: 0 mg 0%
- Sodium: 170 mg 7%

Index

213

Conclusion

Thank you again for downloading this book!

I hope you enjoyed reading about my book!

If you enjoyed this book, please take the time to share your thoughts and post a review on Amazon. It'd be greatly appreciated!

Write me an honest review about the book – I truly value your opinion and thoughts and I will incorporate them into my next book, which is already underway.

Thank you!

If you have any questions, **feel free to contact at:** *healthy@dearbeautydiary.com*

Mia Safra

https://dearbeautydiary.com/mia-safra

Manufactured by Amazon.ca
Acheson, AB

30462662R00122